THE CRITIQUE OF WAR

THE CRITIQUE OF WAR

Contemporary Philosophical Explorations

Edited by
ROBERT GINSBERG
Assistant Professor of Philosophy
Pennsylvania State University

HENRY REGNERY COMPANY · *Chicago*

The translations of Bandeira de Mello's chapter from the Portuguese and Frondizi's chapter from the Spanish were prepared by the Editor in consultation with the respective authors.

Manufactured in the United States of America.
Library of Congress Catalog Card Number: 77–88846

Since wars begin in the minds of men, it is in the minds of men that the defences of peace must be constructed.

Constitution of UNESCO

Table of Contents

IV. THE UNJUSTIFIABILITY OF WAR

V. THE ALTERNATIVE TO WAR

INTRODUCTION

Philosophy vs. War

Robert Ginsberg

I

This volume is a Critique in the sense of being a critical inquiry into the condition of human crisis. It raises and explores the questions that are crucial in the problem of war and searches out and evaluates possible solutions. This book does not win the battle against war, but it does open a frontal attack. And it calls for reinforcements.

The Critique is the fruit of an international project in which 192 thinkers in 40 countries were invited to participate. Eighteen of the world's most distinguished philosophers and scholars in the related fields of law, religion, history, government, and education have worked independently, writing chapters especially for the volume. In many cases their contributions had to be shortened by the editor to fit within the overall scheme of the book. Rather than exhaustive treatments, the chapters are intended to lay the foundations and show the directions for comprehensive study.

War is the greatest human problem. Therefore it is the most important problem for philosophy. Put simply, the problem is that any group of human beings may be destroyed by a war at any moment, and the totality of all human beings may be destroyed by an ultimate war at any time. Conditions are ripe for war, including ultimate war. Thus, not only is whatever men value perpetually menaced by destruction, but man himself, the source and end of every value, falls under the same threat. War is the arch enemy of mankind.

War demands philosophical inquiry and resolution, not only because it is the supreme negation of human value and human existence, but also because it is *human action*, caused by men, executed by men, justified by men. War is the paradox of man against himself. And therefore, as the supreme champion of man for man, philosophy must take the field.

The atomic age has introduced into the world a new human condition: the likelihood of world destruction. Our ingenuity has made it possible to fight ultimate war. Though it may have long been in our dreams, annihilation is now, for the first time, technically within our grasp. We have come to the limit condition of our being. We can either decide that war is no longer possible for us, or that we are no longer possible. As the awful darkness of extermination closes in about us, disheartening men, so the possibility of creating peace for ourselves also dawns and brings with it a resurgence of our energies. And, perhaps for the last time, the establishment of peace may be within our grasp. Whether by default, in despair, out of perversity, or simply unknowingly, we have already chosen and are well advanced upon the route to annihilation. Only by a leap of existence back to life can humanity survive itself.

War is waking philosophers throughout the world to the discovery of their primary duty of service to humanity —which is inseparable from a genuine love of wisdom. Yet philosophy, Eastern as well as Western, has struggled with the problem of war since ancient times, and its history is rich in the analysis and praise of peace. In the late seventeenth and throughout the eighteenth centuries, to take just one example, philosophers all over Europe exchanged treatises outlining the practical steps for the curtailment of war and the institution of lasting peace. These included William Penn's *Essay Towards the Present and Future Peace of Europe;* the Abbé de Saint-Pierre's *Project to Establish Perpetual Peace in Europe,* of which Rousseau published both a condensation and a critique; Bentham's *Plan for an Universal and Perpetual Peace;* and Kant's *On Perpetual Peace: A Philosophical Sketch.* While conditions and facts change, values and arguments often do not. Philosophical treatment of war in the atomic age can make use of the insights and suggestions of past philosophers. At the least we might learn not to repeat their errors. The importance of the work of previous thinkers is evident in the chapters that follow. Kant sought, as do some of the present authors, the governmental framework for the world and for nations in which war would not be needed because politics would have been transformed by morals. William James sought, as do other contributors, the pragmatic alternative to war that could be a moral outlet to vigorous energies. The ideas of Plato, Aristotle, Hegel, Marx, Ramakrishna, Nietzsche, Tolstoy, Lenin, Ortega y Gasset, Iqbal, and Gandhi, as well as of contemporary thinkers such as Buber, Russell, and Sartre, are also subject to critical evaluation in the text. But further exploration is needed of the treatment of war and peace within the long history of philosophy.[1]

War is not a problem that falls under a single branch of philosophy, nor is there just one philosophic method for treating war. Philosophy makes available the full richness of its intellectual techniques and is equipped to take on war successively under its several disciplines. The authors in this volume illustrate the application of linguistic analysis, dialectical reasoning, textual research, history of ideas, legal reasoning, and pragmatic evaluation. They have conducted studies of ethics, political philosophy, philosophy of value, philosophy of history, philosophy of religion, and philosophy of law. They trace the roots and offshoots of war in the fields of biology, psychology, sociology, politics, economics, history, technology, culture, language, religion, and law.

Theories have applications. Arguments illuminate actuality. The particular institutions, actions, and claims of men and nations are accessible to philosophical criticism that proceeds from general principles. The American war in Vietnam, for example, is subjected to scrutiny here through half a dozen philosophic perspectives. From them it appears to be a monstrous crime against humanity, deserving the condemnation of all men of good will and good sense. The American-Soviet Cold War, which currently divides the world into two vast armed camps, is criticized for its lack of necessity and its foundation in misconception and mistrust. Accommodation between capitalism and communism is possible and desirable if based on understanding and a mutual concern for the sufferings of the rest of humanity. The United Nations is evaluated as a progressive yet inadequate institution that could be converted by radical changes into the instrument for world peace. Other applications are also called for and will have to be made by the reader, particularly with respect to the occurrence or prevention of future wars. The philosophy of war is a philosophy of man and his world; it has its value, then, in being used by man in the world. In the long run, there is nothing more practical, more applicable and efficacious, than the powers of reason and value. But we are now threatened by the likelihood that there will not be a long run. Consequently, philosophy, as practiced here, has not renounced the world, as its practice elsewhere has been, but resolved to save it.

What philosophy is called upon for first of all is the recognition of its responsibility for human existence in the face of likely destruction. Then what is needed is a diagnosis of man as the maker of war, which is what unmakes him. The clarification of the causes of war should lead to an understanding of its consequences and place in the world, for a war system of human organization both provokes wars and is their product. War is an activity invariably accompanied by justification; philosophy ought to examine critically the possibility of moral and rational justification applied to war. Since war is human activity, philosophy must propose plans of action to counteract war. To denounce war does not suffice. Philosophy must lead to the practice that will defeat war.

II

There is a professional prejudice among contemporary philosophers, especially in the English-speaking world, that they should keep their hands off the world in order to be left in peace by it. Worldly problems are transitory and particular. Imbued with passion and irrationality, they call for action and decision. Philosophy, on the other hand, deals with theories, universals, and reasons, and it settles its differences by the dispassionate machinery of logic or linguistic analysis. As a consequence of this predisposition, philosophy nowadays is content to illuminate the language of ethical discourse, or metaethics, instead of the problems of ethics. Historical and social conditions also have favored the current fashion in philosophy, for example: technology and the comfortable insulation from the universe offered the philosopher as a university functionary. But certainly one symptom of the world's disease is the indifference of professional philosophy to the fate of the world.

The conduct of philosophy, however, itself presupposes the primacy of human life and value. The leisure and tranquillity needed to pursue metaethics, symbolic logic, or linguistic structure are the result of ethical decisions and human labors. Even to devote oneself to a life of theory indifferent to the world is to commit oneself by an action in the world and therefore to affirm its value. Since the world is the very thing at stake, so is philosophy. It is in our interest to take account of the interests and sufferings of others. Help is needed, and our help is needed not just as citizens but as professional thinkers.

Philosophers have taken stands recently on particular issues in the world, though they have not especially used philosophic resources in making their contributions. The history of philosophic involvement with war in this century is a shaky one, as *Warren E. Steinkraus* reveals in his chapter. When not ignoring war, philosophers have offered naive arguments exhibiting their ignorance of the world, and in some cases they have served as warmongers. Even the stand of philosophers against the American war in Vietnam is largely a reaction against a *particular* war, while most philosophers who have dealt with war in a theoretical way have given arguments favoring war. Steinkraus urges the philosopher to clarify the language of politics, locate its genuine issues, enhance human values, reexamine justice, oppose the military mentality and mythology, and engender a Copernican Revolution in our thinking for positive alternative action.

The nature of philosophical activity, not only the recognition of the importance of war as subject matter, has value for the solution of the problem. *Edwin A. Burtt* warns that philosophers have moved away from the mutual search for enlightenment, characteristic of Socratic dialogue, to arrive at a method of disputation in which they seek victory over one another. If we were to replace this form of philosophical violence with a new striving for truth, then philosophy would serve as an appropriate model for the treatment of social and political differences. Conflict between nations could be replaced by peaceful cooperation once there is a recognition of common interests, an active sharing of different values, and an acceptance of fruitful disagreement. Philosophy can assist the translation of national disagreements into a rational discourse in which resolutions can be sought and may be found by initially competing parties. Philosophy thereby would be the moral alternative to war. At the very least, warn Steinkraus and Burtt, we must not delude ourselves that wars spring from genuine philosophic differences, and philosophers must resist the temptation to be philosophical servants of war.

The *Critique of War* itself is designed to stimulate further philosophical activity, and the editor plans to bring out a second volume of studies on war, continuing this work. But other kinds of steps can be taken too, for example: (1) International Centers for the Philosophy of Peace and War could be established in various places in the world to maintain specialized libraries, hold regular institutes, offer coursework, facilitate and publish research, sponsor public discussions, arrange exchange of personnel, stimulate peace work in each of their regions, and keep in contact with one another; (2) an *International Journal for the Philosophy of Peace and War* could be published by the Centers for the presentation of research, the exchange of news, the discussion of practical applications, and the evaluation of theories; (3) International Philosophy Peace Teams could be set up, composed of thinkers respected in the world who would volunteer to clarify and evaluate the claims and justifications in any armed conflict, to assist the parties involved to opt for a negotiated settlement of their differences, to encourage reevaluation of political principles and methods of any of the parties, and in general to convert conflicts between nations from violence to rational argument. The philosopher is best fitted to be the friend of humanity in its adversity, since he ought to have the broadest grasp of what is real in the human condition, on one hand, and the keenest appreciation of human value and capability, on the other.

III

Alternatives to war can hardly be proposed unless we first make clear what war is, and this condition can be fulfilled in part by inquiry into its causes. Causal study involves more than a description of how wars come about under various circumstances. We need to isolate the principal causal factors and discover the point of human responsibility. Where in human events do men make the crucial decision that is war? What conditions will most probably lead to war? If we knew the answers to these questions, we might also know what can be changed by human action or argument to avoid war. Thus, finding the cause can mean finding the solution.

Knowledge of causes both explains the past and predicts the future. We know what is likely to happen (indeed, it is in the process of happening); namely, wars will continue to occur until an ultimate war destroys us all. But we can prevent wars by counteracting, or diverting, or abolishing their causes. In one manifestation or another, the basic cause of war is the irrationality of man. Armed with reason man ought to be able to master himself.

When war is attributed to man's nature, war is inevitable. Many of the authors challenge that attribution or reveal the resources of human nature that can be mobilized against war. War does have its roots in human nature, *Urpo Harva* discovers, namely, in aggression and the death wish or contempt for life that engender the spirit of self-sacrifice, heroism, and the desire for adventure. But man can take stock of his nature and his environment and then responsibly channel his destructiveness into harmless outlets. An education for peace would provide for what is best in human nature. The analysis of personality development through its biological, psychological, sociological, cultural, economic, and ecological dimensions permits *Howard L. Parsons* to show how the American capitalist society educates the natural aggressiveness in people to war. He warns that men cannot take steps to prevent war unless they recognize how they are responsible for the exploitive human relationships that engender it. One solution is the change from a class-structured economy to a cooperative economy aimed at fulfillment for all men. The usual concept of human nature is outdated and philosophically indefensible, argues *Risieri Frondizi*. Mistaken conceptions, including the one that World War III is inevitable, can nonetheless lead to their actualization in behavior. The principal cause of present-day conflict is ideological, and by combating social injustice we can satisfy the needs that otherwise reinforce such conflict.

In a sense, every critical treatment of war has a cause of war in mind: that which if not acted upon would lead to war. But in another sense knowledge of war's causes is secondary, for an ill can often be remedied without knowing its origin. What we must primarily seek is the cause of war's *abolition*.

IV

Critical understanding of war comes from its manifestations and effects in the world as well as from its origin and rise. We live in a war world. Our personalities, values, myths, ideologies, and even philosophic methods are shaped by a system in which war is an enduring reality. War is caused by the system just as the system is a consequence of war. In this vicious circle men talk of peace and prepare for war. Philosophers seek ways to control the factors of war while participating as citizens in the very system that nourishes them. To reach the causes in the system it seems we must first radically alter society and the life of nations. The question philosophers then raise is: What exactly is the role of war in human life? In answer we find that war values permeate our language, conceptions of history and progress, attitudes toward government and civilization, and daily activities.

A poetic sensitivity to language permits *Thomas Merton* to expose the pathological grounding of our war idiom. It is as if we were trying to speak a new and incomprehensible reality by means of blows. Our language reveals that all *we* understand is force. We have abandoned the possibility of communication and dialogue. The study of integral history has revealed to *John Nef* the interrelatedness of nations and the common menace to mankind now posed by war. Though we are inclined to think that progress in technology and civilization is due to war, in fact progress has occurred in spite of war. To balance technological invention with its increased power of destruction we need a new moral inventiveness. The present world crisis takes the form of a capitalist-communist confrontation, based largely on an American misunderstanding of Marxist doctrines, argues *John Somerville*. Our ideological blindness has kept us from seeing the broad common ground sufficient for peaceful coexistence. International law is nonexistent, warns *Paul Arthur Schilpp*, because the highest law recognized by a state is its sovereignty. The idea of national sovereignty has been entrenched in our minds since infancy so that international relations remain anarchic despite our professed brotherhood. And only by breaking the emotional attachment and moving to a world government that recognizes the sovereignty of mankind can we be saved from such destructive anarchy. War is the activity of killing by organized groups for self-defense, and where there is no government over men, as is the case internationally, the differences between groups are settled by violence, argues *Carl J. Friedrich.* Even world government would be open to the threat of civil war, during which groups seek to impose their power on opponents.

Underlying these features of the war system is a common value: though it may sometimes be wrong, war is right. It is wrong when waged against Us, and right when we wage it against Others. Our waging of war is right because history says it is so, or because our government says it is so, or because we say it is so. Since other people as well are convinced of the rightness of their waging war, the system of the world provides a bloody spectacle of righteous extermination.

V

War is wrong. Whatever men take to be good is subject to destruction by war. Killing and maiming people are surely the greatest evils in human conduct. And since war is evidently unjustifiable, men have to justify waging war by appeal to exceptional circumstances and overriding principles. But the exception becomes the rule, and every party to all wars has indulged in a justification for its participation, usually that of self-defense. The theory of "just war," worked out by philosophers in the past to separate the mass of improper wars from the few admissible ones, has subsequently been used to rationalize whatever war one was prepared to embark upon.

In recent times, however, it has become clear that any

"just war" can easily lead to ultimate war, in which all human purposes will be defeated, since all humans will be defeated, observes *Barrows Dunham*. Thus, the probable outcome of war negates any value war may have to men. But we may also ask if our actions are right regardless of consequences. The younger generation protests our war-making as a violation of what is categorically moral; we ought to treat people as ends to be served and not as objects for profit or destruction. War is an activity incompatible with rational practice, *A. C. Genova* discovers in his inquiry. Physical violence cannot make sense as a rational alternative for action in the solution of disputes. Since war amounts to getting one's way at all costs, it destroys all rational standards, including the pursuit of inquiry. Philosophy as the foundation of inquiry and of all rational activity is the antithesis of war.

To prove that war is wrong is not to prevent it, but it does show us what we ought to do, and if we can instruct men to do what they ought, then they will prevent war. Our hope lies in the youth who implore us to obey the imperative of morality, and in philosophers who implore us to use our heads to discover the irrationality of violence.

Though theory argues war is evil, there come times in the actual course of events when not to go to war in defense of oneself or others is to allow great evil to be done. The philosopher can argue that self-defense necessitated by such desperate conditions cannot be classified as war. Sometimes it is agonizingly difficult to judge whether it is better to resort to arms to oppose war or to refrain from arms so as not to be party to war. If we renounce self-defense, the war system wins an easy victory, but so it does in a sense if we resort to defense. All wars are justified when labeled "defensive," and if we are to stay alive in the war system, we will have to be ready to justify our wars. Yet as nations continue to offer justifications for their own protection, they are rapidly advancing to mutual destruction. Hence, if we are to be moral *and* alive, we will have to change the whole world.

VI

The heart of the philosophic problem of war is action: what steps ought we to take to stop, control, minimize, prevent, or eliminate war? What actions are those that create peace? A theory of world peace is worth nothing to the world unless it includes the method of its implementation in the world. The time for the method is now, the place for it everywhere, the practitioners of it ourselves. The steps specified must be ones that we can actually put into practice; they must be efficacious, especially when opposed by violence; and they must not violate the fundamental value of humanity which we seek to protect. We may take steps on the cosmic level, intensifying our spiritual bonds with men and God. We may instigate action at the world level, assisting the world community to institute world government. We may bring action to bear at the national level, obliging states to obey law and morality. We may start work for peace at the level of the individual, by conquest of the self.

Though war is a natural instinct of life, applicable within as well as between species, claims *Lydio Machado Bandeira de Mello,* man has the means of defending himself against it, namely, law and government. These are rational instruments of order and cooperation supported by collective force. The same instruments in use for nations must be applied to the whole world. Only a world state will keep the peace between nations, regulated by an international law enforced by a world police force. But if there is to be peace, a change in human nature will be needed, argues *Swami*

Nikhilananda, and religions that point the way to God can provide that change. We are following different paths to the same goal, and the realization of the oneness of existence, that is, of the solidarity of all men, is the metaphysical foundation of peace. Each of us, then, should seek to deepen his religious consciousness. This solidarity, or "being with," *C. A. Qadir* recognizes as the dialectical answer to pessimism and the opposition between men. The idea of the stewardship of man on earth provides the context for human interrelationship. A world government founded on this idea and recognizing the sovereignty of God might not totally abolish war, but it would help man to live up to his trust in peace.

The pacifist conscience is most fit for the maturation of societies, argues *Harrop A. Freeman,* and the nonviolent method can accomplish the revolutions needed in institutions. Pacifism has the same goal as law, namely, living in peace, whereas violence and war are the opposites of law. Nonviolent resistance, *satyagraha,* claims *R. Balasubramanian,* can effectively bring about whatever war is supposed to achieve but without the violence. This moral equivalent of war can also work in the atomic age, since it recognizes a human nature sensitive to love even in a Hitler's breast. The individual is supreme, and the first step toward peace is the recognition of his moral responsibility. The revolution in science that has built and yet menaces the modern age must be matched, pleads *Robert S. Hartman,* by a revolution in values affirmative of life. The intellectual challenge to the philosopher is to build a science of value that will account for the existential interdependence of men of which the youth of the world have already shown awareness in their protests.

Solutions to the problem of war call for a new humanity: a humanity that lives together under one world government, that shares one world of the spirit, that accepts a common trust under God, that recognizes nonviolence as the only moral action, that gives sovereignty to the value of man over the realm of things. Since war is radically evil, the war system must be radically altered and the causes of war silenced. The philosopher has his special duty in the struggle for peace as educator, planner, critic, and leader. He must find the causes of peace and set them into operation. He must outline the peace system and train men to build it. He must praise the steps that others take that are right, and he must take the right steps himself though he fall into disfavor in his own nation.

A philosophy of war is only completed by a philosophy of peace. The tone of the philosophy of war is deceptively negative, since it works *against* what is destructive of human beings. Yet this work is clearly affirmative of the worth of human beings. Without war, it is easily said, people would be able to live in peace. But peace is not simply the negation or absence of war. Rather, war should be thought of as the violation of peace, which itself has been found to be of the highest value by prior philosophical inquiry. But the question may then be posed: How can we have peace or study and evaluate it before the problem of war has been solved? Or the question can be recast: How can we study and criticize war and seek to defeat it if we have not first assured ourselves of the identity, dignity, and dynamism of peace?

In answer, a variety of positive concepts of peace are proposed: peace of mind in which a mature personality reaches its fulfillment; fraternal peace wherein men cooperate and share in the fulfillment of life; divine peace in which culminating oneness with the highest values and existence is achieved; peace as a form of love, as a system of law, as a method of understanding. Peace, in fact, is the realization of what man ought to be. Philosophy is preeminent among the arts of peace in that its primary concern is identifying and implementing what man ought to be.

The first step in the variety of actions proposed to institute peace is philosophical: we must stipulate the meaning of law for our life, put in order our conscience and soul, discover our connection to man and God, create our values as men. Self-awareness, self-regulation, self-motivation—these are the springs of action for the conquest of war and the construction of peace. Peace has to be waged. It calls for work, courage, sacrifice.

In the final analysis, the only moral equavalent to war is peace, since peace is the fulfillment of man and war his destruction. Philosophy makes the challenge clear to us: It is possible for man to make himself, that is, to create his fulfillment. But if he does not choose to do so now, there is little doubt that he will soon destroy himself.

NOTE

1. Peter Mayer has edited a valuable collection of writings from the history of philosophy on war and peace, *The Pacifist Conscience* (Chicago: Regnery, 1967), which includes selections from the works of Lao-Tzu, Motse, Buddha, Tertullian, Erasmus, Kant, Penn, Emerson, Thoreau, Tolstoy, James, Gandhi, Alain, Einstein, Freud, Reinhold Niebuhr, Buber, Simone Weil, Russell, A. J. Muste, Martin Luther King, and Camus.

I

The Philosopher and War

CHAPTER ONE

War and the Philosopher's Duty

Warren E. Steinkraus

Professor of Philosophy,
State University College of New York at Oswego

Though the problems of war and peace have never been foremost in the minds of philosophers, thinkers from the earliest times to the present have occasionally addressed themselves to the questions. Some have reflected on war as a part of their general theory of society and without any particular war in mind. Others have given their attention to war and the war method only when it became an immediate problem—their country was at war or war was imminent. Of those who incorporate talk about war and peace in their general social philosophy there are very few who repudiate war entirely, while those who consider the problem under the pressure of an actual war seem almost uniformly incapable of doing anything more than provide a justification for their nation's behavior. The great bulk of philosophers who have spoken on the question of war have supported and defended it as an instrument of social change. The number of thinkers who have directly opposed the war system either in theory or under empirical circumstances is very small. Only in the present decade has vigorous opposition to specific wars been voiced by some philosophers, and only in the nuclear age have a few outspoken thinkers condemned war in theory as well as in practice. No philosopher has been awarded the Nobel Peace Prize, though two men with a basic philosophical orientation have won it, Albert Schweitzer and Martin Luther King, Jr., but their views have hardly been popular with philosophers.

We need not review at length the positions of those who consider war a necessary, even desirable, aspect of their theory of the state. Plato held that the state must be organized to engage in violence in order to preserve itself in an anarchic world. Christian philosophers after Constantine[1] introduced the idea that wars fought in self-defense and for the preservation of the state could be viewed as just, and they laid down requirements for a "just war." Thinkers such as Machiavelli and Hobbes saw war as basic to the state's existence, even inevitable, while Hugo Grotius, the founder of international law, sought to humanize war, reduce its savagery, and accelerate its extinction by promoting congresses of powers to seek peaceful solutions to conflicts. Fichte saw war as a stage contributing to the movement of civilization. Hegel's justification of war as a function of an evolving state culminated in German thought in such extreme glorifications of war as one finds in Treitschke and Bernhardi. The Marxian analysis sees war as inevitable in capitalist society and looks to a warless communist world. Recent and current philosophical treatments favoring war neither glorify it nor assert its inevitability but view it as a necessary way to prevent injustice and preserve "freedom."

There is no comparable line of philosophic thinkers who have unequivocally opposed war in theory and actuality though some, such as Grotius, sought to remove the conditions of hostility, and others, such as Kant, to provide the grounding for an international structure to prevent war. Kant did not oppose war categorically but urged that it be fought with decency if at all—which means he would be against modern warfare. Some early Christian writers before Augustine viewed all war as ethically wrong. Notable was Origen,[2] though the same view is found in Tertullian, Clement of Alexandria, and Cyprian. Similarly, there are aspects of Buddhist, Hindu, and Jain teaching that oppose violence unconditionally and in any form. No modern Western philosopher of prominence, save Bertrand Russell, has ever taken an uncompromising anti-war or pacifist stand. William James came close in his famous essay, "The Moral Equivalent of War," and there have been a few studies of a semi-philosophical character in the East and West that have not only denounced all war but proposed alternatives. Best known of the Western thinkers perhaps are Leo Tolstoy and Aldous Huxley,[3] though Richard B. Gregg's *The Power of Non-Violence* presents a more systematic and better reasoned account.[4] Joan V. Bondurant's *Conquest of Violence: The Gandhian Philosophy of Conflict*[5] is the best recent treatment. Besides Gandhi himself, other Eastern thinkers who have developed philosophical defenses of nonviolent alternatives to war include A. C. Das Gupta, R. R. Diwakar, and K. Shridharani.[6] European and American philosophers seem hardly aware that there is such a point of view let alone that there are viable arguments for it.

Most philosophers, then, who have dealt with the question of war in a general, theoretical way have felt it their duty to provide arguments favoring war and the war method. Their views are better known than the positions of those who treat war empirically and specifically. Their arguments, as A. C. Knudson has acutely shown,[7] reduce to three: (1) the argument from human nature, war is justifiable because man is a warlike animal;[8] (2) the argument from the nature of the state as a power, to preserve sovereignty and avoid anarchism, a nation must engage in war (the theory follows inevitably from the dynamic nature of the state itself); (3) the argument from the positive value of war, war contributes to the human race, ennobles character, and promotes culture.

There is no need to evaluate these arguments here. It is doubtful if anyone today would make serious use of them. An apologia for war based on them is, as Knudson says,

> at bottom a phase of philosophical irrationalism. It is a surrender to the tyranny of the past, a passionate devotion to a fading ideal and a blind faith in mere power arrayed against a rational and moral philosophy of state and human life.[9]

Among the varying responsibilities philosophers felt they had with regard to specific wars, one may detect the following: (1) studied aloofness—which invariably means tacit acceptance; (2) overt defense of a particular national policy; (3) reluctant and even hesitant justification; and (4) direct criticism with or without a consideration of alternatives. No systematic study or tabulation of philosophers' attitudes has been made,[10] but we can cite some interesting examples of each of these positions.

1. A look at the standard philosophical journals of the various war years is revealing. G. F. Stout and G. E. Moore edited *Mind* during World War I and World War II, respectively. There was not a single essay or discussion of war in that journal during those periods. Nor were there any articles directly on the topic of war and peace in the *Philosphical Review* between 1914 and 1918,[11] and only four appeared in the same journal between 1939 and 1945. The *Journal of Philosophy* carried three specific articles on war during each world war, and the *Journal of Philosophy and Phenomenological Research* contained nothing on war or peace during its first years, 1940–1945. *Philosophy* carried twelve articles on war during that period and editorially supported the war, as did the *Personalist,* which had eleven of similar nature between 1939 and 1945. As might be ex-

pected, more sustained discussion of war and peace occurred in the *International Journal of Ethics* during both wars, with thirty-six and ten articles, respectively. Earlier there was discussion of the Spanish–American War.

2. Open support for specific national policy in wartime has been forthcoming from a number of philosophers. In 1813, for example, Fichte delivered a lecture entitled "*Ueber den Begriff des wahrhaftigen Krieges*" to encourage the Prussians fighting Napoleon. (This particular defense was of course linked with Fichte's overall philosophy of state.) Prominent Harvard philosophy professors openly supported the Allied cause in both world wars. At the beginning of World War I, Josiah Royce considered ways to prevent war in his *War and Insurance* but was so stunned by the fall of Belgium and the sinking of the *Lusitania* that he became an active opponent of Germany and saw the struggle as "the cause of mankind,"[12] exclaiming:

> But now, while the war lasts, and Belgium bleeds, and mankind mourns, let us aid the allied enemies of Germany with sympathy since the cause of the allied enemies of Germany is the cause of mankind . . . let us be ashamed of ourselves that we cannot even now stand beside Belgium, and suffer with her for our duty and for mankind.[13]

Ralph Barton Perry wrote and spoke in defense of both wars, attacking Russell's pacifism[14] in the first and writing three books on behalf of the second, the title of one being *Our Side Is Right*.[15] (Heidegger would probably have been willing to write under the same title for Germany in the 1940's.) William E. Hocking devoted considerable time to the support of both world wars, busying himself with problems of morale in the first,[16] during which he gave lectures in the trenches, and participating in the second by lecturing at the Naval War College and writing semipopular essays seeking to convince Americans of their duties in the perspective of history and the thought patterns of the world.[17] Thus, he wrote:

> One difference between this war and the last is that this time there is a whole planet to be put in order . . . What we require now is to turn our native characteristics and qualities of temperament into a positive policy and keep our present appointment with destiny.[18]

Numerous other philosophers wrote in defense of their nations' stand in either or both world wars and on both sides.

3. Reluctant and hesitating justification of various wars has been expressed by some philosophers who did not feel that either of the world wars was doing very much for mankind in general but thought that particular enemies should be stopped as a "lesser evil." John Dewey, sympathetic to the views of his friend, Quaker pacifist Jane Addams, saw World War I as the lesser of two evils, not as some great cause for humanity.[19] And Bertrand Russell lent his support to World War II but had no illusions about it as humanity's great struggle.

4. Direct general criticism of war and the military method has been uncommon. The most famous case was, of course, that of Bertrand Russell in World War I. He charged, "no single of the combatants is justified in the present war."[20] Earlier, Felix Adler vigorously examined United States policy and conduct in the Spanish-American War and opposed it.[21] Similarly, Herbert Welsh openly criticized his country in "The Ethics of Our Philippine Policy," noting "we have here every condition which justifies the assertion that this was a war of criminal aggression."[22] Morris Cohen branded the war with Mexico as "indeed as brazen a bit of imperialism as can be found in the history of any nation."[23] In 1927, Hans Driesch affirmed:

> Practically, war today must always unconditionally be avoided, even that for the defense of neutrality. There are morally praiseworthy means which are much more effective than it, namely passive resistance and boycott.[24]

Fever was so high during World War II that there was little open opposition to it by any philosophers anywhere. There may have been philosophic opponents of the holocaust in Japan, Germany, the U.S.S.R., and France, but I never heard of any. I do know of at least eight American philosophers who were unyielding in their opposition, and some of them suffered abuse.

Only in the sixth and seventh decades of the twentieth century have philosophers in any number in the West begun to make fundamental criticisms of the war method. Lord Russell has spent recent years in opposing nuclear armaments and warning men of the doom to come if international tension issues in armed conflict. He sounds an urgent note in his *Common Sense and Nuclear Warfare* and *Has Man a Future?* A nonogenarian, he has forthrightly opposed the Vietnam War, though perhaps more as a pamphleteer than as a philosopher.[25] Jean-Paul Sartre's anti-war stand is well known. Abraham Heschel has taken a stand against all war and has written specifically on "The Moral Outrage in Vietnam."[26] In an unprecedented action, at its 1966 Christmas meeting, the Eastern Division of the American Philosophical Association approved by a strong majority a resolution criticizing the military action of the United States in Vietnam.[27] In May, 1967, the Western Division passed by a vote of 123 to 42 a strongly worded resolution characterizing the Vietnam War as "a moral crisis in the history of our country."[28] Never before in human history have philosophers united in such strong numbers in opposing their nation's war activity. The attitude for centuries has been mute acceptance of one's country's military adventures or overt defense of them. But the

Vietnam War and the threat of nuclear war have stimulated such an awareness of the issues of war and peace among philosophers that it is unlikely that they will ever again assume their previous stance. Yet even this is not a repudiation of war as such. It reflects a certain revulsion against a particular war.

One might well ask here why it is that philosophers have been so long in becoming critical of the institution of war and why some are still reluctant to repudiate all war. This question takes on more significance when one realizes that philosophers have long ago repudiated such other institutions as slavery and duelling. Apologias for the former could be heard just over a century ago and for the latter, two centuries ago. Some philosophers today accept the war system even though they do not glorify war or see it as a natural process of a sovereign state.

Why, then, has there been such an unwillingness to examine war critically and why have philosophers in such numbers tended to favor war with a unanimity that is not found in any other areas of interest? A number of factors may be involved, and we must enter cautiously into the arena of social and historical causality. We can get some illumination by noting a parallel case. Two of the most eminent minds of all history, Plato and Aristotle, never raised to the level of sustained reflection and criticism the established institution of slavery. They lived in a civilization that had slavery as its economic base. Legally, slaves were not regarded as persons and had no rights. Though Aristotle wrote in his will that his slaves should be freed upon his death, it was unheard of to question slavery itself. As Whitehead astutely remarks:

> But neither the humane slave-owners, nor the inspired Plato nor the clear-headed lawyers initiated any campaign against slavery. They accepted it as a matter of course. It was pre-

supposed in the very structure of society; and such necessity limits the scope of all generalities.[29]

The same is true of the method of war and the institution of the military. Reliance on armed might as a way of dealing with real or pretended enemies of the state is as deeply rooted and persistent in Western culture today as slavery was in ancient times. "War is as much a social pattern as is the domestic slavery which the ancients thought to be an immutable fact," notes John Dewey.[30] And military ways of doing things have not ordinarily been viewed by most philosophers with any more alarm than that slavery occasioned Plato or Aristotle. Philosophers began speaking out against slavery in the eighteenth and nineteenth centuries, and it is virtually gone today. There has been no comparable opposition or even sustained critical examination of the institution of the military. Nations as well as philosophers still continue to assert that military solutions to political and economic problems are the soundest and in the last resort the most effective way to stop the encroachment of hostile values. Military metaphors and language are commonplace in philosophical writing. Military units inhabit college campuses. And at least one American philosopher offered a defense of Universal Military Training, "which could be led up to from the sixth or seventh grade of the elementary school."[31] It is instructive to note the disdain with which what might be called "Establishment" philosophers greet the assertions of Bertrand Russell about nuclear armaments and the Vietnam War. Yet while his views are, to be sure, controversial, they spring from a passion for humanity and an apparently rational perspective on nationalism and war.

Of course when the intellectual leaders of organized religions, namely, Judaism, Christianity, and Islam, have sanctioned and still do sanction the use of armed violence in self-defense and for the sake of dearly held values,[32] it is hard to expect philosophers to assume leadership in critically judging war.

Again, philosophers themselves have been involved with the military system. Some such as Fichte, LaMettrie, Helmholtz, and Descartes were directly engaged in military activities. German general Hans Speidel, a professor at Tübingen, was one of Rommel's officers in the last war. More famous was Jan Christian Smuts, a general with marked philosophical interests. In his quest for a peaceful "Holistic" universe he was able to view World War I as "at bottom a struggle for the Good, a wild striving for human betterment. . . . Holism is at work even in the conflicts and confusions of men. . . . Immeasurable sacrifices have not been in vain."[33] Numerous philosophers now at work in Britain and America gave their allegiance to their nations in wartime. Some participated in both wars, joining in the wave of national fervor without much critical questioning. Having participated nobly in war is a prestigious thing, and it is an item of some modest commercial value in book advertisements. It is hard to imagine that current American, British, Soviet, Italian, German, and Japanese philosophers who took an active part in recent wars, enjoy the prestige of the veteran, draw military pensions, and perhaps retain "reserve status" can look with unjaundiced eye at the military and the war system itself. The late T. V. Smith, who took leave as coeditor of *Ethics* in order to serve in World War II, openly supported the war system during the time of the Korean conflict, even with a dash of romanticism.[34] And while others may not offer apologias for war, they do not come forward with fundamental ethical criticisms, either. War is not a precluded topic for them; it is just not preferred.

Of course there is always a personal risk involved in subjecting national military policies and practices to critical reflection, particularly if one's country is at war and especially if one's homeland does not have a free market in ideas. When Bertrand Russell struck out against the Great War in 1915, he did not increase his popularity.[35] If there were others, they lacked his courage. There may be some little truth in Porter Sargent's observation about intellectuals in wartime:

> Some seem lacking in the vitamins that bring intellectual courage and are inclined to see the thing, hear the thing, speak the thing that will preserve their immediate security and bring them immediate reward.[36]

Honest timidity is surely understandable—but then one thinks of Socrates. It may be that the unexamined military way of dealing with things is not worth supporting under any conditions.

But we should ask whether it really is the philosopher's duty to consider the problem of war. Interest in social and political questions has not been a dominant feature in the thought of most historic figures in philosophy. Some have avoided such discussions—and not without reason. The desire both to see things under the aspect of eternity and to engage in careful conceptual analysis does not seem compatible with interest in problems of national policy or specific courses of action. When philosophers give their efforts to some immediate social problem, they tend to subordinate philosophical perspective to social necessity. The result might be injurious to philosophy itself. Accordingly, philosophers in their professional capacities often wish to remain free from involvement in political or social criticism.

Any professor of philosophy knows what this tension means in the area of individual ethics. An academician cannot hope, or try, to help students solve their own specific problems, telling them how to vote, how much to invest, or what to do when arrested. Practical exigencies cannot dictate philosophical activity or philosophy itself disappears. At the beginning of World War II, Elijah Jordan cogently wrote: "The role of philosophy in times of crisis is the same as its role at any other time."[37] One cannot press philosophy into specific service for some urgent need. And yet such a course of action has been followed, and in the case of war philosophers have usually become spokesmen for the military.

A philosopher worthy of the name cannot omit from consideration depth issues that are raised by immediate human needs and problems. Though he may not be expected to pass explicit judgment on specific matters, he may reasonably be expected to point out underlying issues, call attention to the type of questions that are relevant, and suggest some of the social and practical implications. It is obviously better to deal with actual historical examples in discussion than it is to manufacture textbook conundrums about proposed cannibalism in isolated lifeboats. C. E. M. Joad once noted that philosophers

> should occupy themselves with topical concerns not . . . take up a topical attitude . . . [for] some of the problems which lie at the root of our contemporary discontents are in the strict sense philosophical problems.[38]

Now, the fundamental problem of the day is how to avoid nuclear war, which would eventuate in the death of civilization. Cool-headed scientists are seriously worried, but philosophers have not shared their concern. The war issue is crucial. It may well be, as John Somerville has said: "We may not have much time in which to solve it. We ought to put it in the center of our work."[39] We must demur from Sidney Hook's odd question-begging prescription for philosophical wisdom in this matter. Hook proposes that to be wise about war and peace the philosopher "must study military technology and the theory and practice of communism, including its strategic exploitation of peace movements to disarm the free world."[40] Philosophers' duties regarding war and peace are broader than this, and we must turn now to an examination of several areas of responsibility that are germane to the philosophic vocation.

1. One duty the philosopher has is to clear up the confusing and misleading language of politics and value that surrounds war and the war method. Each war, of course, has its propaganda backing, and logicians might well engage in propaganda analysis, but this is more the province of the psychologist and social scientist. The philosopher needs to explore the concepts used by thoughtful people as they talk about war. In World War I, the Allied powers talked about making the world "safe for democracy," and since the beginning of World War II, there has been unending talk of freedom. President Roosevelt spoke of the "Four Freedoms," and as the war wore on, we heard that certain towns were "liberated" from nazi, fascist, or Japanese control. Today, there is a good deal of talk about the "free world." Sidney Hook has said that "the very willingness to go down fighting in defense of freedom may be the greatest force for peace when facing an opponent who makes a fetish out of historical survival."[41] But what does freedom really mean? Liberation from capture, abstract rights, economic individualism, a form of government, political structure? Are all types of freedom equally desirable? There has probably never been a military unit anywhere that has not been told it was fighting for freedom of one sort or another. While Britain spoke of "liberating" people from nazi tyranny, it maintained a colonial empire that denied "freedom" to millions of people. While "free" enterprise prevails in South Africa, there is not even "freedom" of movement for blacks in that tragic country. At the same time, nations Westerners hold to be quite lacking in "freedom"

declare themselves to be democracies and their armed forces are viewed as "liberators." Totalitarian states that favor the West are seen to be part of the "free world." A nation may spend billions defending "freedom" thousands of miles from its shores while its own citizens are not free from harassment because of skin color or free from the encroachments of a military-industrial complex—which regards itself as a "bulwark of freedom." One might ask: Does fighting for freedom really mean killing for social change? Can the philosopher come to the aid of ordinary mortals by clarifying such words as "freedom," "honor,"[42] "service," "loyalty," "aggressor," and "patriotism"?

2. Akin to this task is the duty of the philosopher to sift out truth and expose lies and fallacies in times of tension or conflict. What are the real issues and questions dividing nations? This sifting is the general responsibility of all intellectuals, Noam Chomsky claims,[43] and it is a special duty of philosophers. Philosophical perspective maintained in wartime can dispel myths that imply, for example, that the total enemy population is inhuman. J. H. Muirhead saw as one of his responsibilities, during World War II, the clarification of who exactly was the enemy.[44] But philosophers have not always maintained such a perspective. They have behaved naively and without knowledge of the complex factors involved in international conflict. Josiah Royce, in formulating what he took to be the duties of Americans in World War I, spoke of Belgium's "sacrifice for mankind" and of Belgium's "noble and unsparing self-sacrifice for international honor."[45] At the same time, the great Plato scholar Wilamowitz-Moellendorf said quite the opposite, from a German vantage point: "What has come to light out of the Belgian soul? How it has revealed itself as the soul of cowardice and treachery!"[46]

During the heat of World War II, some thinkers held that the war was a battle of philosophies, that philosophers should "come forward unmistakably as protagonists in the cause of humanity."[47] And at least one wrote that "part of philosophical argument is forged not in libraries and before writing tables, but in armament factories, aerodromes and shell proof trenches."[48] From one point of view, it may be possible to say this, and yet must it not be exposed as a verbal gloss to hide the empirical inhumanity and brutality of war itself? Instead of saying that two philosophies are struggling, might it not be wiser to say that two groups are killing each other: each one thinks the other is an aggressor, and each one thinks it is defending civilization? The most efficient killer will win.

It may be that the justification of enormous military establishments today is based on a similar fallacy that great principles are involved and that the only way they can be fostered and defended is by means of war threat. If a war threat is not introduced, hostile values will dominate. That there are military cliques, prestige groups, and industrial interests making capital out of this interpretation goes without saying. Philosophers need to probe deeply before claiming that conflicts between nations are at base philosophical.

3. There is also a need to examine anew and test the validity of the standard arguments that have been used in the past half-century to justify and condone war. Though no one today would suggest that war is intrinsically beneficial, most philosophers still view it as a necessary evil instrument in the attainment of some desirable end, even if that end is only self-defense. This idea of a necessary evil means to a desirable goal is then linked with (a) altruism and (b) idealism.

A. The *altruistic* form of the argument runs: Great harm is being done or is likely to be done to some relatively innocent people (maybe ourselves) by some group ruthlessly bent on selfish ends. We must defend ourselves or others to protect them from the evil force that will destroy or enslave them. Failure to engage in war would violate our duty and result in evils far worse than the temporary evil of war itself. Or to say it differently, one sees his own nation as the champion of humanity fighting against forces that threaten slavery and brutality. One does not fight for markets or for territories or for property but in self-defense or to defend the innocent and weak against an aggressor.

B. When this altruistic emphasis is linked with *idealism*, the argument seems incontrovertible. Accordingly, a given war is seen as the only way to preserve the great ideals and values of mankind. The fight is more than a defense of ourselves or other people. It is a battle for great principles without which "life would not be worth living."[49] There are some values greater than life itself, and these great principles must be preserved no matter what the cost. Currently, some thinkers are quite prepared to risk nuclear chaos in order that ideal principles will not be thwarted. This version of the justification for war is heard so frequently that it begins to have the status of one of those holy truths of mankind no sane person would dare challenge. Whether the argument is relevant anymore, if it ever was, is something that needs to be looked into by a cautious philosophical mind. Philosophers by the hundreds have rushed to the colors, in both East and West, with apologias of this sort. They have often become spokesmen for the military, handmaidens of national policy, providing a rationale and strengthening morale.[50] Even acute thinkers who have recognized how philosophy in the past has been used often as a tool to sanction support for the church and theology fail to recognize that their uncritical rallying to the cause of the nation-state amounts to the same thing. Apparently it is easier to recognize philosophy as a tool of the church than it is to identify it as a tool of the warring state.

We may ask a few questions of both the altruistic and idealistic apologias for war. The argument from altruism is based on an individualist analogy. Surely a neighbor would rush to the aid of an innocent child who was being attacked by some brute? And might he not be willing to use any force necessary to quash the molester? But is it the same between nations? Bertrand Russell once wrote: "We all recognize the need to restrain murderers and it is even more important to restrain murderous states."[51] But does this analogy hold? The dynamics and motives of nations are not as patent as the ruffian's, but the very language of aggression and defense is used by all nations and perpetuates what is evidently a false analogy.

The idealistic facet of the argument assumes that there is little or no relation between means and ends, that certain shocking acts such as the bombing of Coventry or Dresden or the dropping of atomic bombs are ethically defensible if they bring about some desired goal. Does the means used affect the goal sought? Can one further democracy by undemocratic means? Has any war been "successful" in promoting the ends its intellectual defenders proclaimed it was seeking? All that success seems to mean in war is that the opponent has been stopped, not that any ideals have been preserved. Indeed, wars ruin ideals for both sides.[52]

The retort can be made that the real reasons for war are not altruistic or idealistic but that one fights out of necessity.[53] And we hear the disjunctive proposition: Either we will militarily oppose the hostile force by threat if not by action or we will have to acquiesce in his totalitarian control. Proponents of the proposition, however, seldom seriously raise the question of further alternatives.[54] The same either/or approach is heard repeatedly, and there is little recognition of other options. The doctrine of nonviolent resistance is discounted before it is studied, often being falsely equated with mere passivity. It may not be the answer, but the greater number of non-Oriental philosophers know very little indeed about active nonviolent resistance, the techniques of the general strike, boycott, massive civil disobedience, and the like.

One needs to ask those who believe in dying and killing for abstract ideals such as honor and freedom whether the preservation of values in general is really more important than the continuation of civilization, where while values may indeed be halted for a time they then possibly may evolve again. If we take a moment to think the unthinkable with Herman Kahn, we quickly see that a major war now would mean the virtual end of life and civilization. What would really be left after a nuclear war? I suppose some wonderful values would remain. Honor would be around; men would have died and killed in the noble effort to preserve freedom; but there would be no human life to indulge these cherished values. Force would have been met with force; great heroes would have arisen; evil would have been thwarted, the innocent defended, the right vindicated, and so on. But to what end?

4. Another duty of the philosopher is to give fresh attention to the problem of human values. In the past, wars have been justified because they allegedly promote worthwhile values or forestall evil. Is this really so? Modern war violates all personal values, as do the very preparation for war and the very institution of the military. When a nation's economy is geared for war rather than toward peace, the outlook on the rights and value of the individual suffers. The purposes of the warfare state take precedence over the fulfillment of the individual's needs and longings. Personal values become subordinated to the machine of the state. Moral sensitivity is blighted. The arms race distorts the moral sense.[55]

The use of anti-personnel bombs or of napalm on civilians, practices of present-day war, would have been utterly abhorrent to apologists for World War I in 1914. But in the name of "necessity" and "freedom" and "self-defense" nations have not only contemplated and threatened the use of nuclear bombs and missiles but are contriving and experimenting with techniques of biological warfare by means of which populations would be decimated by disease. Those who know of such things firsthand, the scientists, have become in some countries the outspoken critics of their governments. Indeed, scientists more than some philosophers and even religious leaders have become intensely concerned with human values and have tried to alert the citizenry to such goings on in such publications as *The Bulletin of the Atomic Scientists, The Minority of One*, or periodicals from the Council for a Livable World.

C. Wright Mills suggests that the duty of the intellectual in these days is to "cultivate moral sensibility and to make it knowledgeable. . . . [and] they should confront the whole attitude toward war, they should teach new views on it."[56] There is room for philosophical activity and perspective here.

5. There is also the duty to examine the meaning of justice in the context of war. Does the threat of nuclear annihilation change the meaning of justice and responsibility? What of the individual's obligation to the state in such a situation? How many Continental philosophers have given serious attention to the ethical questions of the right to conscientious objection and civil disobedience? Nations long enamored of military prowess that boast about the loyalty of conscripted young men tend to be conservative on such matters.

Wars have often been defended on the ground that they were for the cause of justice. Is it conceivable that justice will be a fruit of any future war? John Somerville asks:

"What concept of human justice would be compatible with the total annihilation of all actual and potential human values?"[57] And what now of the idea of a "just" war?[58]

Similarly, the deeper question of international justice and international tribunals for those who allegedly commit crimes against humanity needs fresh treatment. It is hard to think that loyal soldiers of one's own nation could ever be guilty of "war crimes," but it is easy to think that dutiful members of an enemy nation could well be culprits.

6. It behooves philosophers to review the ethical and value presuppositions of the so-called conventional wisdom of military deterrence and to raise doubts about the time-honored means of dealing with enemies. It is not at all clear, as Sidney Hook has maintained, that the "balance of terror" may be less tragic than other alternatives in opposing the "enemies of freedom."[59] Must not the philosopher engage in some clear-headed thinking on what an enemy is? Perhaps *war* is a greater enemy of man than any nation. Might he not give consideration to nonmilitary alternatives? The military method is a "given" in almost every social order. Its ethical implications need to be examined in a sustained and critical way. To be sure, there have been long discussions of international law and international organizations, even federations, but the resort to armed violence seems always to be an intrinsic part of such considerations. It may be that a Copernican Revolution is needed in the philosophy of war and peace, though the prospects do not seem immediately forthcoming.

In writing on war some years ago, John Dewey gave high praise to William James's essay "The Moral Equivalent of War" and added: "Certain basic needs and emotions are permanent. But they are capable of finding expression in ways that are radically different from the ways in which they currently operate."[60] And Dewey held out hope that insight into the psychological, sociological, and economic conditions producing war would yield to new methods of treatment. There is room for experiment.

It is unfortunately true that many philosophers have evinced considerable naiveté on social causality and have not as a group gone much beyond the simplistic analysis of human events one finds in the pages of *Time* magazine. The ease with which they oversimplified the issues in World Wars I and II illustrates this. The duty to examine alternatives to the military approach seems ineluctable.

7. There remains another responsibility philosophers have on the question of war. In one of the few systematic treatments of the problem, A. C. Knudson remarks that the apologetic for war

> has given the warlike spirit a theoretical right of way which has led peoples to drift or plunge into war when a less acquiescent or fatalistic attitude toward the war system might have enabled them to avert it.[61]

If this is the case, then, in a sense, the war method too often wins by default. Into the stream of culture and the ways of thinking of ordinary citizens the philosopher must introduce the products of his reflection. He must perform the service of destroying myths that tend to sanctify the war system, and he must assist in promoting constructive ideas for meeting conflicts creatively and without violence.

It is difficult to assess how a culture changes. Kant believed there was inherent in nature a principle of moral progress making for peace. But we do not wish to get involved in the knotty problems of the philosophy of history. It is true that institutions and practices once accepted socially and regarded as quite natural, even necessary, have been eradicated in a span of years. It is unimaginable that anyone anywhere today would defend the practice of slavery or the custom of duelling. Similarly, capital punishment is becoming harder to justify and penal systems that are primarily punitive and retributive are losing ground. What factors bring about such changes?[62] Surely philosophers cannot claim much credit. Nevertheless, W. T. Stace once wrote "their ideas, secretly infiltrating among the masses are among the forces which drive civilization. Plato has had more influence on the destiny of men than the inventor of the steam engine."[63]

Failure on the part of philosophers to discuss war and its alternatives critically makes it easier for unthinking prejudice and mindless practices to succeed. One wonders how things would have fared in Germany four decades or so ago if leading philosophers had openly challenged and debated the presuppositions of incipient Hitlerism.

Contributions that philosophers may make to the question of war may be modest, but to refuse the endeavor seems likely to ensure that thinking will be done by others who have neither the training nor the skills to deal with the problem creatively. Customary ideologies win by default.

Doubtless other reasons could be adduced to establish the philosopher's duty to treat the problem of war. What rejoinders could there be? One could urge that philosophers are not social reformers, and this of course is true (but the proposals we have set forth deal with issues and attitudes, not specific plans for reform). Or it might be said that philosophers should not consider topics better left to experts in political and military matters (but are there really any experts on fundamental moral issues such as war?). Again, it might be said that no matter what philosophers say or think, the deeply entrenched military method will still operate in the real activities of men (besides being defeatist, this is also question begging).

Naturally there is some risk involved when a philosopher seeks to view the war method with a critical eye and in broad perspective. There is the minor risk of being unnerved and upset by controversial discussion and the major risk, particularly in some parts of the world, of being subject to investigation, penalty, and even punishment. Centuries ago scientists took risks for the sake of truth and were regarded sometimes as enemies of the people. Philosophers who dissect the military might also be so regarded. Galileo would have been better off personally if he had confined his attention to terrestrial physics rather than to astronomy. It takes little effort to see why philosophers today find more satisfaction in abstract technical questions than in considering the ethics of social change. If novels and even symphonies are criticized in some lands today because they do not purvey a proper political perspective, how much more likely is it that philosophic treatises that challenge the "geocentric" view of war will get into trouble?

To the thinker who avers that the war question is not a fit subject for philosophical investigation, we have no answer. He divorces himself from humanity. And it may be that he has confused professional responsibility with timidity.

NOTES

1. G. J. Heering claims that the fall of Christianity began with the acceptance of the war method after Constantine. *See* his *The Fall of Christianity*, trans. Thompson (New York: Fellowship Publications, 1943). Originally published in Dutch in 1928.

2. *See* his "Against Celsus," in C. J. Cadoux, *Christian Pacifism Re-Examined* (Oxford: Blackwell, 1940), pp. 232–240. *See also* the more accessible "Origen Against Violence," in Mulford Sibley (ed.), *The Quiet Battle* (Garden City, N. Y.: Doubleday, 1963), pp. 16–17.

3. *See* Leo Tolstoy, *The Law of Love and the Law of Violence*, trans. Mary Koutouzow Tolstoy (New York: Rudolph Field, 1948), *and* Aldous Huxley, *Ends and Means* (New York: Harpers, 1937).

4. Rev. ed. London: Routledge, 1938. First published in 1935, revised again in 1944. A similar volume is Clarence M. Case's *Non-Violent Coersion* (London: Allen & Unwin, 1923).

5. First published by the Princeton University Press in 1958. Rev. ed., Berkeley: University of California Press, 1967.

6. *See* the bibliography of *ibid.*, pp. 250–255.

7. A. C. Knudson, *The Philosophy of War and Peace* (New York: Abingdon, 1947). These arguments occur on pp. 20 f, 28 f, and 36 f, respectively.

8. Even while otherwise justifying war, Julian Huxley says: "War, far from being a universal law of nature or even a common occurrence, is a very rare exception among living creatures; and where it occurs, it is either associated with another phenomenon, almost equally rare, the amassing of property, or with territorial rights." *On Living in a Revolution* (New York: Harpers, 1942), p. 77.

9. A. C. Knudson, *op. cit.*, pp. 47 f.

10. One specific study was made by George W. Hartman in an article entitled: "The Strengths and Weaknesses of the Pacifist Position as Seen by American Philosophers," *Philosophical Review*, 53 (1943), 125–144. The findings showed that those quizzed were definitely on the side of war, and observations of the following type were reported: "If there weren't soldiers there wouldn't be any chance to be a pacifist." *See also* Merle Curti's interesting article "The American Scholar in Three Wars," *Journal of the History of Ideas*, 3 (June, 1942), 241–264. Curti detects four basic attitudes of scholars toward the Revolution, the Civil War, and World War I and points out how pugnacious scholars were in 1917. "Before we formally entered the war, American scholars by and large were already in it." (p. 247)

11. There were two articles on the state and its authority and in some issues there appeared reports from A. Lalande on philosophical activity in France—which was primarily anti-German.

12. J. Royce, *The Hope of the Great Community* (New York: Macmillan, 1916), p. 12. He also wrote: "I should be a poor professor of philosophy and in particular of moral philosophy if I left my class in the least doubt as to how I view such things." (p. 16)

13. *Ibid.*, pp. 12 f. He even urged "a rupture of all diplomatic relations between our republic and those foes of mankind." (p. 13) On the other hand, Bertrand Russell wrote: "Our sympathy with Belgium should make us hate war rather than Germany," "The Ethics of War," *Ethics*, 25 (1914–1915), 131.

14. R. B. Perry, "Non-Resistance and the War," *Ethics*, 25 (1914–1915), 307–316.

15. Harvard University Press, 1942. The others were: *Shall Not Perish From the Earth* (1940) and *On All Fronts* (1941). Later Perry wrote: *One World in the Making* (New York: Current Books, 1945). Perry was a major in World War I.

16. Cf. his *Morale and Its Enemies* (New Haven: Yale University Press, 1918).

17. Cf. his "A New East in a New World," *Fortune*, 26 (Aug., 1942), 107–131.

18. W. E. Hocking, "America's World Purpose," *Life*, 16 (Apr. 17, 1944), 112.

19. *See* the biography of Dewey in Paul A. Schilpp (ed.), *The Philosophy of John Dewey* (New York: Tudor, 1939), p. 30.

20. Bertrand Russell, "The Ethics of War," *op. cit.*, p. 127.

21. Felix Adler, "The Parting of the Ways in the Foreign Policy of the United States," *Ethics*, 9 (1898–1899), 1–12.

22. In *Ethics*, 10 (1899–1900), 314.

23. Morris Cohen, *American Thought* (New York: Collier, 1962), p. 16.

24. Hans Driesch, *Die sittliche Tat* (Leipzig: Reinecke, 1927), p. 117. I owe this citation to E. S. Brightman, *Moral Laws* (New York: Abingdon, 1933), p. 240.

25. *See* the pamphlet issued by *Liberation* magazine in New York, "Appeal to the American Conscience," 1966.

26. A. Heschel, in *Fellowship*, 32 (Sept., 1966), 24–26.

27. The resolution, introduced by Gregory Vlastos and Hilary Putnam, read: "The traditions of our vocation make it appropriate that we express our concern on issues of great moral urgency. We feel that the war in Vietnam is such an issue. Accordingly, we deplore any attempt to settle the fate of Vietnam by purely military means and strongly oppose further escalation." *Proceedings of the American Philosophical Association*, 40 (1966–1967), 90. At their meeting at the same time, the Pacific Division solicited signatures for an anti-war petition.

28. *Ibid.*, p. 108.

29. A. N. Whitehead, *Adventures of Ideas* (New York: Macmillan, 1933), p. 17.

30. John Dewey, *Problems of Men* (New York: Philosophical Library, 1946), p. 186. One might also call attention to racism as a more subtle presupposition of culture in the United States. The number of professional philosophers among blacks is probably not even two score.

31. This neo-Prussian aberration appeared during the Korean War and was proposed by H. M. Kallen in "UMT and the Nation's Schools in the Religion of Democracy," *Ethics*, 62 (1937), 9.

32. It is interesting to note that these three religions categorically oppose suicide, but not the killing of other persons in wartime. *See* E. S. Brightman, *op. cit.*, p. 217.

33. Jan Smuts, *Holism and Evolution* (New York: Macmillan, 1926). Reprinted by Viking in 1961, p. 344.

34. T. V. Smith, "Ethics for Soldiers of Freedom," *Ethics*, 60 (Apr., 1950),

157–168. This article includes the statement: "I have made bold to advise soldiers, under defined circumstances, to forget ethics." (p. 160)

35. In his *Autobiography* (Boston: Little, Brown, 1967), Russell notes how McTaggart disliked him for his opinions on the war and eventually took a leading part in removing him from his lectureship at Cambridge. (p. 84) Bosanquet was more open and wrote to Hoernle in June of 1916: "I wonder where Russell will end up. . . . His views about the war are not unreasonable I think; but the steps he has got involved in are undesirable." Muirhead (ed.), *Bernard Bosanquet and His Friends* (London: Allen & Unwin, 1935), p. 190.

36. Porter Sargent, *War and Education* (Boston: Porter Sargent, 1943), p. 357.

37. Elijah Jordan, "Philosophy in Social Crisis," *Ethics*, 51 (1940–1941), 379.

38. C. E. M. Joad, "Appeal to Philosophers," *Philosophy*, 15 (1940), 410.

39. John Somerville, "Democracy and the Problem of War," *The Humanist*, 27 (May–June, 1967), 4. This paper was read at the Seventh Inter-American Congress of Philosophy in Quebec (June, 1967).

40. Sidney Hook, "Pragmatism and the Tragic Sense of Life," *Proceedings of the American Philosophical Association*, 33 (1960), 8.

41. *Ibid.*, p. 25.

42. Over fifty years ago, Bertrand Russell wrote: "It is perhaps not too much to hope that the day may come when the honor of nations, like that of individuals, will no longer be measured by their willingness to inflict slaughter." "The Ethics of War," *Ethics*, 25 (1914–1915), 141.

43. N. Chomsky, "The Responsibility of Intellectuals," *New York Review of Books*, 8 (Feb. 23, 1967), 16–26.

44. J. H. Muirhead, "With Whom Are We at War?" *Philosophy*, 15 (1940), 3–6. After World War I, Bosanquet similarly opposed popular appeals to "punish the Germans."

45. J. Royce, *op. cit.*, p. 12.

46. I owe this quotation to G. J. Heering, *op. cit.*, p. 141.

47. Sydney Hooper, "Why We Are at War," *Philosophy*, 14 (1939), 385.

48. P. Kohnstamm, "Personalism and the World Situation," *Personalist*, 20 (1939), 360.

49. With a complete lack of philosophical perspective, R. T. Flewelling wrote in 1918: "Men know full well that if Germany were in any sense to win this war, no spot on God's earth would be worth living in." *Philosophy and the War* (New York: Abingdon, 1918), p. 38.

50. Note Julian Huxley's remark: "The truer our philosophy, the more complete and the more efficiently it is applied to the circumstances of war . . . the more it will help us to formulate peace aims which will be not merely satisfying, but themselves an efficient weapon of war." *Op. cit.*, p. 56.

51. B. Russell, *Unpopular Essays* (New York: Simon & Schuster, 1950), p. 44.

52. "The common doom of opposite ideals is the usual though not the invariable penalty of supporting ideals by force," said Russell, "The Ethics of War," *Ethics*, 25 (1914–1915), 137.

53. Necessity is another idea that merits examination. Senator Fulbright notes that the United States has fought wars that were unjust, unnecessary, or both and suggests "The War of 1812, the Civil War and the Spanish–American War as examples of wars that were at least unnecessary." *The Arrogance of Power* (New York: Vintage, 1967), p. 36. J. Narveson in "Pacifism: A Philosophical Analysis," *Ethics*, 75 (1964–1965), 259–271, makes some striking observations about the matter of self-defense and the defense of others.

54. This is the case in F. S. Northedge's article, "Peace, War, and Philosophy," in *The Encyclopedia of Philosophy*, Vol. VI (New York: Macmillan & Free Press, 1967), p. 66.

55. Bertrand Russell, *Has Man a Future?* (Baltimore: Penguin, 1961), p. 34.

56. C. Wright Mills, *The Causes of World War Three* (New York: Ballantine, 1960), p. 151.

57. J. Somerville, *op. cit.*, p. 4.

58. E. I. Watkin has observed: "If the rules laid down by Catholic theologians in the past are true, no war can in future be justified on whatever issue. For it can be waged only by a method so immoral that a more immoral method can hardly be conceived." In Rufus Jones (ed.), *The Church, the Gospel and War* (New York: Harpers, 1948), p. 117.

59. S. Hook, *op. cit.*, p. 25.

60. J. Dewey, *op. cit.*, p. 189.

61. A. C. Knudson, *op. cit.*, p. 49.

62. For an interesting treatment of this question, *see* A. N. Whitehead, *op. cit.*, ch. ii, §§7, 8.

63. W. T. Stace, "The Philosophical Issues Involved in the War," *Philosophy*, 16 (1941), 242.

CHAPTER TWO

Philosophers as Warriors

Edwin A. Burtt

*Sage Professor of Philosophy,
Cornell University*

How should philosophic truth be sought?

This fundamental question has challenged philosophers throughout the history of their enterprise. The answers explicitly offered vary, and usually the answer is implicit only—it is revealed by their way of philosophizing. An answer almost never explicitly acknowledged, but very influential over the centuries, is that philosophic truth should be sought by fighting for it. Philosophers have tried to fill their role in life and thought by becoming successful warriors.

Since such a view of philosophic method is rather unfamiliar, evidence for it is needed. Let us prepare the ground for presenting it by a quick survey of the evolution of philosophic methods in Western thought.

Passing over the early methods that were not explicitly avowed, the first method to gain conscious articulation seems to have been the Socratic dialectic, immortalized in the dialogues of Plato. A simple statement of its distinctive character appears in the opening book of *The Republic*. When discussion about the central theme of justice got under way, the question was raised as to how the discussion should be carried on. Is it to become a contest for debating supremacy between Socrates and Thrasymachus, or should it be guided by a different aim, and if the latter, what ought that aim to be? The following statement is made by Socrates as an answer to that question:

> If we give him speech for speech, recounting all the advantages which the just man enjoys, then letting him make another speech, and after that making a further speech ourselves, we shall have to count and weigh the advantages claimed in each of the speeches; and then we shall need judges to decide the matter. But if, as before, we come to an agreement between ourselves, we shall be ourselves both pleaders and judges. (I, 348.)

In the subsequent history of thought, this statement has failed to catch the attention it deserves. Part of the reason lies in the fact that in the dialogues (with one exception) Socrates easily overwhelms the other participants and appears more as an authoritative teacher of philosophic truth than as one arguer among others. Consequently, the significant ideal underlying the dialectic has been almost lost from sight: the ideal of a free discussion among seekers for truth, in which all take part and which leads, step by step, to a conclusion wholly convincing to each participant. That ideal has exercised some influence in the later course of philosophic history, especially its emphasis on free discussion, but what it implies as a solution to the problem of method is more illuminating than has as yet been generally recognized.

To be sure, as Plato portrays it, the ideal presupposes a conception of philosophic truth and of the rational mind of man that in certain important respects proved to be unjustified. The crucial mistake in the underlying conception of truth lay in the assumption that on the ultimate issues that philosophers like to discuss, as well as on those that can be settled by mathematical reckoning or common sense observation, there is a single truth capable of being demonstrated. The primary mistake in the conception of man's rational faculty lay in the assumption that it can overcome all obstructive motivations in the mind of any sincere seeker, so that he will accept such a single truth when it has been clearly presented. Largely because of the presence of these unjustified assumptions, the Socratic dialectic has been widely misinterpreted and a very significant presupposition that may be fully justified has almost escaped the attention of philosophers. They have adopted, with few exceptions, the conviction that truth should be pursued by the method of open discussion with all viewpoints having their innings. But the presupposition that the essential token of successful progress is agreement freely attained needs far more serious consideration than it has been given.

Our further survey can take the form of answering, as best we can, two questions: Why was this presupposition so easily lost? What are the essential conditions of progress toward uncoerced agreement?

The crucial answer to the first question seems to be that the history of thought has been dominated by a conception of the relation between science and philosophy such that, while the method of open discussion was in general practiced, the criterion of success was found in what appeared at any given time to be the specific requirements of science. It has been taken for granted that voluntary agreement can be dependably won only by respect for these requirements. Philosophers have played a decisive part in discovering and formulating the requirements, and when they have been formulated, for example, in logical systems and theories of empirical method, philosophers have felt under strong pressure to exemplify them fully in the philosophies proposed. Their eyes have been focused on these trusted methods rather than on the ulterior criterion of free agreement. Hence the second question, What are the essential conditions of progress toward such agreement? has been almost completely ignored, instead of occupying the center of philosophic concern as otherwise would very likely have been the case.

In this situation it is not surprising that a method has been practiced by most philosophers that preserves an arena for open discussion but in other respects is far from conducive to the winning of voluntary agreement. It is the method that in international relations is called "war" (either hot or cold). Philosophers have sought the goal of ultimate truth by becoming warriors. That this has not been more obvious is due to their special way of waging war. The belligerent art they try to practice successfully takes the form, in their field, of argumentative debate.

The words "argument" and "debate" are not pejorative terms, and that is why they are usable at this juncture. "Debate" as such is simply organized discussion of controversial topics, in which any number of concerned debaters may take part. When it is "argumentative," each debater's part is presented in a systematic logical sequence aimed at convincing those who listen or read that if certain plausible premises are accepted certain important conclusions follow. Philosophers have carried on their discussions through the centuries in this fashion; their meetings, journal articles, and books consist mainly (and often wholly) of argumentative debate.

Any contribution to the debate will be on the whole either constructive or destructive. At one extreme, it can be an expression of sincere search for truth; at the other, it can express belligerent hostility toward all who disagree. Various other motives can play a part—some in harmony with truthfulness, some not—and these motives can be mixed in various ways in any debater's mind. Hence it is difficult to pass judgment with confidence on any particular piece of argument. But when one looks at a well-selected sample of philosophical discussions with these possibilities in mind, he can hardly avoid sensing that the dominant note is more often destructive than constructive, he finds each participant acting like a fighter whose primary aim is to put his opponents to rout.

Take an argument at random. How does the author typically proceed? The overall atmosphere of tolerance for diverse viewpoints requires that established standards of courtesy be respected. So he will begin his argument with an outline sketch of the position or doctrine he is attacking. This sketch may vary all the way from a just picture, quite acceptable to those who hold that viewpoint, to a distorted portrayal, but today a high model of fair-mindedness has come to prevail. The reader or listener soon realizes, however, that this sketch is preparatory to the main purpose of the argument. The transition to its vital sector comes with the bellicose words (or some synonymous phrase): "But this will not do!" What follows that peppery pronouncement reveals the author's main aim, which is to destroy the opponent's philosophical position or at least to weaken its foundations. The underlying motive, as consciously seen by the author of the argument, is the urge to overthrow falsehood wherever it rears its head and make sure that it gets no firm seat on the philosophic throne.

What are the presuppositions behind this kind of argument?

There are many, of course. Let us focus attention on two fundamental presuppositions the unsoundness of which would be seen at once if they were clearly recognized. They are: (1) there is a universally accepted criterion of philosophic truth with which *my* viewpoint is in accord while that of my opponents is not, and (2) by aggressively attacking a fallacious viewpoint, I can show it up as such and prevent it from extending its influence. The first presupposition reveals a lack of awareness on the part of the arguer that his own unavowed premises are just as subject to critical questioning as those of his opponent, and that no ultimate criterion is presently available to serve as an impartial court of appeal. The second presupposition reveals a lack of awareness that the hostile and pugnacious urge, which cannot be wholly hidden if it is there, instead of cowing people into submission provokes a similar urge in response. Not only is the opponent almost sure to remain unconvinced, but thinkers on the sidelines are moved to find some way to reject a position defended in this cantankerous fashion. To reject it is not difficult for anyone with a modicum of logical cleverness, for plausible alternative premises are always to be found if one looks for them. Experience constantly confirms the truth of the familiar proverb that "he who is convinced against his will is of the same opinion still." Likewise, it confirms the truth of the maxim that even when a debater thinks he has won a shrewd argument he has fewer friends as a result.

Now compare this jousting form of philosophic debate with prevailing methods of dealing with disputes in other areas. And when international disputes are considered, it will not be long before the analogy of war will present itself. The similarities are striking.

Of course the differences are important, too, especially in an age when war can easily become nuclear devastation for the whole world. Where combatants are restricted to the use of verbal weapons, the tragic consequences of widespread physical destruction are avoided, and it may be, as debates in the forum of the United Nations lead us to suspect, that some of the passionate animosity that would otherwise find physical expression is thus siphoned off. But if one is tempted to say "harmlessly" siphoned off, he would do well to pause and survey the natural effects of contentious debate. Hostile words can cut as deeply as swords, and the sharpest cuts are sometimes made when the hostility is camouflaged by a surface show of gentility and reasonableness.

At any rate, we must reflect scrupulously on the basic similarities between war and this kind of philosophical argumentation. In both cases, there is the strong and dogmatic belief that "my position is wholly right and any opposing position is wrong." In both cases the strategy is that of forcing the opponent to submit, in his own eyes if possible, but at least in the eyes of onlookers who, it is to be hoped, can be kept by clever argument from allying themselves with him. A skillful probing of his Achilles heel can reveal unpalatable implications in his doctrine. While he casts about for a better way to defend himself, the attacker can concentrate on a forceful presentation of his own alternative. The way these characteristic features are revealed in the prosecution of war is familiar to everyone. A third similarity is not so obvious, but it may be equally important. It is blindness to the changes taking place in world opinion, which may be passing from a state of awe before proficiency in destructive coercion toward a state of respect for constructive leadership. Through this change, possession of a vast nuclear arsenal is becoming a sign of impotence rather than of power, and shrewd national leaders are finding ways to circumvent the aims of those who continue to trust in such a futile force. In the philosophical arena a parallel change is taking place. Readers seem to be less fascinated by an author's dexterity at outwitting others and more moved by admiration for competence in the wise illumination of whatever issues challenge thinkers.

In the light of these similarities, must we not say that while philosophical controversy is more like cold war than hot war, it exemplifies essentially the same method of settling disputes? Perhaps the difference between cold and hot war is not as crucial as people are inclined to suppose.

It has become sharply clear, especially since the world entered the nuclear age, that if the human race is to survive into the future, war must be left behind. And it may be that what this involves in the long run is a very deep-seated change. Already there is a reluctant but widespread recognition that armed conflict can no longer be safely embarked upon, and leaders who see no other way to gain their ends are searching for strategies that will minimize its perils. Toward what conclusion is this altered orientation tending? The preamble to the UNESCO Constitution says, "Since wars begin in the minds of men, it is in the minds of men that the defences of peace must be constructed." Western thinkers need to remember that the word "mind" here includes "heart" as well as "intellect"; this would be taken for granted in the East, where it has perennially been realized that a person's intellect is never separated from his resources of feeling or his orientation of will. The preamble implies, then, a radical idea. For war to be really renounced it must be renounced within as well as in action without. Peace in the minds and hearts of people needs to be widely won before world peace can be securely established. Put in negative terms, as long as man's spirit harbors violence, he is likely to resort to violence in his relations with the outside world, and any overt expression of violence can easily escalate into a larger scene of destruction. The bearing of this idea on philosophical discussion is quickly apparent. When a philosopher is moved by an aggressive eagerness to knock his opponent down, is he not exhibiting the presence of violence within—violence restrained from expressing itself in an undisciplined pugnacity that is still violence? What needs to be done about this kind of violent aggression if a peaceful world is to be securely established?

Consider the international scene with this question in

mind, before we come back to philosophy. By what does inner readiness for the armed violence that is war need to be replaced?

First, by a genuine toleration of all the tolerable differences among men. The present self-righteous urge to divide the world into black and white, of seeing oneself and one's associates as wholly on the side of the angels and under mandate to subdue all who refuse to submit to the rule of righteousness, must give way to a realization of the various shades of gray that are the reality everywhere and a charitable acceptance of the right of all of them to exist. Such an attitude of toleration would provide the needed foundation in men's minds for the reign of law in international affairs. Nothing less can end the anarchy that is inevitable when national leaders assume it as their duty to suppress those whom they regard as evil demons at large in the world.

But there is a second step, without which world peace cannot be wholly secure and its positive possibilities remain incapable of being realized. When it has been taken, that fact will be evident in a welcoming attitude on the part of each people toward progress by others, in a ready sharing of one another's experience, in a wholehearted willingness to learn from each other. An important presupposition behind taking this step is that tolerance is not enough, that beyond acknowledging the right of all countries to their place on the stage and to the privileges one demands for his own country there must come this active sharing, through which the gains won by each group's experience are added to the resources of all people. Is it not clear that the future lies with the countries that are most responsive to the opportunities for this sharing? They will learn more of the lessons needed for survival and progress, and will learn them more quickly, than those that are less responsive. Their part in building the future will be a larger part.

In this regard it is interesting to look at the stance characteristically taken by the United States and the Soviet Union as they view each other today. Once the rulers of the Soviet Union left behind their bondage to a dogmatic Marxism they have been quite ready to learn advantageous lessons from the practice of "free enterprise" in the United States, although there must be strong resistance on the part of those who regard capitalism as an unqualified evil. The ruling group is thus building an economy able to profit from proven success anywhere[1] while retaining the socialist vision of human well-being in all respects that have a good chance to succeed. Of course, what is learned is presented to the Russian people in disguised form, so that public condemnation of the other side may continue. The United States is also learning from the experience of socialism, but very reluctantly and therefore much more slowly. Its leaders and their fellow citizens are so confident of the rightness of the present American way that they are almost unable to learn anything important elsewhere. The deep roots of this closedmindedness are revealed in the typical reaction of Americans when they see this or that capitalist technique adopted in Russia: "So, they are confirming the rightness of our free economy!" A wiser reaction would be: "How hopeful it is that they are ready to learn, even from those they regard as enemies! Let us learn all the lessons we can from their experience, so that our resources for building the world of the future will be equally competent with theirs."

How now do these considerations bear on philosophy? In its field the first of these two steps has always been taken for granted, to the extent that the right of all viewpoints to be freely presented and discussed has been respected. What would it mean for the second step to be taken, practiced in the arena of philosophical discussion?

Lest the varied delights of controversy and conflict where

no physical destruction is caused be needlessly lost, the first questions would seem to be these: What forms of philosophical debate are likely to be convincing to readers and hearers? What forms tempt us to use them but are likely to be futile? An impulse toward aggression against the minds of our fellow men is in all of us. It would be desirable to know under what conditions argumentative aggression in philosophy achieves its ends, and how it needs to be channeled if it is to fill a wholly constructive function. It is rather astonishing that these primary questions are almost never raised. Our spontaneous, unreflective answers to them may be very wide of the mark. The main reason they are not raised is no doubt that when thinkers are in the mood of controversial argumentation, they are only marginally interested in learning how to argue better. Their energy is almost wholly spent in the effort to put something across.

It is not difficult, however, to glimpse one philosophical orientation that fully meets the conditions of success and can therefore guide one's participation in the debates of philosophers constructively. It is a natural application to these debates of what has been described as the second step in the elimination of war between nations. A philosopher who takes this step would leave behind not only the consuming urge to destroy competing philosophies but also the grudging willingness simply to tolerate their presence. He would see other philosophies as a valuable resource in his effort to fill his role adequately; he would be fully open to their positive possibilities. When he sets himself to discuss the position of a fellow philosopher, instead of saying to him, in effect, "How can I overthrow your argument most successfully?"—which of course is said unconsciously more than consciously—he would be saying: "What true insight have you found that I might share?" In a debate reflecting this orientation, each participant would realize that his own philosophy rests on presuppositions that need to be questioned and would seize the opportunity provided by discussion to become aware of them and to see how they might be wisely revised under the challenge of other philosophies. There would still be a place for negative criticism, but it would take a more effective and more reasonable—not to say, generous—form when it is offered in the setting of this open sensitivity.

Progress in this direction is being slowly made. Not many centuries ago even an exposition of a rival philosophy was apt to be prejudiced rather than impartial; it would unblushingly fit the ideas expounded into the framework of the expounder's viewpoint. Now such a twisted portrayal is rare in philosophical argument. As for critical appraisals, a blithe rejection of the claims of all other philosophies and a dogmatic insistence on the unqualified adequacy of one's own used to be fairly frequent. Three-quarters of a century ago, F. H. Bradley could bumptiously affirm:

> With regard to the main character of the Absolute our position is briefly this. We hold that our conclusion is certain, and that to doubt it logically is impossible. There is no other view, there is no other idea beyond the view here put forward. It is impossible rationally even to entertain the question of another possibility. Outside our main result there is nothing except the wholly unmeaning, or else something which on scrutiny is seen really not to fall outside.[2]

Now such an arrogant self-righteousness in attacking other philosophies and defending one's own would be avoided. Not only is it in bad taste, but it exemplifies an unfortunate blindness to the inevitable limitations in the position one has espoused. The philosophical arena no longer welcomes expressions of this bizarre dogmatism; it expects participants to show a greater awareness of the realities in which discussion of controversial issues goes on. But there is room for a more radical transformation in this direction.

When the arena is permeated by an atmosphere of receptivity to truth from every quarter, philosophy will have clearly freed itself from the spirit of pugnacious violence and will have set its own house in order for the nuclear age. Nothing needs to be lost that any perceptive thinker would not be glad to lose. There will be a testing of one's intellectual powers to the limit, with plenty of opportunity to display one's acumen, adaptability, and alert responsiveness. What will have faded from the scene is destructive argumentation—argumentation that in the long run is ruinous to the prospects of the would-be destroyer as well as to the health of philosophical discussion.

With this metamorphosis established in their own field, philosophers will have a magnificent opportunity to lead the way toward a nonviolent creative community in all fields of thought and experience. Then their own practice will provide an inspiring model of the method of truth-seeking that intrinsically fosters such a community.

NOTES

1. One reason, of course, is that communist thinkers uniformly recognize American leadership in industrial know-how.

2. Cf. his *Appearance and Reality* (London: 1899), p. 518.

II

The Causes of War

CHAPTER THREE

War and Human Nature

Urpo Harva

Professor of Adult Education,
University of Tampere, Finland

To those who subscribe to Darwin's theory of evolution, it is clear that throughout their entire existence human beings have practiced manifold violence upon one another. There is in humanity a prominent animal element, and this involves violence and conflict. The struggle for existence is an essential part of life. We have no answer to such metaphysical questions as why life does develop at all and why do the laws of development involve strife as a dominant feature. We must content ourselves with the observation that the course of development is disharmonious and tragic.

The emergence of culture has brought no end to the struggle. On the contrary, in cultured societies violence has been organized into wars, wars that may embroil the whole world. Kant writes: "Peace among men living side by side is not a natural state; natural to them is rather a state of war, if not always open hostilities at least the eternal threat of them."[1] The frequency of outbreak has remained more or less the same over the millennia; no tendency to diminish is to be perceived. On the contrary, it might be maintained that the present century is more restless than others in this respect.[2] War is a permanent feature of our life, surviving from one historical period to another regardless of all change in social and political systems, in religions, ethics, intellectual and technical standards. These systems have simply altered the nature of war.

Whence does war derive its vital energy? Will there always be war in spite of all cultural development? Is strife an inseparable part of life, so that the only peace for man is the peace of the grave?

Two mutually conflicting answers have been given to these questions. First, war springs from human nature, the basis of which is biological and hereditary and cannot thus be changed. We are biologically determined. The dream of a permanent peace is but a beautiful illusion. In any case, the effort to realize that dream can only mislead us and bring unhappiness. Second, war arises by reason of our social and cultural environment, that is, from things that we can change. We may recreate our surroundings in such a way that war will lose its source of energy. Even if war did derive from human nature, from our gene structure, we may be able, as biological knowledge expands, to change even our nature. Man creates himself through work, as Karl Marx puts it. Man may change himself from a warlike to a peaceable being. If we regard war as being inevitably implied by human character, we shall never be rid of it. To create the kingdom of eternal peace we must free ourselves of the illusion that strife is eternal. We are determined no more to one than to the other; our biological and cultural development depends upon ourselves.

We may consider these conceptions more closely from three points of view: the sociological, the biological, and the psychological.

The Marxist theory of war is sociological. It maintains that the original human society was a communistic brotherhood, but that with the division of labor and the establishment of the private property principle this community became a class society. Ever since, history has been above all the history of class struggle. The conflicts between the classes lead to wars among citizens and nations. These conflicts, again, are basically economic. Once the economic structure of society is reformed to the communist principle, once the class divisions are removed, war will be a thing of the past. The classless society of the future will be the realm of eternal peace.

Auguste Comte taught that the expansion of the natural sciences promotes the technical development of society. With this comes such a development in the efficacy of the weapons of war that war becomes too destructive to be countenanced. Comte was of the opinion that the Napoleonic Wars were the last great outbreak Europe would see.

Of the accuracy or otherwise of the Marxist prognosis there is as yet no empirical evidence. Comte's prophecy, on the other hand, has already proved false. Our present century has seen the dawn of Friedrich Nietzsche's "classical era of war."

All theories that regard war as a function of social conditions are obviously one-sided. The bias of Marxism derives from its view of the individual as being no more than a product of society, a gathering of social relations. It does not take sufficient account of what biology and psychology have to say of human nature.

Biology has now revealed some illuminating aspects of the instinct structure of animals. There is a powerful instinct of aggression, and this is directed not only against members of other species (interspecific, as Lorenz[3] puts it) but expressly within the respective kinds (intraspecific). Lorenz has shown that aggressiveness promotes the preservation of the species; it is a selective factor that ensures that the more powerful members survive and procreate. Darwin himself realized this. More recent research has shown intra-specific aggressiveness to be of particular significance from the ecological point of view. Individuals of the same species striving against each other push each other further apart. In this way there is an even spacing over their "territorium" —which ensures that they are sufficiently provided for. On the other hand aggression has its drawbacks. Since it is the most powerful who survive and continue the species, aggressiveness becomes ever more marked, as has been the case in rats. "It is quite possible that the party hatred prevailing among the various strains of rats is truly nothing but 'an invention of the devil' out of which no good can come."[4] Change in environment may mean that inherent modes of behavior lose their equilibrium. The aggressiveness that in certain conditions functions to the advantage of a species may in others prove disastrous.

Likewise, in man the aggressive instinct is a legacy from distant times when it was of advantage in preserving the race. By the process of selection there have developed in us "warlike virtues." Above all, development in the technical field, particularly in the production of weapons, has now rendered aggression so dangerous that the survival of the human race itself is in jeopardy. It is frequently maintained that the atom bomb has made possible for the first time in history the self-destruction of the entire human species. This is not quite true. Man has always, or at least for a very long time, been a creature capable of suicide. The atom bomb has simply made it possible for the suicidal aggressiveness of a very small group of men to destroy us all.

Freud assumed that alongside the instinct for self-preservation there is a death urge, for he could not otherwise explain why millions of men in World War I submitted so willingly to their fates. He was presumably wrong. Man has a love of life, but he does not love it indiscriminately. He must derive satisfaction from it. The Greek philosophers taught that man's fundamental desire is to be happy. If he does not succeed in this aspiration, he may come to love death (necrophilia). Fromm writes: "Man has a potential for destructive and sadistic violence because he is human. . . . because he must try to destroy life if he cannot create it."[5]

Aggression and necrophilia are the two deep sources from which war derives its motive energies.

Biology reveals that the structure of life is frequently such that a species may survive only if its individual members fight to the death to protect their progeny. In other words, the instinct to preserve the race is more powerful than the instinct of self-preservation. This same phenomenon is seen in man. Man experiences a profound need to sacrifice himself for others. Down the ages this has been held to be among his noblest virtues. Self-sacrifice may, on the one hand, lead to martyrdom (for example, Jesus); on the other, it may bring the hero's laurels. Man sacrifices himself not only for his children and his friends but also for his nation, his culture, his religion—in short, for all that he holds to have absolute value. As Jean-Paul Sartre has written, "A man is not really a man until he has found something for which he is prepared to die."

People who live the dull life of everyday are not in a position to satisfy the urge to self-sacrifice. Ordinary life in poor communities, as in welfare states, may easily become egotistical. Individuals and groups seek their own, often most trifling, interests and derive no profound or complete satisfaction from them. The militarists have ever been aware of this and have known how to appeal to man's self-sacrificing and heroic instincts.

A life of quiet and monotony, offering no adventure or excitement, may ultimately become insufferable. And when life becomes passive and mechanical it holds no stimulus for the creative impulse and inspiration. From such gray, shallow existence, war offers an escape. "Many are happier in war than in peace," Russell remarks.[6]

Here again, then, is a favorable soil for the roots of war, in the spirit of self-sacrifice, in heroism, in the craving man has for adventure. The assertion that "the nations do not want war" can in fact only be made by those who fly in the face of what the biologist and the psychologist tell us of human character.

"Man fears nothing so much as death." If this were true, we could not explain why wars are so widespread. Of course, man is afraid to die, but his fear is determined by the kind of death he is faced with. For many the most dreadful death is a prolonged and painful process—for which reason euthanasia is so much discussed—or else a death of loneliness and vanity. Death in battle does not usually come in this fashion. It is frequently swift. Moreover, the collective character of war makes death collective. Thus, throughout the ages, society, in paying tribute to or worshiping its heroes, has given its assurance that "they did not die in vain." The hero's death is in fact, by reason of the collective nature of war and its exhilaration and moral sublimity, one of the easiest ways to die.

Some philosophers say that life is the highest value. In actual fact, contempt for life is general. If this were not so, the enormous number of motor accidents would be inexplicable. To many, the thrill of speed and the admiration of technical ingenuity are more important than their own lives or the lives of others. War, too, feeds upon necrophilous contempt for life.

War, then, has its roots in human nature, even in its profoundest depths. Is war thus an inevitable part of man's fate?

It is to be noted that though the roots of war lie in the nature of man, war itself does not pertain to man's nature. There is no urge or need for war, as there is a sexual urge or the need for food. For example, aggressiveness does not of necessity lead to war. Man is not merely an animal whose behavior is determined by the same laws as govern the lives of the beasts. Man is also self-aware, rational, and spiritual. He can, for example, conceive the consequences of aggression and can change his environment in such a way that this element in him may find a harmless, even a useful outlet.

For thousands of years, individuals have preached the gospel of nonviolence and also lived by it. They have assumed enormous importance in witnessing to the possibility of man's freeing himself of the fascination of war and of living in friendship and love. In their case the energies of war are exhausted and love of peace has taken their place.

The road to peace can be found only if we have a realistic picture of war. This involves a diversity of scientific research and philosophical thought. In the first place, we must rid ourselves of certain general misconceptions. One was exposed above, namely, that war derives inevitably from human nature. A second, however, is that war is absolute evil and peace absolute good. If we define war as killing, wounding, and destroying certain values, war is absolutely unconscionable. But this is too narrow an interpretation. War also involves some purpose other than the destruction of these values, and this may be something precious, for example, the establishment of peace, the defense of freedom. Hence the Catholic Church centuries ago developed the doctrine of justifiable and unjustifiable war, a line of thought adopted also by the Marxists. In itself the idea is sound, but its practical value becomes increasingly problematic. In the first place, no neutral authority has been created to determine what wars are righteous and what are not. The individual must thus in most cases simply believe what his own government tells him. Secondly, the destructive power of modern weapons makes it questionable whether war can ever again be justified. And for these two reasons pacifism is gaining ground.

It is further to be noted that war also evokes noble forces. This is pointed out not only by inhumane militarists but also, for example, by such a profound thinker as Dostoyevsky.[7] And again it must be admitted that not every kind of peace is good. A peaceful community may be so ridden with injustice, oppression, and deprivation of liberty that the situation may well be considered worse than war. And where such a state of affairs is only to be corrected by means of a most destructive war, the only alternative, at least from the standpoint of Christian ethics, is patiently to await the time when the powers of evil will play themselves out and good come into its own.

Wars arise of themselves, but peace demands great effort. In fact, of course, the first part of this statement is not quite correct, for war is man-made and not to be compared, for example, with natural disasters. Men are responsible for wars, whereas they cannot be called to account for the consequences of an earthquake. But the initial assertion is correct in the sense that aggressiveness is a spontaneous instinct.[8] Peace movements are sterile, even dangerous, if the difficulty of constructing peace is not appreciated (for example, the medieval *Pax Dei* movement was turned through a strange process of dialectic into militarism). And Kant wrote: "On the cultural level hitherto attained war is an indispensable means of promoting culture; only when the perfect cultural state is reached (God alone knows when) will peace be a blessing to us, indeed, only then will it be possible."[9] Peace is thus not a means toward the perfection of culture but a fruit of it. The building of peace is the building of culture. This involves change in society, on the one hand, in man himself, on the other—a fact not realized by those peacemakers who believe in the efficacy of demonstrations and agreements.[10] Positively dangerous, again, are such peace propagandists who seek to arouse moral indignation or hatred against those whom they brand as immoral warmongers, in other words, those who see evil only in others. Such strategies appeal to aggressiveness and are thus a danger.

Sociologists, psychologists, and biologists have already to some extent investigated the social background to war and peace. Fromm, for example, holds that love of life emerges best in a society enjoying security (that is, one that provides its citizens the opportunity to satisfy basic material needs), justice, and freedom. Russell emphasizes that mere security is not enough, because man also longs for the thrill of adventure, and Lorenz points to the dangers latent in a competitive and commercial society.[11] Although such researches are as yet incomplete, it is possible to see now that human society would have to undergo a radical change before the forces of war can be weakened and the effort for peace gain way.

Very little research has been done on the question of changing human nature in the direction of peace, that is, on education for peace. On the basis of biological and psychological knowledge, however, a number of educational principles can now be conceived. It is, for example, clear that aggressiveness must not be suppressed, for this is impossible. Lorenz emphasizes that aggressiveness is essential; even though it might be eliminated by influencing the genes, the elimination of aggression should not be attempted. Lorenz holds it a serious mistake on the part of American educationists to think that by sparing the child from frustration and allowing it to behave without restraint they will produce a less aggressive individual.[12]

Since destructiveness is a consequence of lifeless existence —a suppressed love of life—education must concern itself with the development of the whole personality. It is in conflict with this principle, for example, that emphasis is placed exclusively on vocational considerations and on adaptation for social life. Attention must be equally divided over the entire range of human values: intellectual, aesthetic, moral, and religious. The roots of war spread wide, and education for peace must likewise seek to embrace every facet of human nature.

It is incomparably easier to plan a community and an education to promote peace than to realize them, for all societies are strongly oriented to war. It is difficult to believe in lasting peace (without the threat of war) without also inaugurating fundamental changes in society and man, at least in those men who exert the decisive influences upon social and cultural life. However, I believe, as does Lorenz, "that something better and higher may yet come of this human race."[13] Only I fear that this too will be a painful birth. One thing is, however, sure: our age, too, has its pacifists, perhaps more than ever before. Already about twenty nations have legislation providing for conscientious objection; elsewhere, the refusal to kill human beings is still regarded as a crime, even as serious a crime as homicide. The pacifists have no political influence at present. But these envoys from the realm of Peace are perhaps a symptom of the search of an even greater number among us anxious to explore all possible roads to peace.

NOTES

1. Immanuel Kant, *Zum ewigen Frieden* (1795), Cassirer Edition, Vol. VI (Berlin: 1923), p. 433.
2. Pitirim Sorokin, *Social and Cultural Dynamics*, Vol. III: *Fluctuation of Social Relationships, War and Revolution* (London: 1937).
3. Konrad Lorenz, *Das sogenannte Böse* (Vienna: 1965).
4. *Ibid.*, p. 236.
5. Erich Fromm, *The Heart of Man* (London: 1965), p. 32.
6. Bertrand Russell, *Authority and the Individual* (London: 1949), p. 18.

7. F. M. Dostoyevsky, *Der Krieg: Politische Schriften* (Munich: 1920).

8. Lorenz, *op. cit.*, p. 77.

9. Immanuel Kant, *Mutmaßlicher Anfang der Menschengeschichte* (1786), Cassirer Edition, Vol. IV (Berlin: 1922), p. 340.

10. Hans Zbinden, *Die Moralkrise des Abendlandes* (Berne: 1947), p. 160.

11. Lorenz, *op. cit.*, p. 351.

12. *Ibid.*, p. 78.

13. *Ibid.*, p. 322.

CHAPTER FOUR

Some Human Roots of Inhuman War

Howard L. Parsons

Bernhard Professor of Philosophy,
University of Bridgeport

I

War (a form of aggression) is in the most general sense a conflict of values between any two parties expressed through the instrumentality of physical weapons (arms) and forces (prisons, concentration camps, blockades, bacteria, etc.) that injures or destroys, partially or totally, human bodies, persons, interpersonal relations, social institutions, societies, intersocietal relations, and the ecological environment.

Thus war in its specific sense is a physical expression of conflict between two persons (quarrel), between families or clans (feud), between a person and society (delinquency, crime), between a group of citizens and the police power of government (civil disobedience, riot), between workers and owners (class war), between large groups within a nation (civil war), between nation-states ("defensive" war), and between alliances of nation-states (international or "world" war).

To survive and to achieve certain values, men show dominance (activity that maintains or controls things and persons). Dominance may be nonexploitation (e.g., control of epidemics) or exploitation (dominance for one's own selfish advantage) . Exploitation in turn may be nonaggression or aggression (self-advantageous action aimed at injuring or destroying things or persons). Aggression may be expressed in nonwar (e.g., verbal attacks) or in war. The general problem in understanding war is to determine how dominance becomes exploitation, exploitation becomes aggression, and aggression becomes war.

In its most general sense, war is the use of physical weapons and forces in a conflict that may be expressed without the use of such weapons and forces. Ideas, propaganda (emotive and directive language), manipulation of expectations, roles, and institutions, words that cut, looks that kill, an ideology that enslaves the mind, a system of classes that dehumanizes men—all can be injurious and destructive of human life, both directly and indirectly. If a person is told repeatedly that he is subhuman and if he adopts such an evaluation and role for himself, then his sense of worth, initiative, and responsibility is injured (traumatized) and his freedom and power of action are crippled and may be eventually destroyed. "Psychological warfare" as practiced by the Nazis, for instance, was aimed at preparing the psychological ground for subjugation of peoples—or, in the case of underfed and regimented concentration camp inmates, preparing the psychological ground for the extermination of peoples.

War in both the general and specific senses is a tangible expression of a conflict of values. Thus the problem of war on the negative side is how to deal with conflicts of values in ways that minimize or eliminate human injury and destruction. On the positive side, it is the problem of peace: How to express conflicts of values in ways that maintain and fulfill human beings. War creates and sustains many human values, personal and social: liberty, equality, fraternity, pride, loyalty, resourcefulness. Many of the values held high by modern men were conceived and implemented in revolutionary struggles. Unless a man struggles or "fights" for the great human values, he cannot maximize for himself and others those great values. But while war creates and fulfills, it simultaneously destroys and frustrates; one man's victory becomes another man's defeat. And in a thermonuclear age in which war is likely to mean universal destruction, the moral equivalent for war must be a universal fight for world peace and the fulfillment of values for all people.

A conflict of values is a direct clash of values that are or seem to be incompatible (the subjection of nation to nation, the freedom of nation from nation). Or it is a contest to obtain or protect a value or values cherished by both sides (food, land, factories).

A value is anything preferred in the overt behavior of a person. Things may also be preferred conceptually or verbally. But unless men "really mean" what they say about values, that is, unless they seek values that they do not have or maintain values they do have (or are prepared to do so), they ordinarily do not seriously conflict with other men over values.

Thus, to the extent that wars are conflicts between men—and not conflicts between impersonal divine-demonic, cosmic, or historical forces, or conflicts caused by conditions that we cannot understand and control, conflicts that are "inevitable"—the roots or causes of all wars lie in men. Men are causers of wars to the extent that men conflict in their values and express such conflict by using physical instruments and forces that injure and destroy human life (not merely the life of the other but also their own life). This holds true whether or not one believes that some things or forces condition men's behavior apart from their conscious knowledge and control. It is men whose values conflict; it is men who seek to resolve such conflicts through the use of weapons and force; and it is men who make such weapons. Wars cannot be known, controlled, and prevented unless the main agents of war, namely, men themselves, begin to recognize their own role in making wars. For whatever may be the causes of war in nature or history, such causes operate through man, and man (and none else) is ultimately responsible for knowing and controlling such causes. If man turns out to be the decisive factor in preventing wars, then it is man who has been the decisive factor in causing wars. Whether we will prevent wars remains to be seen. But we will not prevent war unless we struggle to locate the causes in our human situation in the world.

The human causes of wars are divisible into biological, psychological, cultural, social, economic, and ecological factors. These factors (variables) operate in a whole complex and in interaction with one another.

The biological causes are the needs (drives) of the human body that move it toward the world of things, relations, and persons in order to create some form of satisfying (value-giving) adjustment to them. Such bodily needs as hunger, thirst, and the need for satisfactory bodily temperature, while they vary among physiques, cultures, and ecological environments, are constants in all human bodies. In addition, in this process of adjustment, the body has needs to be acted upon, to *receive,* and to be *dependent* on those objects, relations, and persons; to act upon and be *dominant* with regard to them; to *detach* themselves from the valued things and selectively to choose and organize the data relevant to its action; and *sensuously to enjoy* the valued thing. These drives are expressed in the whole organism and in the corresponding specialized structures: the receptors; the skeletal structure, muscles, and glands; the nervous system; and the centers of pleasure. Thus the primary bodily needs and value-sources, wherein originate both behavioral and verbal values, are dependence (receptivity), dominance, detachment, and sensuous enjoyment.[1] Overt conflicts concerning values, and hence wars, arise where the dominance drives of the two parties clash and where recourse is taken to physical weapons or force to resolve the conflict.

"Dominance" as such does not mean "domination" or "domineering." It is simply the disposition or action of the human being to exercise control over something in the environment, either to maintain it or to change it in some way. There is no evidence that man has a domineering or aggressive or warring instinct.[2] But every human body has a need-disposition to be active in the control of selected portions of its environment in its process of adjustment and survival. Only under specific conditions of society and nature is this disposition transformed into aggression, that is, the use of physical weapons or force to achieve that control; into acquisitiveness, that is, aggrandizement toward property, territory, and power over others; into possessiveness, that is, a tendency to control what has been acquired; into revenge, that is, a desire to retaliate for lost control; into blaming others, that is, holding others responsible for one's lost control; and into egotism, that is, judging things by the criterion of whether they satisfy the controlling self alone. Since some of these attitudes are normally ingredients in the warring person, it seems evident that the attitudes necessary for war are acquired rather than inborn. The action tendencies or vectors of man develop in a bio-social-ecological situation, for example, rejection, reception, acquisition, construction, conservation, expression, transmission, elimination, destruction, defendance, and avoidance. But these do not predestine man to war.[3]

The mode of dominance, like other modes of the human adjustive process—dependence, detachment, and sensuous enjoyment—is a basic, ever-present process of the human being's behavior. Like other modes, too, the mode of dominance is a basic value, that is, it is something sought and maintained for its own value, just as it is directed toward objects that it seeks or maintains. Also, in relation to the other modes, dominance functions as a means. It is by means of dominant activity in the environment that the values necessary to survival are obtained and used (food, other persons). And by means of dominance the ideas of detachment may be carried out while the values of dependence and sensuous enjoyment may be facilitated. Thus after appropriate dominant action, a person may more effectively enter into a relation of dependence and sensuous enjoyment with regard to the food or the other person.

Where the dominance drive of one party using weapons or force expresses itself with no resistance or counter-dominance from the other party, such a relation, in the definition above, is not strictly "war." Such concession or appeasement toward the dominance drive of others occurs frequently in the relations of child to parent, spouse to spouse, and nation to nation. It is a common procedure that under certain conditions appeasement tends to reduce or extinguish the injurious and destructive force of a dominance drive of a party and to bring the party into noninjurious and nondestructive relations with the other party. Appeasement is criticized (as in Chamberlain's concessions to Hitler's demand for the Sudetenland) when it seems to forsake or destroy more of human value than it preserves and creates. Pacifists or those who believe in passive resistance, on the supposition that "it takes two to make a fight," have simply developed this common procedure into a technique for redefining and redirecting the warring, aggressive relation between men. This procedure probably has its origin in the appeasement gestures that appear in a great variety of species of social animals.[4]

The kind and degree of dominance are functions of numerous factors: internal stimuli to action, such as glands, musculature, skeletal structure, sex, and age; amount and kind of food available; the meanings of the culture, for example, whether the prevailing ideas and values stimulate and reinforce aggressive or nonaggressive settlement of conflicts; the patterns of social institutions, for example, whether they provide outlets for dominant activity through peaceful activity, as among the Hopi Indians and Hindus, or outlets through aggressive activity, as among the Apaches and Americans; the economic system, for example, whether it favors individual dominance, as in early laissez-faire capitalism, or social dominance, as in socialist systems; and the ecological environment, for example, the plant and animal life and the ways necessary to obtain it for food, the soil, the terrain, the fuels, the metals, the climate (temperature, rainfall, storms, etc.), the oxygen in the air, etc.[5]

II

The psychological causes of human behavior (and hence of wars, under certain conditions) are divisible into those of temperament and personality. "Temperament" here means an inherited and relatively constant set of behavior traits associated with bodily constitution. Endomorphy (soft roundness of physique) is associated with temperamental traits of dependence; mesomorphy (bone, muscle, and connective tissue), with dominance; and ectomorphy (linear fragility of body), with detachment.[6] Other conditions being equal, a person with a high degree of mesomorphy and hence temperamental disposition to dominance is more likely to make war than a person with less mesomorphy and temperamental dominance. To put it negatively, persons low in mesomorphy tend to cope with deprivation and conflict in the nonaggressive ways of detachment and dependence. The religious ideals of Vedanta, Buddhism, Taoism, and Christianity, which give an important place to nonviolence, are probably correlated in a significant way with a low degree of mesomorphy in the populations that have adopted them. Again, somatotyping[7] and the history of warfare indicate that men, more mesomorphic than women, are probably more disposed to warfare than are women.

But the functioning of the innate structures of physique (the specific expression of innate temperament) is conditioned by culture, society, the economy, and the ecological environment. Warfare generally requires the suppression or subordination of the needs of dependence, sensuous enjoyment, and detachment, in favor of the demand for dominant action. And it requires ordinarily a person of greater than average endowment in the physical and psychological traits of dominance in order to sustain its disciplines. A common type in the western European and American world from feudal times to the present is the "robber baron"; his musculature, freeing itself from the settled restrictions of an agrarian economy, has equipped him for dominant activity in industry, commerce, maritime exploration, land pioneering, and warfare against all opponents, including other Europeans, the American Indians, the African Negroes, and the Asiatics. The robber baron not only created a new economy, but that economy in turn created the conditions favorable for his further predatory activity. The fact that the most devastating wars of aggression have originated from the free enterprise system of mesomorphic men indicates a serious imbalance in hereditary tendency and social environment. It indicates a demand to transform the dominance drive of men into constructive channels by transforming the social environment from one of predation (imperialism, racism, oppression) to one of constructive cooperation.

The body and temperament of the person are continuously subjected to the influence of the social and physical environment. A certain kind of interaction of body and environment produces personality—a relatively stable and unified pattern of need-dispositions, emotions, purposes, instrumental actions, satisfactions, ideas, idealized values, etc. The formation and transformation of personality occur at those points of intersection between the body and those acculturalized bodies (persons) who make up the society. In a discussion of the psychological causes of war, therefore, it is necessary to look at the major social causes as they operate upon the individual person.

The significant factor in personality formation is signs and the capacity of the individual body of *Homo sapiens* to hear signs, to articulate and to write signs, to manipulate them into new combinations, to respond to signs as others do whether expressed by himself or others.[8] "Sign" here means any stimulus disposing expectant response to what is not the stimulus; it is the initiator of meaning, so that the sign-response-signified defines the "meaning." "Culture" is any shared system of signs and meanings functioning in a society. A "society" in turn is a system of relatively stable interactions or institutions, which are systems of roles. And "roles" are systems of mutual expectations or sign-processes.[9]

The formation of personality is the internalizing of others' signs and meanings in the disposition and behavior of the individual body, so that the individual body learns to communicate with others (acquires a "mind"), learns how to "take the role of the other" and to initiate and direct his own behavior in response to the expectations of others (acquires a "self"), and successively acts out the roles expected of him by others (becomes a "child," a "boy," a "student," a "husband," an "engineer," etc.).[10]

If we confine our analysis to Western societies and in particular to U.S. society, with which the writer is most familiar and for which he feels most responsible, we can understand some of the sources of aggression in the formation of personality in society.

Since the child acquires his sense of identity, his concepts of the roles he is to play, and the significance (value) of his actions from his relations to others in his immediate family, any serious disturbances in these relations produces insecurity and malfunctioning: frustration, anxiety, and tendencies toward aggression. The biological basis for the child's relations to others is his prolonged dependence, sensitivity, and responsiveness. Born as a helpless and hairless mammal, the child needs, in order to survive, the food, protection, stimulation, and loving care that only others can provide. If his needs are not fulfilled from the beginning in appropriate measure and kind, the result is retarded development and passivity, withdrawal and aggression.[11] If he receives love and then the love is withdrawn, or if love is ambivalently alternated with hostility or negligence, the consequence is deep anxiety: a diffuse and unconscious fear of loss of support. In this event, the child gets two conflicting sets of signs: the first leads him to expect care, support, and the satisfaction of his needs; the second leads him to expect noncare, nonsupport, and nonsatisfaction. The first leads him to respond by a trusting movement toward harmonious cooperation with the other; the second leads him to respond by a distrustful movement away from or against the other. Trapped in this ambivalence, the child is thrown into a state of acute anxiety, which may pass on into neurosis or psychosis.[12] In any case, the generation and nurture of the love-need in relation to others produces frustration and a tendency to aggression when the love is withheld and the need is thwarted in its satisfaction. This mechanism holds not only for children but also for the adult human being who never really outgrows his need for love:

> *Heaven has no rage like love to hatred turned,*
> *Nor hell a fury like a woman scorned.*[13]

But the child is small and dependent, and if he has been conditioned to expect love and to respond trustingly to it, he will not, when ambivalently faced with its withdrawal, respond by aggressively injuring the person who has proferred it. Instead, his aggression will be repressed or find its outlet in some other defense mechanism, such as fantasy. The pattern of insecurity, anxiety, and repressed aggression may thus form the foundation of character and carry over into the life of youth, adolescence, and adulthood, where it is more likely to find an overt and socially sanctioned expression. A child reared permissively or neglectfully, having learned to get what he wants by physical assault, will tend to act out his aggressive tendencies.

The conflict between the love-needs and the action-needs, or between the dependence-receptivity-needs and the dominance-needs—to state the matter generally—is aggravated by the child's and adult's situation in the "isolated conjugal family" and in a highly individualized and competitive society. In family and school and the occupational world (or marriage, for the women), the person is continuously expected to "succeed" and to "win"—in short, to be dominant in an efficient way over things and persons. The damage to self-esteem and frustration that ensues for most under this press produces an aggressive reaction. One's identity, status, and value are uncertain and must be repeatedly proved; love is precarious and must be forever earned from the parents who are the principal persons who can distribute it. At the same time, the child or adult is expected to be affectionate to members of his family and kind and mannerly to those outside the family. The Judaic-Christian ethic of love is juxtaposed to the capitalist dog-eat-dog philosophy. Thus the child and adult are locked once more into an ambivalence whose usual effect is aggression that must be repressed.

The ambivalence, anxiety, and aggression take different

forms in boys and girls.[14] The general masculine role in the society is that of the independent, self-made, dominant, aggressive "he-man," with a "tabu on tenderness"[15] identified with the feminine. This ideal has deep historical roots in the revolt of American merchants and farmers against the mother country, in the traditions of the pioneer and the Wild West, and in the expansion of capitalism in the late nineteenth and twentieth centuries. Though today small business enterprises and farms have greatly diminished and most men work in large impersonal organizations,[16] and though the frontier has long since been closed and the opportunities for world expansion and conquest limited (as witness the Vietnam War), the masculine ideal still persists. The small boy in America is driven by a "compulsive masculinity," which expresses and perpetuates his sense of ambivalence and insecurity. While he views his mother as the surrogate of a moral, disciplined, responsible society, a society he needs but which threatens his sense of adequacy, she is also the source of sensuous and emotional love, a value he needs but which threatens to become the dependent tie that binds and prevents his own free development and "masculinity." Later, aggressive sexuality may be his way out of this ambivalence.[17]

Why must the boy move so obsessively toward identification with the father and so fearfully away from identification with the mother? Largely because of the traditional transmission of the sex role from father to son and the historical factors we have mentioned. The agricultural and industrial development of the country has demanded a continuous supply of young men with the qualities of dominance—initiative, resourcefulness, the ability to overcome obstacles, efficiency, industriousness, aggressiveness, etc.—to "do the job." Hence at an early age American boys have pointed in the direction of an ideal symbolized variously by Benjamin Franklin, George Washington, Daniel Boone,

Abraham Lincoln, Ulysses S. Grant, Andrew Carnegie, John D. Rockefeller, Jesse James, Thomas A. Edison, Theodore Roosevelt, Henry Ford, Charles A. Lindbergh, and Babe Ruth. The rigors of exploiting and settling a continent and expanding a new capitalism called for a sharp segregation of masculine occupational life from feminine domestic life, and hence a segregation of the qualities of dominance from the qualities of dependency-receptivity and detachment.

Although the character of the economy is quite different today from what it was in 1776, 1865, 1890, and 1918, the masculine orientation still has a pervasive influence. From 1920 to 1950, some 75 per cent of U.S. corporations got only 5 per cent of the national income; the great proportion of business was done by large industrial corporations rather than by small retail or service firms.[18] In the early nineteenth century, probably 80 per cent of the occupied population were self-employed entrepreneurs; in 1870, about 33 per cent were; in 1940, about 20 per cent.[19] This has meant a great increase in white collar workers employed by large organizations. In the "post-industrial" society of contemporary America, most men are engaged in service occupations: trade, finance, real estate, sales, government, education, health, recreation, travel. Professional, technical, and scientific groups are next largest to the semi-skilled workers and are growing much more rapidly than the labor force.[20] Hence the ancestral ideal of pioneer, captain of industry, and self-made man no longer fits social conditions. The aggressiveness induced in the young male by the ideology of dominance and violence, in television, cinema, and literature, must later, in the adult world, be restricted and trimmed to suit the demands of large-scale, impersonal organizations. The result in the competitive, status-seeking anxiety-producing world of business is still more disappointment, frustration, and accumulation of repressed aggression. This syndrome carries over into the world of social relations outside business, where, as in business, politeness is the rule and aggression tends to be contained.

The Hippies, those drifting waifs of the wealthier classes, are symptoms that this contradiction between the inherited ideology of individualism and the actual fact of large, impersonal, economic organizations has reached a crisis stage. The male Hippies have no strong masculine identification with their fathers, of whom they have seen little and whom they regard as the faceless symbols of a faceless society. They have taken up with feminine qualities, more out of protest than out of positive identifications with their mothers, and their identities are confused. They have sublimated their aggressive tendencies into the pathways of alienation and the gospel of "flower power" and "love." The Hippies reject the masculine-aggressive expectations of society, but lacking an alternative ego structure, they have difficulty constructing a positive and enduring set of expectations. They are symptoms that the economy of mass organization has not yet generated an ideology that, replacing that of rugged individualism, will facilitate the cooperative and peaceful development of individuals. They realize that a society at war with itself and other societies cannot survive. They do not realize that the constructive corrective for that is not anarchism but a genuinely democratic and political movement toward socialism.

All the while boys and girls continue to be subjected to the fare of violence in television, radio, movies, popular literature, and daily headlines. Crime is featured and implicitly glamorized; the outlaw in American folklore wears a kind of evil halo. Warfare, the national glorification of the aggressive theme that runs through all or nearly all of our institutional life,[21] is represented by the government and by many in the mass media as the highest form of man's devotion to country and mankind. Military toys, enabling the small boy to act out and mechanize his aggressive tendencies, provide him with the opportunity to emulate the role of the hero who he sees portrayed on television and in comic books. Accordingly, the "bad boy" role of physical prowess and aggression receives powerful social reinforcement. The boy increasingly anticipates the time and place when he will be able to realize the childish aggressive impulses and fantasies so fully nurtured and cultivated by the culture. Thus the military-industrial complex generates that fund of aggression, that set of expectations and roles, by which it will eventually feed its own nationalistic purposes.

The young girl undergoes different pressures and frustrations. Identified with the role of her mother from early childhood, she finds, gradually or suddenly, that she must subordinate that apparently central role to the dominant role of the male in wider society and in her own courtship, marriage, and family. The role of the adult female, moreover, is ambivalent. Shall she be mother or sexual playmate? Subordinate or equal or superordinate in relation to male? Active career woman or passive auxiliary to a male career? Competitor, companion, or servant of man? All of these conflicting expectations and roles operate in the life of the growing girl and the adult woman and produce feelings and impulses of aggression directed against both men and women. The general competitive motif of the institutional life, moreover, compounds this aggression, and in the case of the married woman is channeled back into her family life, where her covert aggression is expressed in ways that perpetuate the pattern of the occupationally isolated husband, the openly aggressive boy, and the conforming daughter. All of these roles, while giving some satisfaction to the mother, are also resented and thus add to her frustration and aggression.[22]

We are speaking very generally. Each individual personality is the intersection and resultant of diverse forces: constitutional need-dispositions, temperamental traits, familial and kinship expectations and roles, cultural meanings, social institutions, and economic and ecological factors. Thus each person constitutes a variation on the general pattern described.

Some analysts of the causes of war have stressed the cultural and ideational factors.[23] They have pointed out how, through the manipulation of the press and other media of ideas, men in a given society have been deceived about the real causes and motives for a war that they were lured into waging. Such an explanation, however, places undue emphasis on the power of ideas. If men were not psychologically disposed to aggressive activity in some form, if they were not essentially unfulfilled and fearful of their own freedom and the judgment of others, it would be difficult if not impossible to conscript them for killing in an aggressive war. Men have gone to war from a variety of motives: excitement, recognition, security, comfort, dignity,[24] wealth, revenge, adventure, prestige, glory, power, plunder, better lands, higher wages, feminine approval, sadism, escape from problems or boredom, loyalty to others and nation, anxiety about self, etc.[25] But such motives are not inborn and inevitable; only certain general dispositions are genetically given in men. Specific motives must be traced to the system of social relations into which an economy casts men. The view that war is due to motives and ideas is not incorrect; it simply fails to acknowledge that motives and ideas are largely the consequence of the power and decisions of the ruling groups as they determine the ruling structures and processes of society. Such motives and ideas cannot be changed except as the class structure of a society is changed. Such change is both ideational and material: men educate one another as they change circumstances. Capitalism as we have known it in the United States produces competitive, anxious, aggressive men and hence dispositions toward aggressive war; a cooperative economy that meets the basic needs of men does not produce such dispositions.

In addition to the economic sources of aggression already mentioned—the occupational segregation of the male, the competitive and anxious press to succeed at the expense of others for the sake of social approval and livelihood, the "antagonistic cooperation" of large-scale business organizations, the glorification of warfare—one other source should be discussed: the dynamic, unstable, and disruptive character of our economic system. Such has been the case since the commercial revolution of the eleventh century challenged the securities of European feudalism. The result has been a transformation of values, a secularizing, naturalizing, humanizing, rationalizing, and empiricizing of institutions and attitudes. In the face of this revolution, "all that is holy is profaned,"[26] and the solidities of family, industry, and other institutional forms, as well as those of philosophy and religion, shift and melt under its impact. The mode and method of this economic revolutionizing power is experiment, or, more exactly, science. But science is dynamic; it takes nothing as sacred or fixed; it corrodes established expectations, roles, and institutional ways of doing and thinking.[27] In the United States the consequent insecurity has produced many persons who aimed their frustration and repressed hostility at targets both at home and abroad,[28] targets chosen on the basis of the authoritarian personality's "violence, anarchic impulses, and chaotic destructiveness in the unconscious sphere"[29] and elicited by the presence of communism on the world scene.[30]

This brings us to our final source of aggression in American society: the ecological. Ecology has to do with the mutual relations of individual organisms, their group or society, and their environment. We have already discussed ecology under cultural, social, and economic categories. But there is a larger environment implicated in man's life: waters, foods, plants, animals, soils, terrain, materials for clothing and buildings and tools and weapons, fuels, metals, temperature, rainfall, sunshine, storms, seasons, ozone, climatic cycles, disease, density of population, etc.[31] A spacious, virgin land in a temperate climate of stimulating cyclonic storms, abundant in natural resources and occupied by relatively few Indians, the continent offered a "golden" opportunity for immigrants from Europe seeking freedom of enterprise and material wealth. The rigors of entrepreneurial, commercial, and pioneer life tended to subordinate or eliminate the weaker, more sensitive portions of the population. Strong mesomorphic persons such as Daniel Boone, Peter Cartright, and Andrew Jackson held sway. Later in the nineteenth century, the robber barons added to their predatory principles the endomorphic "gospel of greed." In this process, American society, led by an industrial-political (now also military) élite has aggressively and radically changed the physical and social environment in its own country and the world: genocide of Indians, soil erosion, deforestation, extinction of animal species, enslavement and genocide of Negroes, imperialism and foreign wars, urban ghettos, widespread hunger, water and air pollution, and an environment of violence in action, feeling, and thought.

III

We have reviewed the major human causes of wars, particularly in United States society. All wars are inhuman insofar as (1) they injure or destroy human life and values of the warred-on, and (2) they deny the generic compassion and reason of the warrior. A warring man, like a buying or selling man, sacrifices some of his humanity. The only possible justification for war would be that, in the light of all realizable alternatives for a given problem, the alternative of war produces the least inhuman consequences. If he fails to bear this in mind, the warrior may discover that, in the long run, in warring against certain inhuman values he has been overtaken by the inhuman values of warring itself.

> *Even anger against injustice*
> *Makes the voice grow harsh. Alas, we*
> *Who wished to lay the foundations of kindness*
> *Could not ourselves be kind.*[32]

Whatever the human ideal may be, the fact is that men have ameliorated or eradicated injustice throughout history by warring against it. Even knowing that they might fail in that, some men have chosen to die warring for the right rather than to die suffering under the wrong. Such warring, whether or not it removed the oppression, might evoke human qualities of courage and dignity, and so inspire others. And it might thus far, at least, be justified. Few there are who would deny a man the right of self-defense against war or a people the right of national liberation.

But all these considerations pale in the blinding light of the atomic bomb. Aggressor, defender, neutral nation; oppressor, oppressed; base, noble—all will be wiped out in a thermonuclear war. Principle and consequence, the two great criteria for human moral decision, will not matter. Such war has become the ultimate in inhumanity, for it will mean the end of all humanity. If we can prevent that, we might secure the breathing space for solving all the other problems.

NOTES

1. Charles Morris, *Varieties of Human Value* (Chicago: University of Chicago Press, 1956). I have somewhat modified Morris's dimensions of action and of value.

2. Geoffrey Gorer, "Man Has No 'Killer' Instinct," *New York Times* Magazine (Nov. 27, 1966), pp. 47 ff. Sally Carrighar, "War Is Not in Our Genes," *New York Times* Magazine (Sept. 10, 1967), pp. 74 ff. Both these articles deal with the claims of Lorenz's book (*see below*), and the latter answers Robert Ardrey, *The Territorial Imperative* (New York: Atheneum, 1966).

3. Henry A. Murray & Clyde Kluckhohn, "Outline of a Conception of Personality," in *Personality in Nature, Society, and Culture*, ed. Kluckhohn & Murray, 2nd ed. (New York: Knopf, 1955), p. 23.

4. Konrad Lorenz, *On Aggression* (New York: Harcourt, Brace & World, 1966), ch. vii.

5. Ellsworth Huntington, *Mainsprings of Civilization* (New York: Wiley, 1945).

6. Charles Morris, *op. cit.*, p. 130. W. H. Sheldon, *The Varieties of Human Physique* (New York & London: Harper & Brothers, 1940), pp. 5–6.

7. *Ibid.*, p. 66.

8. George H. Mead, *Mind, Self and Society* (Chicago: University of Chicago Press, 1934).

9. Talcott Parsons, *The Social System* (Glencoe, Ill.: Free Press, 1951), p. 11.

10. George H. Mead, *op. cit.*

11. John Bowlby, *Maternal Care and Mental Health* and *Deprivation of Maternal Care* (New York: Schocken, 1966).

12. Jules H. Masserman, *Behavior and Neurosis* (Chicago: University of Chicago Press, 1943).

13. William Congreve.

14. In what follows the role of the female in American society is not discussed so fully as is that of the male, but her role in contributing to a warfare society should not be minimized.

15. Ian D. Suttie, *The Origins of Love and Hate* (New York: Matrix House, 1966).

16. C. Wright Mills, *White Collar* (New York: Oxford University Press, 1956).

17. Talcott Parsons, "Certain Primary Sources and Patterns of Aggres-

sion in the Social Structure of the Western World," in *A Study of Interpersonal Relation*, ed. Patrick Mullahy (New York: Hermitage, 1949), pp. 269–296.

18. C. Wright Mills, *op. cit.*, p. 24.

19. *Ibid.*, p. 63.

20. Herman Kahn & Anthony J. Wiener, "The Next Thirty-Three Years: A Framework for Speculation," *Daedalus* (Summer, 1967), p. 720.

21. Frederic Wertham, *A Sign for Cain: An Exploration of Human Violence* (New York: Macmillan, 1966).

22. For a discussion of the frustration of the middle-class woman, *see* Betty Friedan, *The Feminine Mystique* (New York: Norton, 1963).

23. E.g., Quincy Wright, *A Study of War*, Vol. II (Chicago: University of Chicago Press, 1942), chs. xxx, xxxvii.

24. Donald A. Wells, *The War Myth* (New York: Western, 1967), p. 179.

25. Quincy Wright, *op. cit.*, p. 1200.

26. Karl Marx & Friedrich Engels, *Manifesto of the Communist Party*.

27. Talcott Parsons, "Certain Primary Sources and Patterns of Aggression in the Social Structure of the Western World," *op. cit.*, pp. 287–288.

28. Seymour Martin Lipset, "The Sources of the 'Radical Right,'" in *The Radical Right*, ed. Daniel Bell (Garden City, N.Y.: Doubleday, 1963).

29. T. W. Adorno, *et al.*, *The Authoritarian Personality* (New York: Harper & Brothers, 1950), p. 675. Some of the extreme proponents of Black Power display similar traits, but it is only conjectural at this time what relation is between the authoritarian personality and the proponent of Black Power. It is significant that both are products of American culture, the one seeking to conserve the status quo, the other to smash it.

30. For a discussion of some of the causes of anticommunism in the United States, *see* Howard L. Parsons, "The Influence of Marx's Thought in the United States," *Praxis*, 2 (1967), pp. 264–275.

31. Ellsworth Huntington, *op. cit.*

32. Bertolt Brecht, "To Posterity."

CHAPTER FIVE

The Ideological Origins of the Third World War

Risieri Frondizi

Visiting Professor of the Philosophy of Education, University of Texas at Austin

Today two different philosophical attitudes exist. One takes human life as its point of departure; the other ignores the problems of man and is more interested in the form and validity of knowledge than in its subject matter.

If it is not accompanied by linguistic and logical rigor and if it does not rest on experience, the first attitude runs the risk of turning into mere fanciful speculation. In its turn, if the second attitude continues to narrow down its interests, analyzing away the fundamental problems of man because they do not fit into its limited linguistic pattern, it may "retreat to formal trivialities and exact nonsense," as C. Wright Mills has said.[1]

I believe that the philosopher must not ignore the fundamental problems of man. His concern and contribution as a citizen are not enough; insofar as he is a philosopher he ought to work hard to clarify the problems that trouble him and his fellow men. The great scope of his concern need not lead him to superficiality and vagueness. Conceptual clarity, linguistic precision, rigorous reasoning are not incompatible with the analysis of the dramatic conditions of man; indeed, they ought to be at the service of man in order to clarify his situation.

What should I do? is one of the constant questions of man. It must also be so for the philosopher, even if the question takes on a different meaning for him. No semantic analysis can analyze away this question, much less the human and dramatic concern that it expresses.

What should I do? is a question millions of men today ask themselves with respect to the most diverse problems and circumstances. One of these troubles is war; the war in Vietnam, for example, either by itself or as a symptom of a possible World War III. There are many philosophers who—as men—are profoundly affected by the drama of this war; I believe they ought to have the same concern *as philosophers* and use their intellectual faculties to illuminate this terrifying situation.

War cannot be avoided if we do not understand the complex mechanism from which it springs, and if we do not dispel confusion, misunderstanding, and prejudice of every kind. One of these prejudices is the belief that war in general, or the next war in particular, is inevitable. Individual and social psychology can bring to light the origin of this prejudice, which, in some cases, has its root in philosophical errors. Thus, the inevitability of war is sometimes attributed to "human nature" or to man's "instincts," both of which are obsolete concepts in the fields of philosophy and psychology. In other cases, the inevitability of war is attributed to forms of determinism that cannot support philosophical analysis, or to cyclical conceptions of the philosophy of history which appear outdated.

We cannot go deeply here into the analysis of these errors and the philosophical root that nourishes them. It will suffice merely to underscore the danger involved in the erroneous doctrines and predictions when they refer to human conduct. We are accustomed to the fact that prediction of the weather does not necessarily coincide with what actually happens. The behavior of the weather is not dependent upon meteorologists. But this is not the case with human behavior. If people are convinced that the price of gold, or any other object, will climb, the rise in price really occurs, since many people start to buy gold out of fear of the rise occurring. The same thing happens in the realm of individuals. Whoever becomes convinced, owing to erroneous reasoning, that he will very soon go crazy will probably end up in a madhouse. Today's error can turn into tomorrow's tragic truth.

There are many people who are convinced that World War III is inevitable. If this false belief is not dispelled, it is probable that the war will take place. In the last twenty-five years we have witnessed a real armaments race based on the belief that sooner or later war will break out. The meteorologists of war are very dangerous; they can turn a puff of wind into a hurricane.

War is a complex phenomenon. We will not avoid it with simplistic solutions. Pacifism, with all the sympathy that it might inspire, is a clear example of naiveté and oversimplification in solving a complex problem that cannot be solved by wishful thinking and goodwill. Goodwill can contribute to the solution of a problem when the latter is due to bad will, but not when it falls outside the field of volition.

Nor can a lasting peace be achieved by means of treaties and agreements if the difficulties from which conflicts originate have not been previously solved. Such agreements might postpone but not eliminate a possible war. The legal and diplomatic organization is instrumental in character; it serves interests and aspirations that escape its own rule. We have to get to the heart of the matter, to the profound causes. But we cannot get at them without first getting them out into the open. The suggestions that follow, then, are intended to indicate the principal—though not the sole—causes of a possible World War III.

It is an old concern of man to investigate the causes of war. Throughout history, the most diverse causes have been indicated. In primitive societies, war appears as a common fact. When concern first arose, supernatural causes were singled out, ranging from divine will to certain spirits that penetrate the soul of the individual and obey the voice and will of supernatural beings.

Moving on to natural causes, the quantity and diversity increased. War is attributed to biological, psychological, economic, and other causes. The point in common—and the error—is the attribution of war to *one* cause, without taking note of the complexity of factors that contribute to the occurrence of an event as complex as a war. The second error is that the cause of war in general is sought as if it were a unique phenomenon.

The truth is that *war* does not exist; what exists are *wars*, in the plural, ranging from tribal skirmishes to World War II. "War" is a generic term that applies to certain bellicose acts that have in common the use of force and violence. If war is not a unique event but a multiplicity of events, or of types and classes of events, it seems logical that they are initiated by different causes. A diversity of causes must correspond to the diversity of phenomena.

Wars recorded by history have had different causes. Some have originated in religious conflicts; others in conflicts of economic interest. And wars have also not been lacking caused by personal rivalries and even conflicting pretensions to the same lady. When we speak in such cases of *the* cause, we mean the principal cause. Usually there is a convergence of different, although interrelated, kinds of cause. We have to remember that besides the so-called causes, there exists a development of conditions that permit such causes to produce a certain effect.

It is not our intention to investigate the problem of the causes of war in general. In the first place, we do not believe that general explanations can be given to events that are particular. Furthermore, many books are devoted to the causes of war, from psychological, sociological, economic, and other points of view. Nor do we wish to get into the thorny problem of the notion of "cause," a complex notion in itself that poses major difficulties when transferred from physical to social phenomena.

I am troubled, as are many other people, by the possibility of a war that has not yet occurred but which increasingly menaces us. My worry about World War III does not have an exclusively theoretical or academic motive. I am troubled as a human being, although I notice that the possible conflict has its roots also in profound philosophical questions related to metaphysical, ethical, and epistemological problems. My ultimate interest, in fact, is of a pragmatic character: knowledge of the possible causes of World War III could serve to diminish the probabilities of its outbreak.

In my opinion, the principal cause of a third world war is ideological conflict. In the second place, although conditioned by the previous factor, is the struggle for power. In the third place, fear and suspicion.

In the past, wars were brought about by causes quite different from the three mentioned above. Today, we need not consider a war of worldwide proportions generated by national vanity, quarrels over boundaries, or conflicts of a personal order between rulers. If a war did occur from such causes, there would be no danger at all that it would spread, since man, along with the increase in his destructive power, has acquired greater prudence and responsibility. He knows very well that a third world war will leave the victor in bad shape, if one can speak of a "victor" in a nuclear war.

Religion was the cause of many wars in the past; today, however, not religious issues but ideological conflicts divide the world. If a war did originate because of religious conflicts, the possibility of its spreading would be in direct proportion to the ideological implications it might have. Limited to a strictly religious matter, a war of this kind could not turn into World War III.

I discard the economic factor as an important cause of the outbreak of the new war. Before World War II, the economic cause was very important: conflicts of economic interest and the search for markets and for raw materials of great strategic or economic significance motivated more than one war. But the principal cause of World War II was not economic in nature but political: Hitler's mad desire to gain power and the Allies' fear of such an increased expansion led to armed conflict. Certainly, the Allies, and particularly the United States, benefited economically from the war, but this was only a consequence, a by-product, of the war. We have to be careful not to confuse "consequence" with "cause" and "motive."

The next world war will have very different characteristics; it will not correspond to the traditional notions. It will be a new event; actually, it will be a world civil war. Since I wish to concentrate full attention on what I consider the principal cause of World War III, I will first treat the other two causes mentioned.

The present armaments race—and many other similar ones that previously ended in wars—has its origin in fear and in suspicion, fear's offspring. Fear requires us to have as many cannons as the enemy *plus one*. Since the enemy thinks exactly the same way, a continual increase of armaments occurs as the result of reciprocal suspicion.

The possibility of a surprise nuclear war has increased fear and suspicion. As is well known, the United States keeps jet planes loaded with nuclear bombs in perpetual flight; I assume that the Soviet Union does something comparable. The danger in this game of suspicion is all the greater because of the possibility that a technical error or a mistaken interpretation of an insignificant fact will lead to war. But the psychological factors of war should not be overemphasized. After all, fear is based on the fact that the other party is our enemy, and he is, in this case, because he has the opposite ideology.

It has been said and often repeated that war erupts first in the minds of men and that that is where we must build peace. The proposition is true, although misleading, because it suggests that man's mind dwells apart from his body and the physical and social environment. The truth is that the mind of man has aspirations and desires that differ according to the needs of the body and the requirements of the physical and social environment.

To make an appeal exclusively to the feelings of men is a naiveté of pacifism, or else a theoretical error concerning the motives of man's feelings and will. Instead of hoping to bring about a change in men's feelings as a result of mere preaching, it is preferable in some cases to change the physical or socioeconomic conditions that give rise to such feelings.

Many wars have come about from lust for power and from the fear of losing it or falling behind the enemy's power. The balance of power is a factor that appears with increasing frequency as a cause of war. It would be foolish to deny its importance. What we contend is that the "power" factor here, as well as fear and suspicion, is the manifestation of a more profound cause, namely, ideological conflict. If Great Britain had the power that the Soviet Union possesses, the possibilities of war would be enormously reduced. The United States would not feel its capitalistic way of life threatened, since the watered down socialism that exists in Great Britain does not aim at enlarging its quasi-leftist influence, nor is it incompatible with the American way of life.

Power, or the covetous preservation and increase of it, should never be completely discarded as cause or factor of a possible war. One could argue with some reason that lust for power is a perpetual cause of war and that such lust disguises itself in different fashions according to the circumstances. "Ideology" could be the disguise that lust for power adopts in our time. Or it can be said that the increase of Soviet power—and not the ideological discrepancy—is what really worries the United States. The Soviet position is similar, with appropriate changes: the Russians are worried about American power and its expansion, and not about the capitalistic regime.

This kind of reasoning has its basis in a philosophical doctrine that serves as an assumption in many discussions of human phenomena: the doctrine that man has an "essence," possesses a "nature" that is his own and therefore is immutable. It is claimed that the basic forms of human nature are immutable since they belong to the very definition of the essence of man. What changes is the expression of this nature, its exterior forms, its guise or manner of presentation. Fear, pleasure, lust for power, etc., form part of human nature, and they can be found present in every situation. These primary forms of human nature take on different aspects according to the physical and sociocultural conditions in which man lives. But we must not allow ourselves to be fooled by the differences in appearance since the underlying fabric of personality is always the same.

This conception of man has its roots in ancient Greece, took strength in some forms of medieval philosophy, and culminates in modern times with the Cartesian doctrine of thinking substance (*res cogitans*). According to this doctrine, because man possesses a substantial character, he is essentially immutable and independent.

From this doctrine, psychological conceptions have been derived, consciously or unconsciously, that speak of man as if we were really dealing with an immutable being and with permanent psychological forces or activities. According to some of these conceptions, man is a destructive being that bears a fate of war in his soul. He is born to wage war, and he uses his reason and intelligence both to increase his destructive power and to justify his martial inclinations.

In my opinion, this theory is erroneous, but equally erroneous is the contrary doctrine, which claims that man is "by nature" good and that civilization, or something similar, tends to pervert him. Even though contrary doctrines are involved, they both agree in crediting man with a "nature" or "essence" that defines him, while setting aside the sociocultural environment in which he lives.

The fields of cultural anthropology, sociology of primitive society, developmental psychology, and history and our increasing awareness of the influence of economic factors in the process of history and of subconscious factors in the realm of psychology seem to support the contemporary philosophical conceptions of historicism, existentialism, and similar views: that man is always in the making; that his being is becoming.[2]

Cultural anthropology, to restrict ourselves to a single field, has shown the manner in which we acquire our values and ideals from the sociocultural environment. We do not acquire them at once and passively, but in an active interaction with this environment. The influence of the sociocultural and historical environment is today undeniable, and it is unnecessary to insist upon it.

We pointed out previously the tragic consequences that a mistaken doctrine could have for man because it has an influence upon his conduct. If man had an immutable nature, and if parts of it were aggression, the destructive impulse, lust for power, and the martial spirit, we would never be able to change it, for an immutable essence would be involved, and all that is left for us would be resignation. Or in the case of preparation for war to avoid annihilation by an enemy, we are not responsible for any evil we might do since we are the victims of a nature that evades any effort we make to change it. Human progress is reduced in such a case to increasing the power of destruction.

Although the history of military developments and the rapid increase in the power of destruction appear to substantiate this thesis, it is easy to observe that man himself has been and remains the one most responsible for what happens. The historicist and existentialist conceptions emphasize the responsibility of man and also his capacity for progress, not only in the means, but also in the ideals and ultimate purposes of life.

In man existence precedes essence, Heidegger affirmed and Sartre and other existentialists repeated. The existence of man, we can add, does not take place in a vacuum but in a physical and sociocultural medium. Man forms his personality in interaction with this medium. Hence, changes in the sociocultural environment can promote or detract from —if not originate—kinds of reaction or attitude. History shows us the way sociocultural change, brought about by many different situations, in many cases produced profound modifications of attitude, if not behavior. On the other hand, if this were not the case, education would be condemned merely to scratch the outer skin of human personality and would be nothing more than training. And educational psychology shows us that this is not the case, for education does not merely give a veneer to man but is capable of forming his personality.

The above condensed arguments are meant to show that it is not lust for power or any other allegedly permanent characteristic of man that is responsible for war, but that war is the product of social, economic, and cultural factors.

Certainly, in the past many wars had their origin in lust for power or in the desire to safeguard power. Others had an economic origin. But that they had some such origin does not mean that they *necessarily have to* occur that way.

In our opinion, the socialist revolution and the possibilities of its expansion introduced a previously nonexistent factor. This factor not only broke the traditional patterns, but it became the predominant element as cause of military conflict. Ideological difference is now the only possible form of conflict that can lead to World War III. Any conflict originating from a different cause is condemned to quarantine, to start up and die out within its own back yard. On the other hand, if there is an ideological element behind the conflict or a change in the ideological equilibrium, the most insignificant difference can turn into a worldwide conflagration.

Ideological conflict succeeds the rivalry for markets and the lust for power. Previously, the great powers made efforts to dominate their enemies by controlling raw materials, such as oil. Today, in contrast, raw materials are sought as a means to fight against an ideological enemy. Previously, wars occurred in the search for new markets to sell new products; today, goodwill is bought, followers are sought and indoctrinated and hatred is stirred up at the cost of great expenditures. It is incredible how much the great powers squander in ideological propaganda, if not in stalemated war, as is happening in Vietnam. Previously, one wanted to dominate the enemy by increasing one's own power; today, one wants to increase power in order to annihilate the ideological enemy. It would be foolish to think that the war in Vietnam had its origin in the search for raw materials or new markets.

According to responsible authors, billions of dollars are wasted on Vietnam each month. The figure is higher than all the profits that all the American companies could possibly gain in that area. The war does not have an economic objective; it has an ideological objective. Money is not sought in Vietnam; it is thrown away.

The ideological conflict goes far beyond a conflict of economic interest. It is much more profound, encompassing political, social, cultural, and religious conceptions. It is a genuine conflict between two *Weltanschauungen*. Naturally, the political and socioeconomic aspects are the important ones. It is too simple a conclusion to attribute perversity and Machiavellianism to one's adversary or to believe that the combat is to save endangered liberty and civilization. Neither dogmatic spirit nor propaganda started this conflict. The human situation, a real crisis of values that demands solution, and a need to treat new and legitimate aspirations of peoples who have suffered hunger and misery for centuries—these are the underlying causes.

Marxism is not a theory that sprouted in Marx's head as the result of a mere theoretical preoccupation. Marx's pragmatic purpose is clearly announced in the famous *Theses on Feuerbach* (XI) : "Philosophers have only *interpreted* the world in various ways; the point, however, is to *change* it." The need for change, in his view, originated in an unjust socioeconomic situation. The spread of Marxist doctrine, as we will see later, has been due to the existence of social injustice and the need felt by millions of men to remedy this injustice. (We cannot here analyze or evaluate the Marxist doctrine and the suitability or disadvantage of its expansion. Our main concern is war and the way to avoid it, and we do not wish to get off the track. Everything said in this chapter should be interpreted in the light of this main concern.)

Our first point consisted in noting that ideological conflict is the principal factor in the possible outbreak of a third world war. The second point is that the existence, persistence, and increase of social injustice aggravate the ideological conflict and favor the spread of a revolutionary doctrine. It should be shown, in the third place, that social injustice not only exists but tends to increase. The fourth point, which derives from the second, is that as social injustice is diminished, the probabilities of a third world war will diminish. The final conclusion seems evident: *whoever loves peace must fight to diminish the social injustice in the world,* though it goes without saying that social injustice by itself, wherever it is encountered, calls for a fight to eliminate it.

Let us go on to the second point. The existence and increase of social injustice favor the spread of a revolutionary doctrine, aggravate the ideological conflict, and, as a consequence, increase the possibilities for an outbreak of World War III.

This is not the first time that this thesis has been propounded; many authors have done so before me. Josué de Castro, President of the Executive Council of the Food and Agricultural Organization (FAO) for four years and author of various works on the problem of hunger in the world, writes:

> Some people think that Soviet infiltration and material aid are the principal explanation for the victories of the Communists over Chiang Kai-shek's troops. It is my impression that there is a more profound reason. The Communist revolution is winning in China today because, although Chiang Kai-shek has a powerful ally in the United States, the followers of Mao Tse-tung have still a stronger ally. That ally is hunger. . . . The fear of famine has been the great recruiting agent of Mao's armies and the decisive factor in the Chinese civil war has been the strategy of starvation. The successes of Communism in China, in my opinion, are due to the fact that the Communists have promised freedom from the threat of starvation. Starvation is in turn a result of imperialist exploitation of man and the soil. No one can deny that this Chinese hope

is an exceedingly natural one, and that its frustration has been nothing less than inhuman.[3]

Hunger did not exist only in China during the time in which Mao started the revolution, and the impetus that hunger gave the revolution in China may be repeated in any part of the globe. And such will be the case if the causes that provoke famine are not corrected.

Millions of men throughout the world, and especially in Latin America, Africa, and Asia, suffer from hunger, misery, and sickness of every description as a consequence of malnutrition. They suffer constantly from the frustration of not being able to satisfy the most basic needs of nutrition and shelter for themselves and their children. And from frustration, as we will now see, comes aggressiveness.

Some have argued that millions of men have always lived in misery and suffered hunger for centuries. That much is certain, but the conclusion men attempt to derive from this fact is erroneous. The difference between the starving masses of today and those of previous centuries is that formerly the people resigned themselves to such a life of misery because they believed that their condition arose from supernatural forces or from the divine will that wanted to punish man for his sins. Today, these masses have discovered that divine providence has nothing to do with their suffering and that the fundamental cause has its roots in the malevolence of certain men and in the existence of an unjust socioeconomic system. This growth of man's awareness of the reasons for his suffering give to the phenomena a dimension they did not previously have. The man who today suffers is not resigned to his suffering. And from the belief that the socioeconomic regime is responsible for it, he logically concludes that it is necessary to change the regime. And if the doors are locked against peaceful change, it is only natural to consider a violent change.

Today, it is admitted that frustration gives rise to aggression. The relation has been expressed in this manner: "The occurrence of aggressive behaviour always presupposes the existence of frustration, and contrariwise, the existence of frustration always leads to some form of aggression."[4] The relationship was also pointed out by Freud, and it was developed in the United States by J. Dollard and some other colleagues in *Frustration and Aggression.*[5] Dollard defines frustration as "that condition which exists when a goal response suffers interference." Aggression is defined as "an act whose goal response is injury to an organism or organism surrogate."

I believe that this psychological doctrine will be amply confirmed if social injustice continues to persist. The aggressive impulse grows day by day in the oppressed areas. Frustration is constant. It is not the frustration of strange or whimsical goals; it concerns biological goals: the simple and justified desire to eat and to sleep under a roof.

Satisfying his most immediate needs of nourishment and shelter for himself and his family is a natural aspiration in man. When this desire is accompanied by a serious determination and a great effort over several years without the accompanying possibility of improvement, it should not be surprising that the people who suffer such immense frustration develop volatile and aggressive impulses. The aggression may be directed against the boss who exploits him, it may be in opposition to the police who suppress his strikes or rallies, or it may be opposed to the government that does nothing to correct the situation. However, when the people note that bosses, police, and government change while the evil remains, they discover that it is not individuals who are to blame, it is the system itself.

This feeling is normally the result of a slow psychological process. It was slow in its formation, but it cut deep into the soul of millions of people who have suffered hunger and misery for generations. You cannot remove such deep convictions with mere words or excuses. The peasants and workers of Latin America have listened to countless promises over the years; many times they have been deceived by the men who made such promises. The governments have failed with their superficial, demagogic measures of reform. The time has come when only a radical reform of the socio-economic structures can prevent a social revolution in Latin America.

The growing aggressive attitude of the suffering masses is based on the actual existence of social injustice. There is a twofold character to the social injustice that exists in the world. On one side, the injustice reveals itself in the enormous gap, which tends to increase, between the rich and powerful nations and those that have little or nothing. The other form of social injustice is found in the internal structure of nations, especially of the underdeveloped ones. This injustice is even more shocking than the gap between nations because the man who is starving and who lives in the greatest misery can see around him the abundance of riches, opulence, and squandering.

The third point refers to the existence of social injustice. It takes little effort to show, in sheer figures and statistics, the existence of social injustice in the world. The richest countries with 16 per cent of the world population have 70 per cent of the world income. On the other hand, the 15 poorest countries, with 50 per cent of the world population, have less than 10 per cent of the world income. The United States has about 6 per cent of the world population and more than a third of the world productive resources. A handful of American businessmen have holdings and assets surpassing the combined possessions and wealth of one hundred million men in Latin America, Africa, or Asia. This comparison becomes more impressive when one realizes that there are many millions of people in those areas who own absolutely nothing. The importance of this notable difference, between the very few who have much and the very many who have little or nothing, continues to increase. If the present trend is kept, in the year 2000 half of the developing nations will have a per capita income of $170, while the United States will have $4,500. Already the FAO has made the statement that the underdeveloped countries were more ill nourished in 1965 than they were before World War II.

Not only is the unjust distribution of riches or their concentration in the hands of a few shocking, their use in affairs that do not benefit humanity also shocks. The financial fortunes reaped are limited entirely to the few businessmen who participate in the transaction.

No country holds a monopoly on squandering money, yet the condition becomes critically important if money is employed as a threat to peace or used to annihilate other human beings. The amount spent by the United States and the Soviet Union in their military budgets could double the standard of living in several Latin American, African, or Asian countries. At the same time, the cost of the war in Vietnam is more than sufficient to eliminate totally starvation in Vietnam, both North and South.

Similar to the subordination of the poor to the rich on the international order—and sharing the same deplorable effects—is the inequality found in the internal structure of several specific areas, especially of the underdeveloped countries.[6]

Let us now move to the fourth proposed argument. If social injustice is lessened, it decreases in an equal proportion the possibility of a third world war. As we have seen, the existence of social injustice has greatly encouraged the aggressiveness of millions of human beings. It not only occurred before the respective social revolutions in the Soviet Union and China, but it is presently taking place in the areas and to the peoples long accustomed to social injustice—as one can observe by comparing certain areas and populations even in the same country, northeast and south Brazil, for example.

If there exists a relation between the degree of social injustice and the increase of aggressiveness, it becomes evident that with the diminishing of the social injustice, the aggressiveness will decrease as well.

In our case, it is not a matter of increasing or decreasing a radical ideology. The important thing for the preservation of peace is that social injustice tends to favor the development of a belligerent attitude. On the other hand, the conservative groups (at least in Latin America), who are responsible for such injustice, adopt almost as a protective reflex a similar belligerent attitude. Against the background of this radical polarization, we know only too well the possible consequences.

President Kennedy recognized that the revolutionary challenge to an unjust social order in Latin America could no longer be ignored, nor could he ignore the shocking social and economic inequality between privileged and impoverished. On March 13, 1962, referring to Latin America, President Kennedy said: "Those who possess wealth and power in poor nations must accept their own responsibilities. . . . *Those who make peaceful revolution impossible will make violent revolution inevitable.*"[7]

What is happening in Latin America is not peculiar to that area; something similar is occurring in other parts of the world. Each area portrays part of the image of another. India, for example, could become an explosive area in a few short years. Misery, starvation, and social injustice abound. Awareness of the great suffering has been missing, and for this reason silent resignation has been maintained. But religious appeasements have now grown obsolete, and in a short time the sleeping conscience of the people may awake, replacing peaceful resignation with open rebellion.

Many other parts of the world offer similar situations, and social injustice has become the most serious explosive power threatening peace today.

For simple reasons of human solidarity, we must fight social injustice wherever it might be found. Those who do not feel this solidarity should realize, at least, that fighting social injustice is the single most important step in removing the threat of war.

NOTES

1. *The Causes of World War Three* (New York: Simon & Schuster, 1958), p. 125.

2. For a critique of the Cartesian doctrine of substance and its derivatives, *see* my *The Nature of the Self: A Functional Interpretation* (New Haven: Yale University Press, 1953).

3. Josué de Castro, *The Geography of Hunger* (Boston: Little, Brown, 1952), pp. 170–171.

4. Cf. *Psychological Factors of Peace and War*, ed. T. H. Pear (London: Hutchins, 1950), p. 162.

5. New Haven: Yale University Press, 1939.

6. On the Latin American situation, *see* my "Paz y justicia social," *Cuadernos Americanos* (September–October, 1967), pp. 7–27. A dramatic and well-documented discussion of hunger in the world will be found in Josué de Castro's *The Geography of Hunger, op. cit. See also* his *The Black Book of Hunger* (Boston: Beacon Press, 1969).

7. Italics mine.

III

The War System

CHAPTER SIX

War and the Crisis of Language

Thomas Merton

The Romans, to speak generally, rely on force in all their enterprises and think it incumbent upon them to carry out their projects in spite of all, and that nothing is impossible when they have once decided upon it.

POLYBIUS

I

Long before George Steiner pointed out that the German language was one of the casualties of naziism and World War II, Brice Parain in France had studied the "word sickness" of 1940, the mortal illness of journalese and political prose that accompanied the collapse of France. In proportion as the country itself accepted the denatured prose of Vichy—in which peace meant aggression and liberty meant oppression—it lost its identity and its capacity for valid action. It succumbed to "a full armed language without practical application." This, Parain reflected, had already happened before, in World War I, when words meant one thing in the trenches and another behind the lines.[1]

The reflections that follow are random and spontaneous insights—less of a philosopher than of a poet. For poets are perhaps the ones who, at the present moment, are most sensitive to the sickness of language—a sickness that, infecting all literature with nausea, prompts us not so much to declare war on conventional language as simply to pick up and examine intently a few chosen pieces of linguistic garbage. But of course, one does not have to be endowed with a peculiar poetic sensibility, still less with political genius, to recognize that official statements made in Washington, about the Vietnam War, for instance, are symptoms of a national—indeed worldwide—illness. Nor is it very hard to see that race riots and assassinations are also symptoms of the same illness, while they are also (and this is more important) a kind of universal language. Perhaps one might better call them an anti-language, a concrete expression of something that is uttered in fire and bullets rather than in words. And this in itself expresses an acute awareness of the gap between words and actions that is characteristic of modern war, because it is also characteristic of political life in general.

The malaise is universal. There is no need to quote a Swedish poet to prove it. But these lines from Gunnar Ekelöf may serve as an apéritif for what is to follow. He begins his poem "Sonata Form Denatured Prose" in these words:

> *crush the alphabet between your teeth yawn vowels, the fire is burning in hell vomit and spit now or never I and dizziness you or never dizziness now or never.*
>
> *we will begin over.*
>
> *crush the alphabet macadam and your teeth yawn vowels, the sweat runs in hell I am dying in the convolutions of my brain vomit now or never dizziness I and you. . .*[2]

There is no need to complete the poem. It is an angry protest against contemporary, denatured language. Ironically, it declares that ordinary modes of communication have broken down into banality and deception. It suggests that violence has gradually come to take the place of other, more polite, communications. Where there is such a flood of words that all words are unsure, it becomes necessary to make one's meaning clear with blows; or at least one explores this as a valid possibility.

The incoherence of language that cannot be trusted and the coherence of weapons that are infallible, or thought to be: this is the dialectic of politics and war, the prose of the twentieth century. We shall see at the end of the chapter that awareness of this fact has made a crucial difference in the racial conflict in the United States, and everywhere else.

II

Meanwhile, it is interesting to observe that religion too has reacted to the same spastic upheaval of language. I do not here refer to the phenomenon of a radical "God is Dead" theology—which in effect is our effort to reshape the language of religion in a last mintue attempt to save it from a plague of abstractness and formalism. This phenomenon is of course important. And so much has been said about it already—perhaps a great deal more than the subject deserves. I merely want to point out, in passing, that the fifties and sixties of our century have witnessed a curious revival of *glossolalia*—"speaking in tongues." Without attempting to evaluate this as charisma, I will at least say that it is significant in a context of religious and linguistic spasm. It is in its own way an expression of a curious kind of radicalism, a reaction to a religious language that is (perhaps obscurely) felt to be inadequate. But it is also, it seems to me, a reaction to something else. Glossolalia has flowered most abundantly in the United States, in fundamentalist and

Pentecostal sects of white Protestants, and perhaps most often in the South about the time of the Freedom Rides and nonviolent civil rights demonstrations. (I do not have much information on what has taken place most recently.) This was also the time when the Cold War was finally building up to the Cuba Crisis and the U.S. intervention in Vietnam was about to begin. Surely there is something interesting about this. At a time when the churches were at last becoming uneasily aware of a grave responsibility to *say something* about civil rights and nuclear war, the ones who could be least expected to be articulate on such subjects (and who often had solid dogmatic prejudices that foreclosed all discussion) began to cry out in unknown tongues.

At precisely the same moment, the Roman Catholic Church was abandoning its ancient liturgical language, the medieval Latin that was unknown to most of its members, and speaking out in a vernacular that many critics found disconcertingly banal and effete. If I refer to these things, it is not in scorn or in criticism. They are simply further expressions of a universal uneasiness about *language*—a sense of anxiety lest speech become entirely deceptive and unreal.

Can this apply to glossolalia? Of course. Fundamentalist religion assumes that the "unknown language" spoken "in the Spirit" is (though unintelligible) *more real* than the ordinary tired everyday language that everybody knows too well. Whether or not one believes that simple Texas housewives can burst out in the dialects of New Guinea head-hunters, under direct inspiration from God, there is here a significant implication that ordinary language is not good enough, and that there is something else which is at once more *real* and less comprehensible. Has ordinary language somehow failed?

I do not wish to hazard all sorts of incompetent guesses

about something I have not studied and do not intend to study . But one thing is quite evident about this phenomenon. He who speaks in an unknown tongue can safely speak without fear of contradiction. His utterance is *definitive* in the sense that it forecloses all dialogue. As St. Paul complained, if you utter a blessing in a strange language the congregation cannot answer "Amen" because it does not know it has been blessed. Such utterance is so final that nothing whatever can be done about it.[3] I wish to stress this unconscious aspiration to *definitive* utterance, to which there can be no rejoinder.

III

Now let us turn elsewhere, to the language of advertisement, which at times approaches the mystic and charismatic heights of glossolalia. Here too, utterance is final. No doubt there are insinuations of dialogue, but really there is no dialogue with an advertisement, just as there was no dialogue between the sirens and the crews they lured to disaster on their rocks. There is nothing to do but be hypnotized and drown, unless you have somehow acquired a fortunate case of deafness. But who can guarantee that he is deaf enough? Meanwhile, it is the vocation of the poet—or anti-poet—*not* to be deaf to such things but to apply his ear intently to their corrupt charms. An example: a perfume advertisement from the *New Yorker* (September 17, 1966).

I present the poem as it appears on a full page, with a picture of a lady swooning with delight at her own smell —the smell of *Arpège*. (Note that the word properly signifies a sound—*arpeggio*. Aware that we are now smelling music, let us be on our guard!)

For the love of Arpège . . .
There's a new hair spray!

The world's most adored fragrance
now in a hair spray. But not hair spray
as you *know it.*

A delicate-as-air spray
Your hair takes on a shimmer and sheen
that's wonderfully young.
You seem to spray new life and bounce
right into it. And a coif of Arpège has
one more thing no other hair spray has.
It has Arpège.

One look at this masterpiece and the anti-poet recognizes himself beaten hands down. This is beyond parody. It must stand inviolate in its own victorious rejection of meaning. We must avoid the temptation to dwell on details: interior rhyme, suggestions of an esoteric cult (the use of our product, besides making you young again, is also a kind of gnostic initiation), of magic (our product gives you a hat of smell—a "coif"—it clothes you in an aura of music-radiance-perfume). What I want to point out is the logical *structure* of this sonata: is is a foolproof tautology, locked tight upon itself, impenetrable, unbreakable, irrefutable. It is endowed with a finality so inviolable that it is beyond debate and beyond reason. Faced with the declaration that "Arpège has Arpège," reason is reduced to silence (I almost said despair). Here again we have an example of speech that is at once totally trivial and totally definitive. It has nothing to do with anything real (although of course the sale of the product is a matter of considerable importance to the manufacturer!), but what it says, it says with utter finality.

The unknown poet might protest that he (or she) was not concerned with truth alone but also with beauty—indeed with love. And obviously this too enters into the structure and substance (so to speak) of the text. Just as the argument takes the form of a completely self-enclosed tautological cliché, so the content, the "experience," is one of self-enclosed narcissism woven of misty confusion. It begins with the claim that a new hair spray exists solely for love of itself and yet also exists for love of *you*, baby, because you are somehow subtly identified with Arpège. This perfume is so magic that it not only makes you smell good, it "coifs" you with a new and unassailable identity: it is you who are unassailable because it is you who have somehow become a tautology. And indeed we are reminded that just as Arpège is—or has—Arpège, so, in the popular psychology of womens' magazines, "you are eminently lovable because you are just *you*." When we reflect that the ultimate conceptions of theology and metaphysics have surfaced in such a context—hair spray—we no longer wonder that theologians are tearing their hair and crying that God is dead. After all, when every smell, every taste, every hissing breakfast food is endowed with the transcendental properties of being . . . But let us turn from art, religion, and love to something more serious and more central to the concerns of our time: war.

IV

A classic example of the contamination of reason and speech by the inherent ambiguity of war is that of the U.S. major who, on February 7, 1968, shelled the South Vietnamese town of Bentre "regardless of civilian casualties. . . . to rout the Vietcong." As he calmly explained, "It became necessary to destroy the town in order to save it." Here we see, again, an insatiable appetite for the tautological, the definitive, the *final*. It is the same kind of language and logic that Hitler used for his notorious "final solution." The symbol of this perfect finality is the circle. An argument turns upon itself, and the beginning and end get lost: it just goes round and round its own circumference. A message comes in that someone thinks there might be some Vietcong in a certain village. Planes are sent, the village is destroyed, many of the people are killed. The destruction of the village and the killing of the people earn for them a final and official identity. The burned huts become "enemy structures"; the dead men, women, and children become "Vietcong," thus adding to a "kill ratio" that can be interpreted as "favorable." They were thought to be Vietcong and were therefore destroyed. By being destroyed they became Vietcong for keeps; they entered "history" definitively as our enemies, because we wanted to be on the "safe side," and "save American lives"—as well as Vietnam.

The logic of "Red or dead" has long since urged us to identify destruction with rescue—to be "dead" is to be saved from being "Red." In the language of melodrama, our grandparents became accustomed to the idea of a "fate worse than death." A schematic morality concluded that if such and such is a fate worse than death, then to prefer it to death would surely be a heinous sin. The logic of warmakers has extended this not only to the preservation of one's own moral integrity but to the fate of others, even of people on the other side of the earth, whom we do not always bother to consult personally on the subject. We weigh the arguments that they are not able to understand (perhaps they have not even heard that arguments exist!). And we decide, in their place, that it is better for them to be dead—killed by us—than Red, living under our enemies.

The Asian whose future we are about to decide is either a bad guy or a good guy. If he is a bad guy, he obviously has to be killed. If he is a good guy, he is on our side and he ought to be ready to die for freedom. We will provide an opportunity for him to do so: we will kill him to prevent him falling under the tyranny of a demonic enemy. Thus we not only defend his interests together with our own, but we protect his virtue along with our own. Think what might happen if he fell under communist rule *and liked it!*

The advantages of this kind of logic are no exclusive possession of the United States. This is purely and simply the logic shared by all war-makers. It is the logic of *power*. Possibly American generals are naive enough to push this logic, without realizing, to absurd conclusions. But all who love power tend to think in some such way. Remember Hitler weeping over the ruins of Warsaw after it had been demolished by the Luftwaffe: "How wicked these people must have been," he sobbed, "to make me do this to them!"

Words like "pacification" and "liberation" have acquired sinister connotations as war has succeeded war. Vietnam has done much to refine and perfect these notions. A "free zone" is now one in which anything that moves is assumed to be "enemy" and can be shot. In order to create a "free zone" that can live up effectively to its name, one must level everything, buildings, vegetation, everything, so that one can clearly see anything that moves, and shoot it. This has very interesting semantic consequences.

> An American Captain accounts for the levelling of a new "Free Zone" in the following terms: "We want to prevent them from moving freely in this area. . . . From now on anything that moves around here is going to be automatically considered V.C. and bombed or fired on. The whole Triangle is going to become a Free Zone. These villagers here are all considered hostile civilians."
>
> How did the Captain solve the semantic problem of distinguishing the hostile civilian from the refugee? "In a V.C. area like this there are three categories. First there are the straight V.C. . . . Then there are the V.C. sympathizers. Then there's the . . . There's a third category . . . I can't think of the third just now but . . . there's no middle road in this war."[4]

"Pacification" or "winning the hearts" of the undecided is thus very much simplified. "Soon" says a news report,[5] "the Government will have no need to win the hearts and minds of Bensuc. There will be no Bensuc." But there are further simplifications. A "high ranking US Field commander is quoted as saying: 'If the people are to the guerrillas as oceans are to the fish . . . we are going to dry up that ocean.' "[6] Merely by existing, a civilian, in this context, becomes a "hostile civilian." But at the same time and by the same token he is our friend and our ally. What simpler way out of the dilemma than to destroy him to "save American lives"?

V

So much for the practical language of the battlefield. Let us now attend to the much more pompous and sinister jargon of the war mandarins in government offices and military think-tanks. Here we have a whole community of intellectuals, scholars who spend their time playing out "scenarios" and considering "acceptable levels" in megadeaths. Their language and their thought are as esoteric, as self-enclosed, as tautologous as the advertisement we have just discussed. But instead of being "coifed" in a sweet smell, they are scientifically antiseptic, businesslike, uncontaminated with sentimental concern for life—other than their own. It is the same basic narcissism, but in a masculine, that is, managerial, mode. One proves one's realism along with one's virility by toughness in playing statistically with global death. It is this playing with death, however, that brings into the players' language itself the corruption of death: not physical but mental and moral extinction. And the corruption spreads from their talk, their thinking, to the words and minds of everybody. What happens then is that the political and moral values they claim to be defending are destroyed by the *contempt* that is more and more evident in the language in which they talk about such things. Technological strategy becomes an end in itself and leads the fascinated players into a maze where finally the very purpose strategy was supposed to serve is itself destroyed. The ambiguity of official war talk has one purpose above all: to mask this ultimate unreason and permit the game to go on.

Of special importance is the *style* of these nuclear mandarins. The technological puckishness of Herman Kahn is perhaps the classic of this genre. He excels in the sly understatement of the inhuman, the apocalyptic, enormity. His style is esoteric, allusive, yet confidential. The reader has the sense of being a privileged eavesdropper in the councils of the mighty. He knows enough to realize that things are going to happen about which he can do nothing, though perhaps he can save his skin in a properly equipped shelter where he may consider at leisure the rationality of survival in an unlivable world. Meanwhile, the cool tone of the author and the reassuring solemnity of his jargon seem to suggest that those in power, those who turn loose these instruments of destruction, have no intention of perishing themselves, that consequently survival must have a point. The point is not revealed, except that nuclear war is somehow implied to be good business. Nor are H-bombs necessarily a sign of cruel intentions. They enable one to enter into communication with the high priests in the enemy camp. They permit the decision makers on both sides to engage in a ritual "test of nerve." In any case, the language of escalation is the language of naked power, a language that is all the more persuasive because it is proud of being ethically illiterate and because it accepts, as realistic, the basic irrationality of its own tactics. The language of escalation, in its superb mixture of banality and apocalypse, science and unreason, is the expression of a massive death wish. We can only hope that this death wish is only that of a decaying Western civilization, and that it is not common to the entire race. Yet the language itself is given universal currency by the mass media. It can quickly contaminate the thinking of everybody.

VI

Sartre speaks of the peculiar, expert negligence of the language used by European mandarins (bankers, politicians, prelates), the "indolent and consummate art" they have of communicating with one another in double-talk that leaves them always able to escape while their subordinates are firmly caught.[7] On others, ambiguous directives are imposed with full authority. For others, these are final and inescapable. The purpose of the language game is then to maintain a certain balance of ambiguity and of authority so that the subject is caught and the official is not. Thus the subject can always be proved wrong and the official is always right. The official is enabled to lie in such a way that if the lie is discovered, a subordinate takes the blame. So much for European democracy. The same has been true in America in a somewhat different context—that of wheeler-dealing and political corruption rather than the framework of authoritarian and official privilege. But power in America, we find, can become mean, belligerent, temperamental. American power, while paying due respect to the demands of plain egalitarian folksiness, has its moments of arbitrary bad humor. But lest this bad humor become too evident, and lest repression begin to seem too forceful, language is at hand as an instrument of manipulation. Once again, the use of language to extol freedom, democracy, and equal rights, while at the same time denying them, causes words to turn sour and to rot in the minds of those who use them. In such a context, the effort of someone such as Lenny

Bruce to restore to language some of its authentic impact was a service despairingly offered to a public that could not fully appreciate it. One might argue that the language of this disconcerting and perhaps prophetic comedian was often less obscene than the "decent" but horrifying platitudes of those who persecuted him.

VII

Michel Foucault has described the evolution of the dialogue between medicine and madness in the Age of Reason.[8] Therapeutic experiments with manic-depressives in the eighteenth century assumed a certain inner consistency in the delirium of the mad and, working within the supposed framework of this consistency, sought to suggest to the madman an alternative to his madness—or, rather, to push the "logic" of his madness to a paroxysm and crisis in which it would be confronted with itself and "forced to argue against the demands of its own truth." Thus, for instance, in cases of religious mania and despair, patients who believed themselves damned were shown a theatrical tableau in which the avenging angel appeared, punished, and then gave assurance that guilt was now taken away. Patients who were dying of starvation because, believing themselves dead, they would not eat were shown representations of dead persons eating and were thus brought face to face with an unexpected syllogism: you claim you are dead and cannot eat, but dead men can eat. . . . The beauty of Foucault's book is that we become fascinated by the way in which the "reason" of the Age of Enlightenment unconsciously shared so much of the madness with which it was in dialogue.

Reading of this dialogue between reason and madness, one is reminded of the language of power and war. In the deliberate, realistic madness of the new language we find an implicit admission that words, ordinary discourse, won't do—not exactly that language itself has broken down, is no longer valid as such. But the enemy is at once so perverse and so irrational—such a psychopathic liar in fact—that he has to be cleverly treated as a beast or as a maniac. We all know that it is customary for one who resorts to violence to do so on the ground that the adversary "does not understand anything else." The "language of escalation" is a more sophisticated application of this principle, but on a massive scale implemented by the threat of a nuclear strike. It seems, indeed, that since the adversary understands nothing but force, and since force means everything up to and including the use of H-bombs, we will eventually get beyond the mere threat of a nuclear strike: one of us will actually strike. This will demonstrate that if you face an enemy with the conviction that he understands nothing but force, you will yourself necessarily behave as if you understood nothing but force. And in fact it is highly probable that if you say he understands nothing but force, it is because you yourself are already in the same plight.

In any case, it is quite obvious that the military on whatever side must be quite convinced of the superior efficacy of force, or they would not be military. If they worry about this at all, they can always reason that force is necessary because we are faced by various bunches of madmen who understand nothing else. The dialogue then proceeds in a way that reminds us of Foucault:

1. Rational discourse with the enemy is useless. He does not understand rational discourse and makes negotiation an opportunity for lying and pathological trickery. He *has to* cheat.

2. Therefore he has to be dealt with solely in the framework of his madness and wickedness, his propensity to lie and cheat. One does not bargain with such a one, because

bargaining implies the acceptance, on both sides, of conditions. He must be pushed to the point where his surrender is unconditional in terms of his own madness. To grant him reasonable conditions would be to treat a madman as a rational being, which would be the worst possible kind of mistake and indeed (if you believe in sin) a sin.

3. His madness has roots in guilt, because he is, after all, wicked. He understands *punishment*. But the punishment must be shown to him in terms of his own madness. He must see that his own destructive violence will lead inexorably to one consequence: his own annihilation. But to translate this into words would lead to confusion. The message must be got to him in the unmistakable language of force itself. Of course, verbal formulas have to be resorted to, in order to define what force is all about, to set conditions, etc. But the verbal formulas must be kept deliberately ambiguous, unclear. The clear and unmistakable message is not that of the *terms offered* but of the escalation itself. In other words there is an *appearance* of dialogue on the verbal and political level. But the real dialogue is with weapons and may be a complete contradiction of what appears to be said in the prose of politics.

The effect of this, of course, is a vicious circle: it begins with a tacit admission that negotiation is meaningless, and it does in fact render the language of negotiation meaningless. War-makers in the twentieth century have gone far toward creating a political language so obscure, so apt for treachery, so ambiguous, that it can no longer serve as an instrument for peace: it is good only for war. But why? Because the language of the war-maker is *self-enclosed in finality*. It does not invite reasonable dialogue, it uses language to silence dialogue, to block communication, so that instead of words the two sides may trade divisions, positions, villages, air bases, cities—and of course the lives of the people in them. The daily toll of the killed (or the "kill ratio") is perfunctorily scrutinized and decoded. And the totals are expertly managed by "ministers of truth" so that the newspaper reader may get the right message.

Our side is always ahead. He who is winning must be the one who is right. But we are right, therefore we must be winning. Once again we have the beautiful, narcissistic tautology of war—or of advertising. Once again, "Arpège has Arpège." There is no communicating with anyone else, because anyone who does not agree, who is outside the charmed circle, is wrong, is evil, is already in hell.

VIII

It is a dictum of Marxism that a word is true if it can be verified by being carried out in action. But this idea is not a monopoly of the Communists. It is now universal. It is everybody's property. Modern politics is a matter of defining how you think things ought to be and then making them come out that way by cunning or by force. If you aren't strong enough or smart enough to verify your ideas by putting them into effect, then you have no business saying how things should be in the first place: follow somebody else who has the necessary power! The strange thing is that this idea is not so modern after all. In fact it is quite ancient. Another word for it is magic, or witchcraft.

Of course, the shaman and the medicine man in primitive society did not possess the advantages of a technological skill that would enable them to say that white was black and then prove the point by turning white into black. Yet even unlimited power does not always succeed in making one's own words come true—as the Vietnam War has conclusively shown.

One of the most curious things about the war in Vietnam is that it is being *fought to vindicate the assumptions upon which it is being fought.* Now it turns out that these American assumptions are quite wrong: the White House and the Pentagon have consistently interpreted the war as a military invasion of South Vietnam by the North. In other words it is the Korean War over again, a "conventional limited war" in which the problems are above all military and can be handled in terms of bombing, sending in more troops, wiping out areas in which the enemy tends to concentrate, cutting supply lines, etc. By the escalation of the war and the bombing of North Vietnam (after the "Tonkin Bay Incident," which has now been shown to have been exaggerated if not actually faked) the United States did actually turn the war into the kind of war it was supposed to be in America apart from the fact that the aggression was the other way around. But this did nothing to alter the fact that the war in the South remained essentially a revolutionary guerrilla struggle that could not be adequately handled by conventional military operations.

Alastair Buchan, analyzing this curious fact in *Encounter,*[9] wonders how it was possible for such a policy to be accepted when the U.S. government relies on "a wide range of research institutes and universities to give greater depth and accuracy to its own operational and political analysis." He hazards a guess that the unassailable self-confidence of science somehow contributed to the error: "Probably technology (helicopters, new small arms, infra-red sensors and all the rest) was the element that corrupted judgement, making it seem possible that the Americans could do what the natives (i.e. the South Vietnamese army) or the old colonial powers (v.g. the French) could not." In other words, there is a certain hubris built into technological thinking that encloses it within itself and its own suppositions and makes it fatally ignore decisive realities that do not fit those suppositions.

However, in such a situation, power can still vindicate

itself by *declaring* that its estimate was the correct one and that it is still winning. Since statistics can be made to prove anything, it adduces statistics to show that its words are in fact coming true. Unfortunately, the Tet offensive of the Vietcong in 1968 made it finally clear that no amount of juggling with words or figures could make this "politics of inadvertence" (the words are Arthur Schlesinger's) come out level with reality. Lyndon Johnson is certainly well versed in all the appropriate skills, and yet in this instance he turned out to be a singularly failed witch.

What needs to be noted is that the massive effort of the United States to gain acceptance for its own version of the Vietnam War by doing all in its power to turn that version into accomplished fact has had profoundly significant effects. And these effects are not what was intended. Confidence in the Washington government, in the American political system, in the credibility of American officials, even in the basic human integrity and sincerity of the American Establishment is now seriously undermined at home and abroad. The *political language* of the United States, which was suspect before, has now been fatally denatured. It has probably lost all its value as intellectual currency. The crisis of the dollar is intimately connected with the crisis of human communication that has resulted from the sinister double-talk of the American Establishment about itself, about the war, about the race situation, about the urgent domestic problems that are being ignored or set aside while the government puts more and more money and manpower into the war. The tragedy is not so much that America has come out of its pristine isolationism but that it has decided to rule the world without paying serious attention to anybody else's view of what the world is all about. Language has been distorted and denatured in defense of this solipsistic, this basically isolationist and sometimes even paranoid, attitude.

IX

What next? The illness of political language—which is almost universal and is a symptom of a Plague of Power that is common to China and America, Russia and western Europe—is characterized everywhere by the same sort of double-talk, tautology, ambiguous cliché, self-righteous and doctrinaire pomposity, and pseudoscientific jargon that mask a total callousness and moral insensitivity, indeed a basic contempt for man. The self-enclosed finality that bars all open dialogue and pretends to impose absolute conditions of one's own choosing upon everybody else ultimately becomes the language of totalist dictatorship, if it is not so already. Revolt against this is taking the form of another, more elemental and anarchistic, kind of violence, together with a different semantic code. Space does not permit us to study this other language, but it must be acknowledged as immensely popular and influential all over the world. It is the language of Che Guevara, of Régis Debray, of Franz Fanon: the violent language and the apocalyptic myth of the guerrilla warrior, the isolated individual and the small group, enabled by revolutionary charisma to defy all the technological might of the biggest powers in the world. In spite of the failure of Che in Bolivia—a failure that only resulted in his canonization as a martyr of the post-colonial revolution—the Vietnam War has had the result of awakening revolutionary hopes all over the world, from Harlem to Angola. Che Guevara called for Vietnams everywhere, and the Black Power movement, introducing the language of Fanon into American political life, is set on making the inner cities of the United States "other Vietnams." At the moment, when the full tragedy has not yet manifested itself, this might to some seem an inspiring revolt against the inhuman pride of technological white power. But the hopes of Fanon—which may have some basis in the jungles of Africa—are couched in the same terms of magic and witchcraft that assert something and then proceed to make it so in fact, thereby vindicating their own prophecy. If this went wrong for U.S. power in Vietnam, it may also go wrong in the American ghettos, where, unfortunately, the Negro does not have miles of swamp and jungle to maneuver in but is enclosed in a small and highly vulnerable area in which he can easily be destroyed or arrested and taken off to concentration camps.

However that may be, the revolutionary tactic that tends to harass and immobilize the Goliath of technological military power and bring it down largely by its own elephantine weight has at the same time created a new language that mocks the ponderous and self-important utterances of the Establishment. This new language, racy, insolent, direct, profane, iconoclastic, and earthy, may have its own magic incantation and myth. It may be involved in its own elaborate set of illusions. But at least it represents a healthier and more concrete style of thought. It does not reduce everything to abstractions, and though it is fully as intransigent as the language of the Establishment, it still seems to be more in contact with relevant experience: the hard realities of poverty, brutality, vice, and resistance.

Yet, flexible though it might be in some respects, it remains another language of power, therefore of self-enclosed finality, which rejects dialogue and negotiation on the axiomatic supposition that the adversary is a devil with whom no dialogue is possible.

NOTES

1. *See* Sartre's essay on Parain in *Situations I* (Paris: 1947), p. 192.

2. Gunnar Ekelöf: *Late Arrival on Earth*, Selected Poems, trans. Robert Bly & Christine Paulston (London: 1967), p. 13.

3. *See* I Corinthians 14.

4. *See* Jonathan Schell in the *New Yorker* (July 15, 1967), p. 59.

5. *New York Times*, Jan. 11, 1967.

6. Quoted in the *New Statesman* (Mar. 11, 1966).

7. *Op. cit.*, p. 202.

8. Michel Foucault, *Madness and Civilization* (New York: 1967), p. 188.

9. Jan.–Feb. 1968.

CHAPTER SEVEN

Political, Technological, and Cultural Aspects of War

John Nef

Chairman,
Center for Human Understanding of the University of Chicago

War has taken on a meaning it has never before had. Unless men are able henceforth to limit war once and for all, they will always run the risk of finding this planet suddenly drained of human life and of the civilized monuments and works of art, including books of philosophy and literature, that have given human life a value that life has never had for any other species.

No problem that confronts men and women, divided among many scores of nations, demands solution with such compelling force as the problem of eliminating the danger of total war. Moreover, the powers of destruction unleashed during the past quarter-century have made the constructive handling of almost all other problems more dependent upon a less war-minded humanity than ever before.

The recognition of this new interdependent condition of mankind, in a world where almost all work is increasingly specialized, came to me through my study of integral history, which began forty years ago. I learned that all aspects of the historical evolution of any nation, or of any group of closely interdependent nations, are interrelated. The central position that the problem of war and peace has come to occupy can be understood better when it is recognized how closely the history of war was always intertwined with the rest of history. A better knowledge of the interrelations of war to political, technological, and cultural development among the Western nations since the Middle Ages can help in meeting the overwhelming dangers that for the first time threaten the human experiment with extinction.

Far from diminishing the importance of other issues—individual as well as collective—the unparalleled risks to which war now subjects us give these issues a greater vitality. New possibilities are opened for the enrichment of life. The hope of diminishing the danger of total war depends on the ways in which men and women guide their daily conduct and make their decisions as members of societies. The hope for a constructive development of civilization may well rest with arousing among humankind a desire to become better individuals. Technological progress has brought about material world unity—an interdependence of all societies and all aspects of living—never before approached. Individuals—the life of even the smallest individual, the smallest matters of an individual's life—can influence the way in which mankind responds to this hope for survival, through improvement, in a common humanity.

If the nations are to achieve policies with respect to warfare different from those that have hitherto prevailed, if world community is gradually to supplant nationalism, racism, and communism or anticommunism as a goal, it must be recognized that the course of history is always changing. It has changed in the last quarter-century faster than ever before. We ought not to count (as many in power today do) upon a repetition of what has happened. There are at least three reasons that we cannot be guided by past conflicts in trying to meet the menace of total war. First, the causes for wars change. Second, as has just been suggested, the nature of warfare changes. Third, serious efforts to attenuate, and even to eliminate, wars are of relatively recent origin. Our principal resource in searching for peace among different nations, races, and creeds or beliefs rests in building upon these efforts.

I

Long ago, when I went to college in the United States, history instructors, with an almost monotonous regularity, used to recite the causes of each war that came within the scope of their lectures: the Thirty Years War in Europe, the Civil War in the United States, or any of the almost endless armed conflicts that have so frequently turned sections of this planet into places of organized mutual slaughter. It was not unusual, I seem to remember, for a particular professor to have for every war a settled number of causes. (And then he would usually follow his description of the war with the same number of results.) Six was a favorite figure! Students found it to their advantage to memorize the professor's causes (and results), for they could frequently be served back in answer to his examination questions.

Of course, the perennial cause of organized fighting between nations or within nations lies much deeper than the causes for particular wars, even if it were possible for experts to agree on those. The perennial cause is embedded in human nature itself, in the temptation to settle scores by violence, in the luxury of destruction and self-destruction. If one were to speak in the language of Christian revelation, the fundamental cause of war is the Fall.

Americans and Europeans have a Christian heritage. Most of our ancestors believed, and there are still among us some who believe, in original sin. Although it is stated in the New Testament, the truly Christian way of meeting this weakness, when war is the issue, has never been tried even by those innumerable persons who have sought salvation, during almost two thousand years, in Christian dogma: Christ suggests that we are all brothers and sisters under a common Father, and that the way to peace is for us to love one another. The murderous conflicts that have been the subject of so much history have been the consequence of refusing this counsel. And alas, as we know, persons professing the Christian faith have not been backward in making that refusal.

The further we dig into history, the more we get the impression that, apart from this basic cause in human nature itself, the general factors responsible for war have always varied. A notion that the sources of organized conflicts are mainly economic became prominent before World War I and has been by no means discarded. We derive the notion partly from successors to and opponents of Marx who were obsessed by the belief that history in general is explicable almost entirely in economic terms. As some saw it, wars arose out of the division of society into rich and poor. The rich had the power and got the profits from victory and even sometimes from defeat. So they were chauvinistic.

Obviously the advent of new weapons makes it difficult to argue that even the rich would gain by total war! Indeed, there were already some persons before 1914 who had a premonition that, from an economic standpoint, modern war would be folly. In 1910 a young Englishman, Norman Angell, wrote a book called *The Great Illusion*, which had a wide sale and was translated into many languages. He sought to demonstrate to businessmen and statesmen everywhere that in modern war the victors stood to lose as much as the vanquished. War would ruin both sides.

Time has caught up with this thesis in a hurry. Yet the "illusion" persists. It was strengthened, at the very time that Angell wrote his book, under the influence of a German professor, Werner Sombart, an economic historian of Marxist origin who later accepted naziism and whose books circulated in Germany before and during the 1914–1918 War. His thesis was that, at least since the Renaissance, war among the Europeans and their descendants has been one of the most economically constructive forces, a principal factor in industrial, commercial, and financial progress, as progress is measured by the yardsticks of economists. Large-scale economic enterprise, power-driven machinery, and mass production all owe much to modern war, he argued, because of the concentration of capital and the standardization of products that the preparation and the waging of war entailed.

My book[1] demonstrated that Sombart's thesis is mistaken for the entire period to which he applied it: the early sixteenth to the early twentieth century. During that period the destructive consequences of war outweighed the constructive influences. It was in spite of wars, and because of the new limitations on warfare, that the economic developments that transformed man's condition took place.

In the history of the western European peoples running back to the Crusades, there were immense variations in the underlying causes for which men were brought to fight. And in any war at any time, multiple causes were invariably intermingled. Some think of the Crusades as religious wars *par excellence*, but in fact even the appeal of Pope Urban II for the First Crusade was not without undertones that might today be classed as economic, or at least demographic. The words the pope pronounced at Clermont-

Ferrand in 1095, "God wills it," are said to have echoed through all Europe. But the versions of his sermon by several witnesses reveal a passage wherein the pope alluded to the recent growth in the European population. This had been considerable, as historical researchers now have shown. The pope suggested that conquests in the Middle East could provide an outlet for the increasing inhabitants, a means of diminishing the conflicts between Christians in Europe itself.

Eight hundred years later religious beliefs seem to have played almost no role in the war of 1914–1918. Both sides appealed for victory to the same God. But we should now know what an error it is to assume that beliefs, which have behind them a fanaticism reminiscent of religious wars, could no longer produce total wars. The so-called Cold War of the mid-twentieth century is a conflict between communism and anticommunism, as little founded in the realities of history as were the struggles between Roman Catholic and Protestant sects that tore central Europe to pieces during the Thirty Years War.[2]

This comparison reminds us that once religious (or what are now called "ideological") wars start, the struggle takes on a dialectic of its own. Beliefs are lost sight of, and people are pushed to kill for the sake of killing, and eventually for the sake of eating.

II

When the obvious has become the overwhelmingly dangerous and when people are inclined to become callous to the danger, it is vital to emphasize the obvious. The nature of war has changed in our time much more fundamentally than the causes for wars.

Among our western European ancestors in the later

Middle Ages physical violence was more common than among us, capital punishment much more widespread. Organized war was not subject to the humanitarian conventions established during the eighteenth and nineteenth centuries, conventions that we are menaced with losing. But the means of waging organized war were paltry compared with those now available. While cannons were invented apparently at the beginning of the fourteenth century in Europe, for several generations they were immobile and so feeble in execution that they were used principally to terrify the enemy by the noise they produced. During the fifteenth century armor was perfected; the knights and even their horses were encased in more elegant, heavier, and ever more cumbersome suits. King James I of England, who was notoriously pacifistic in his inclinations, is said to have remarked that armor served a double purpose: it protected those who wore it and at the same time hindered them from disposing of their adversaries. War in medieval times was bloody enough for all that, but the numbers then engaged in organized wars were so small as to seem insignificant. At Agincourt in 1415, a great battle in the Hundred Years' War, not more than six thousand men were mobilized on each side.

Contrast that situation with the one prevailing today. Suddenly, within the lifetime of the generations who fought two world wars, it has become practicable to kill tens of *millions* of people all at once. It has become practicable in a couple of *days* to destroy more persons than the eighty million or so who died as a result of all-out war in the ten *years* from 1914 to 1918 and from 1939 to 1945. The difference in the possible *scale* of organized war now and in the past is so overwhelming as to constitute a difference in *kind*. For the first time, the road to total war has become the road to annihilation.

III

There are those who hold that this change is proof of the constructive character of organized conflict! That could be the case only if the change put an end, once and for all, to war as an instrument of political policies. The persons who have recently vaunted the constructive nature of modern war have adopted an argument they could have derived from Sombart. If their attention is called to the weakness of his thesis for history down to 1914 (when he had already stated it), they either brush aside the evidence or say that while war may have been mainly destructive before 1914, the experience of two world wars has proved how economically constructive war has become.

Let us consider these views, which remain rather prevalent. Let us consider whether initiative would languish, whether happiness would diminish, if total war should cease to play a major role in history, to be replaced by less dangerous outlets for man's belligerent instincts.

Invention is of various kinds. The differences are of great moment in considering these questions of the relations between war and human progress.

There are the inventions of the artist and the craftsman (and the greatest artists must always be skilled craftsmen, though their genius consists in transcending traditional craftsmanship). The goal of both artist and craftsman is not primarily multiplication but quality. It is beauty and the harmony without which there can be no beauty. This goal imposes limits on the number of works produced. A painter may turn his mind and hand to etching, for the sake of increasing the examples of his art, or, like Rubens, maintain a vast establishment in which assistants complete many of the canvasses whose subject, nature, and design are his. But the number of etchings pulled from a plate has to be limited. So do the number of canvasses completed. Else the personal meaning, strength, and perfection essential to a work of art will be lost. Indeed, it may be questioned whether all the pictures from Rubens's studio were works of art, in spite of the genius of the masterpieces he personally completed.

Therefore the purpose of the kind of invention that results in works of literature, of the visual arts, and of music, and also in beautiful furnishings, clothing, decorations, musical instruments, etc., is defeated without restraints on productivity. Genius consists to no small extent in making the right refusals, and prominent among these is the refusal to conform to the demands of the market for quantity. The invention of the artist and the craftsman is not dependent, in the main, on the efficiency recognized by conventional economists. Both the artist and the craftsman often need to waste materials, time, and effort in the cause of beauty. Their invention is illustrative of the utility of the useless.[3] After the eighteenth century, the value of that came to be lost sight of, perhaps mainly under the aegis of the British Empire and the United States.

The second kind of invention that should be distinguished in this discussion is that of the experimental scientist. What such a scientist seeks is truth about the nature of the physical and the biological universes. He is concerned with time, space, motion, and matter, not with human quarrels and conflicts. He is not interested *as a scientist* in the practical uses to which his discoveries are put, and this objectivity and independence offer him his great opportunity. In speculating about the physical or the biological universe, he makes *inventions*, in the sense that he constructs images concerning particular aspects of these universes, which then have to be established as true in the light of tangible evidence.

While the workings of the scientist's mind often resemble those of an artist's, there is a fundamental difference in the nature of the results sought. Scientific invention is less concerned with results that will endure in and of themselves than with concepts that may serve as stepping stones to more advanced concepts. Unlike the artist, unlike even the true craftsman, the scientist creates in the hope that, as a famous Victorian economist expressed it, a pupil of his "in due course . . . will render [his results] obsolete."[4]

A third kind of invention needs to be distinguished: that associated with technological progress. In recent times the word "invention" has most frequently been used in connection with this type of inventive genius. As the phrase is widely used today, "technological progress" is associated with invention for the sake of practical efficiency, with devices for multiplying output, diminishing labor costs, increasing the speed and diminishing the expense of transport and communication. The minds of men who invent devices for such objectives, of men such as Thomas Edison or Alexander Graham Bell, are most resourceful and enterprising. But as engineers their purpose is different from that of scientists' as well as of artists'.

The relations between scientific and technological invention, which have played an increasing part since the eighteenth century in bringing about the conquest of the material world, remain to be fully unraveled. Speaking generally, the greater has been the dependence of practical inventions upon scientific knowledge (and indeed, upon scientific progress), the more spectacular has been "technological progress."[5] Never has the dependence of technological progress upon science been so great as during the technological revolution that has swept across the planet and into outer space since World War II. So it is not unnatural that this progress should often be attributed to the stimuli of organized warfare.

In considering this view, several observations would seem to be of capital importance. When the relations in the West between war and human progress are examined, from the sixteenth century through the twentieth, it becomes evident that the provision of weapons has always tried man's ingenuity. War was always to some degree a source of constructive technological invention. It is the magnitude of the technological progress attributable to the demands of war that has changed in our times.

Since 1914 the constructive technological consequences of war have increased, as statisticians might say, in geometrical progression, but so, potentially, have the destructive consequences. Unless mankind masters war, the latter will outweigh the constructive consequences, as they always have since the revolution in the art of war in the age of the Renaissance, and to an *overwhelmingly greater extent.*

The prevalent and popular notion that the recent total wars have been a great stimulus to the inventive *scientific* mind also requires careful scrutiny. The possibilities inherent in nuclear fission were revealed during the first third of the twentieth century by a few scientists of genius, notable among them Rutherford, the Curies, Bohr, Louis de Broglie. The basic discoveries were all made by persons working quietly, without publicity, and often without adequate financial support, before the sciences had the public acclaim they have since acquired. None of these persons made his discoveries for the sake of building more powerful weapons of war.

They were doubtless aware of the powers inherent in their scientific achievements. Great scientists, in their pursuit of truth, have never been ignorant of the dangerous consequences that might follow from particular scientific discoveries. This was the case as far back as Newton, Boyle, Napier, even Leonardo da Vinci. What changed during and after the eighteenth century was the pessimism scientists felt about humanity. The growing optimism led to a willingness to put scientific results freely at the disposal of technological progress. The stimulus to doing so was less the prospect of bigger wars than the hope mankind might find ways of putting an end to war.

Before the entry of the United States into World War II, the practical possibilities for the release of new sources of energy inherent in recent scientific discoveries were well known even beyond the scientific community, which then existed in comparative quiet and intellectual seclusion. At the end of 1941, a group of eminent experimental scientists under the leadership of the late Enrico Fermi decided to devote themselves to finding whether a chain reaction of sufficient magnitude could be obtained from nuclear fission to make possible the manufacture of bombs of almost infinitely greater destructive power. There can be no doubt that the decision grew out of the war. Nor that it speeded up the practical applications of nuclear power. Yet it is equally clear that nuclear power would have soon been used, if there had been no war, and mainly for ends different from those that were given priority because of the immense sums invested by the United States government in this war project. Herbert Anderson, Fermi's pupil and associate, remembers that before the war Fermi told him: "If you work with me in this field, some day you'll be president of the Uranium Corporation of America and you'll make lots of money!"[6]

The philosophical question that confronts us is whether it was in the interest of happiness to have scientific research move in the directions prompted by war and to have technological progress, under the impetus of such scientific diversions, speeded up to the extent it has been. On both counts, a distinguished scholar who occupies a position of authority in the American scientific community has recently written with reservations. "The stupendous technical achievement in defense made during World War II," says Dr. Caryl P. Haskins,

> was . . . widely believed to be one of science . . . In fact, of course, it was for the most part nothing of the kind. It was, instead, a tremendous effort of application, conducted with almost unbelievable effectiveness and skill and on a scale never realized before, but nonetheless an enterprise basically of technology rather than of science, of technology drawing upon scientific resources slowly built up over many earlier decades.[7]

What seem to have been some of the consequences for scientific invention itself? What seem to have been some of the consequences for human welfare?

The increasing concern of governments with new kinds of armaments and the enormously increased expenditures on armaments that accompanied the employment of scientists in war work and in the preparation for war since 1945 have made science dependent as never before on government support. And government service requires a kind of nationalistic outlook and dedication that cannot be considered as altogether objective and independent.[8] Scientists have become, to a degree that was never true before, the servants and agents of governments. Such service often diverts them from the disinterested search for truth, and disinterestedness is essential for pure scientific invention.

Furthermore, the growing expenditures on "science" in recent years have been accompanied by radical changes in the nature of research. The scientific revolution of the seventeenth century and the subsequent increasingly rapid development of modern science down to World War II were the work of individuals of genius. They derived intellectual stimulus from fellow scientists and from many other sources, including technological inventors. But each scientist did his own work. Each was his own master, or, to put it more accurately, each was the dedicated servant of scientific truth. More recently the tendency has been toward group research with teams of scholars working together. The work of one is dependent on that of the others. The loss of a member of the group requires replacement by another with the same special training, a training that the other members of the team seldom possess. Some of the older scientists regret this trend toward collective investigation. They see it as a blow to the creative invention hitherto characteristic of the experimental sciences.

In short, it is by no means certain that the capital in pure science that is being drawn upon so heavily for practical purposes is being fully replaced. It has been suggested, moreover, that a wise statesman can obtain more helpful advice from scientists who retain their independence of governments. If political policy is ever to be of disinterested service to humanity, that suggestion will have to carry weight.

The conquest of the material world has been speeded up partly under the impact of war. But may we not be making haste too rapidly for human happiness? Speed of change is widely treated (and the public is encouraged to regard it as such) as an unmitigated blessing. Yet even if the world escapes total war, to the waging of which this very speed of change could contribute, the uprooting inherent in the technological revolution of the past quarter-century seems to be one cause for a spreading malaise that should concern humanity. It is therefore questionable whether efforts could not be more fruitfully directed to preparing society everywhere for the social convulsions that are involved in the application not only of the physical but now of the biological sciences, rather than to a helter-skelter promotion of newly invented devices for turning out products in abundance and even for making over the biological structure of men and women themselves.

IV

Our brief inquiry leads to the conclusion that among the supreme needs of humanity today are two which run counter to present trends. One is the need to reduce the speed of technological progress, fed by scientific knowledge, in the interests of a more rounded, stable, and refined life for societies, in which the individual of distinction, whose goals are the good, the true, and the beautiful, will count for more. The other is the need to reduce the threat of total war by strengthening movements toward world community. The two needs may well be interrelated.

The advent since the juncture of the sixteenth and seventeenth centuries of novel restraints on war was partly responsible for the rise of "civilization." That word was first used in the mid-eighteenth century to describe what some distinguished Europeans and Americans believed to be a society more humane in its potentialities than any previously achieved on earth.

Until modern times limits on total war had come, generally speaking, not as a result of restraints on force but by the establishment of absolute power through conquest. Perhaps the most striking example was the Roman Empire. In the Roman peace no one gave up the idea of total victory. On the contrary, it was total conquest resulting from a series of total victories, such as the victory of Rome over Carthage in the Third Punic War, that left all the other people of Europe and the Mediterranean basin subjects of the Roman emperors. The *Pax Romana* was not a peace among free men. It was destroyed when the barbarians found means of defeating the Roman legions.

This example has no utility in the twentieth century.

An attempt to establish an empire of this kind in the future would be likely to wipe mankind off the earth.

Many among the early Christians believed that if the world became Christian, there would be no more wars. Certainly the experiment has never been tried, but the history of those sections of the world where the great majority were professed Christian communicants is far from reassuring.

The widening of the Christian faith in Europe from the fourth to the eleventh centuries brought on a spiritual unity through the Roman Church with its increasingly numerous ecclesiastical foundations. And this unity was accompanied by efforts on the part of successive popes to limit organized war between Christian countries. Indeed, by various decrees the popes sought to define a just war, as they also sought to prevent the use of certain weapons such as the crossbow, to restrict the days for fighting, to prohibit priests from shedding blood. For a time, in fact, the pacific decrees of the papacy seem to have had some success in limiting war in Europe itself, notably during the thirteenth century. But even before the schisms that followed within the Church, and in spite of the immense prestige possessed by the papacy between the eleventh and the thirteenth centuries, the pacifistic principle was grievously compromised insofar as organized religion was concerned in the Crusades. Total war was treated not only as legitimate but as desirable, and the Crusades brought war not only against non-Christians but against the orthodox Christians of Constantinople and Russia. The recent history of the Crusades by Runciman teaches also that, once in the Near East, the Crusaders surpassed their adversaries in violence and cruelty against civilians.

In the innumerable local wars among the Europeans themselves that accompanied much of the crusading, and which multiplied after the Crusades were over, the same language of violence without mercy, employed so freely against the Moslems, was turned on brother Christians. The siege of Ghent at the end of the fourteenth century, as described by Froissard, suggests that there was hardly a limit to the eagerness to kill and burn fellow Christians regardless of sex or age. The same is true of medieval Scottish history before the rise of "civilization," as described by Sir Walter Scott in *Tales of a Grandfather*.

Had there not been since the late sixteenth century and down through much of the nineteenth great changes in manners and customs, the West might never have achieved "civilization" and later the industrialism that was partly founded on "civilization." Without limited warfare, without the hope that humanity might eventually master war and Christ's message of peace and brotherhood become more effective, the abundance that has made many prideful might never have been achieved.

Among the principal brakes on total war was the spread of art and craftsmanship, as both were practiced during the seventeenth and eighteenth centuries. Along with their spread went changes toward a greater gentleness in manners, to which artists such as Callot, Rubens, Velasquez, and Rembrandt contributed. In fact, the first great efforts to diminish violence appeared at the end of the French religious wars, some twenty-five years before the concept of a universal authority to settle quarrels between nations was introduced without stir by a certain Emeric Crucé in 1623.[9]

As a consequence of these new efforts, bulwarks came to be erected in the minds of men and women, including statesmen, against unrestricted warfare. The recent study of the history of science has concentrated attention on the scientific revolution. But the discoveries—we can perhaps call them the inventions—in the domain of morality and the increasing concern over physical suffering were hardly less important for the application, with the coming of "civilization," of the principle of limited warfare.

The consequences of advances in scientific and in technological invention are neutral insofar as the heart is concerned. The great need of humanity today is for inventions that will contribute to peace and to more harmonious material progress. One cannot achieve a shift in the goals of endeavor toward artistic and moral invention by government fiat, or by planning that gives even greater power to men over men. But one can stress the need for such a shift, in the hope that this may help the young of their free will to move in that direction without increasing the role of government in private affairs—which is perhaps already greater than human needs require.

It was the partly successful attempts to impose restraints on war after the Reformation and the Counter-Reformation that prevented war from stopping progress. Now that warfare has suddenly become potentially totally destructive, the road to a securer peace than our ancestors managed to achieve has become, as never before, the only road to progress.

NOTES

1. Nef, *War and Human Progress* (Cambridge, Mass.: 1950).

2. Nef, *The United States and Civilization*, 2nd ed. (Chicago: 1967), pp. 98–110, 413–416.

3. Nef, "L'Universalité française," *French Review*, XXXIX (1956), 383–388.

4. J. M. Keynes, *Essays in Biography* (London: 1933), pp. 253–254.

5. Nef, *The Conquest of the Material World* (Chicago: 1964), ch. vii.

6. Herbert Anderson, "Science in the Defense of Human Dignity," in *Towards World Community*, ed. Nef (The Hague: 1968), p. 21.

7. Caryl P. Haskins, *Report to the Carnegie Institution 1965–1966*, p. 12. Cf. pp. 12–14.

8. Cf. J. de Bourbon Busset, "Letters and Nationalism," in *Towards World Community, op. cit.*, pp. 111–113.

9. Nef, *Cultural Foundations of Industrial Civilization* (Cambridge, England: 1958), esp. chs. iv, v, vi.

CHAPTER EIGHT

Marxism and War

John Somerville

Professor of Philosophy,
California Western University

The central problem of our age is the problem of war, and the central aspect of that problem is the relations between capitalist powers and communist powers. War has become central because developments in physical science and technology have brought into being thermonuclear and other weaponry capable of terminating all life on the planet earth. The capitalist-communist relationship has become central because, in a world where, some fifty years ago, capitalism reigned supreme, communism has come to state power in something like one-third of its territory. These are the chief terms of reference that confront man in the second half of the twentieth century as he struggles with the problem of his survival, now placed in greater jeopardy than at any past period of which we have knowledge.

Both problems that are now central represent stages qualitatively new in man's history. Most of the thought, feeling, and human creativity given in the past to the subject of war were directed at how to fight and win wars. The premises of this past approach were obviously that one side could win, that most of mankind would survive, and that the planet as a whole would remain intact and habitable. Up to twenty-five years ago everyone could count on the empirical truth of these premises—and did so. But now that it is clear that no one can count on their truth any longer, the whole nature of the problem changes, not only in degree but also in kind. A similar change has taken place in the capitalism-communism problem: whereas, up to fifty years ago, it was a debate in which only one side held state power, now both sides have all the physical power inherent in the highly organized modern state system. Ideological theory can no longer be discussed apart from international practice. International relations cannot be carried on profitably without a thoroughly responsible knowledge of social philosophies. The most important facts about contemporary states are their theories.

One very important manifestation of this situation may be seen in the fact that in reckoning the chances of war and the possibilities of peace as between capitalism and communism, the problem, strictly speaking, is not simply that there are unavoidable conflicts of interest at the material level and irreconcilable differences of philosophy at the theoretical level. The war-peace question is whether the means of handling these conflicts and differences must necessarily include large-scale military action.

The answer to this question involves not only the attitude toward war—its acceptability and use—that actually prevails on each side but also the impression prevailing on each side concerning the attitude of the other side; for conflicts between states have this in common with conflicts between two persons as individuals: whether either party will use force depends almost as much upon what each is convinced his opponent will do as upon what each would choose otherwise.

This factor is particularly evident in the present fateful tensions that so plainly exist between capitalism and communism on a world scale, tensions that have already taken the form of protracted, if localized, wars (e.g., Korea, Vietnam). In both the official statement of United States foreign policy at the theoretical level and its implementation at the level of practical action, a central role is played by the idea or thesis that Marxist communist ideology includes an attitude toward violent revolution and armed warfare that not only is basically different from our attitude but is in essence criminal. Put bluntly, the thesis is that communism is committed to the use of illegal and immoral force and violence, in the form of revolution and warfare, to destroy capitalism. Our military actions taken against communism are thus alleged to be essentially defensive and preventive and, hence, morally and legally justified wherever they occur.[1]

The factual record indicates that since the termination of World War II (in which, without doubt, victory for our side was possible only because the United States and Soviet Russia were allied with each other), military actions taken by the executive branch of the U.S. government in the name of "containment," "liberation," "stopping communism," "destroying communism," "dealing with the communist conspiracy" (expressions that, *prima facie*, presuppose criminality in the other party), even when such military actions represent large-scale systematic war initiated unilaterally by the executive without asking for a congressional judgment and declaration on the issue of war, as the Constitution requires, have so far been accepted by a majority of the voting citizens and a majority of the Congress.[2] Domestic legislation curtailing freedom of speech, belief, association, and political action has likewise been accepted by a majority of the voters and the Congress on basically the same ground put forward for the justification of a foreign policy of military intervention: that Marxist communism is essentially a criminal conspiracy because of its alleged commitment to force and violence, by virtue of its very nature and doctrine.

This is an almost unbelievable situation, because the theories, principles, and doctrines of Marxism are so explicit, so readily available in print, and, in their content concerning the conditions that justify armed revolution and warfare, so close to our own principles as a nation. This last mentioned fact should occasion no surprise, as it is historically clear that Marx and Engels had no need to create a doctrine of the right of revolution, the right to overthrow by force any government that the people (the majority) feel is violating their rights, is unwilling or unable to carry out their will. Such a doctrine was already there, explicitly recognized as a corollary of the sovereignty of the people. Clearly, if the people are sovereign, and the government is their agent, then any government, of whatever type or for whatever reason, would have no right to remain in existence and impose its authority on the majority of the people contrary to their will. And, if there is a dispute as to whether the government is carrying out the people's will, it is the people who must finally decide this question, else they would not be sovereign.

Probably the best expression ever given to this right of revolution is in the American Declaration of Independence, which includes among the "self-evident" truths: that people have rights, and

> that to secure these rights, governments are instituted among men, deriving their just powers from the consent of the governed; that whenever any form of government becomes destructive of these ends, it is the right of the people to alter or to abolish it, and to institute new government, laying its foundation on such principles, and organizing its powers in such form as to them shall seem most likely to effect their safety and happiness.

A subsequent passage even goes beyond the "right" of the people to do this and speaks of their "duty": "It is their right, it is their duty, to throw off such government."

This whole concept of the right of revolution, which our founding fathers had derived principally from John Locke, some of the language of whose *Second Treatise of Government*[3] Jefferson borrowed in the passages just quoted, was inherited, accepted, and taken for granted by Marx, Engels, and their followers. In fact, it was developed and made more explicit in several of its aspects by Lenin, in what he termed the doctrine of "the revolutionary situation." In his *The War and the Second International*, it is formulated in this way:

> For a Marxist there is no doubt that a revolution is impossible without a revolutionary situation; furthermore, we know that not every revolutionary situation leads to revolution. What are, generally speaking. the characteristics of a revolutionary situation? We can hardly be mistaken when we indicate the following three outstanding signs: (1) it is impossible for the ruling class to maintain their power unchanged; for there is a crisis "higher up," taking one form or another; there is a crisis in the policy of the ruling class; as a result there appears a crack through which the dissatisfaction and the revolt of the oppressed classes burst forth. If a revolution is to take place it is usually insufficient that "one does not wish down below," but it is necessary that "one is incapable up above" to continue in the old way; (2) the wants and sufferings of the oppressed classes become more acute than usual; (3) in consequence of the above causes, there is a considerable increase in the activity of the masses who in "peace time" allow themselves to be robbed without protest, but in stormy times are drawn both by the circumstances of the crisis and *by the "higher-ups" themselves* into independent historic action.
>
> Without these objective changes, which are independent not only of the will of separate groups and parties but even of separate classes, a revolution as a rule is impossible. The coexistence of all these objective changes is called a revolutionary situation. This situation existed in 1905 in Russia and in all the periods of revolution in the West, but it also existed in the seventh decade of the last century in Germany; it existed

> in 1859–1861 and in 1879–1880 in Russia, though there was no revolution in these latter instances. Why? Because a revolution emerges not out of every revolutionary situation, but out of such situations where, to the above mentioned objective changes, subjective ones are added, namely, the ability of the revolutionary *classes* to carry out revolutionary mass actions *strong* enough to break (or to undermine) the old government, it being the rule that never, not even in a period of crises, does a government "fall" of itself without being "helped to fall."[4]

In other words, while Lenin shares with Jefferson the idea that forcible revolution will not and should not occur "for light and transient causes," but only when unusually sharp and extensive oppressions, abuses, and usurpations have occurred—and then only when the people feel oppressed and abused and react to such mistreatment with an unusual degree of protest and political activity—Lenin adds both an "objective" and a "subjective" precondition. The latter (that the revolutionary classes should have sufficient strength and organization) was no doubt assumed by Jefferson. But the former is new: that objective conditions must have reached a point where the existing government can no longer control them and fulfill its functions. In this regard, Lenin stresses that what he refers to are "objective changes, which are independent not only of the will of separate groups and parties but even of separate classes." Lenin has in view, of course, basic economic changes, problems, and crises. So long as it is possible for a government of the old type to solve and control such problems and developments, it will be able to remain in power and to defeat insurrectionary action, even if the masses "down below" were ready and willing to support insurrectionary action against it.

The reason Lenin adds this qualification is evident in the light of the elementary principles of Marxism: developments in politics are subordinate to developments in economics, and revolutions that represent progress of primary significance are those that reflect and facilitate basic changes in the forces and relations of production. Jefferson does not go into matters of this kind. Although he certainly recognized that economic factors entered into the causes of the revolution of which he was the outstanding ideological spokesman, as the grievances listed in the Declaration show, he did not develop any general theory about the role of the economic factor in revolutions in particular, or in the course of history in general. In dealing with revolution, Jefferson, like Locke, stressed its moral and political aspects.

However, even in relation to these aspects, it is of the greatest significance to note that Lenin is far more explicit than Jefferson in emphasizing the necessity of having the support of the majority, as a precondition of justifiable revolution. Thus he says flatly: "If a revolutionary party has not a majority among the front ranks of the revolutionary classes and in the country generally there can be no question of insurrection."[5] Shortly before the outbreak of the revolution that he led in Russia, Lenin said: "We are not Blanquists; we are not in favor of seizure of power by a minority."[6] Even sharper in its concreteness is the statement Lenin made in September, 1917, about two months before the beginning of the Bolshevik Revolution, in a letter to the Central Committee of the Party. Speaking of conditions as they were in July, 1917, Lenin says:

> However, to have concluded that we could have seized power at that time would have been wrong because the objective conditions for a successful insurrection did not exist. We still lacked the support of the class which is the vanguard of the revolution. We still did not have a majority among the workers and soldiers of the capitals.

But, referring to the time at which he is writing, Lenin adds: "The picture is now entirely different. We have the following of the majority of a *class*, the vanguard of the revolution, the vanguard of the people, which is capable of carrying the masses with it. We have the following of the *majority* of the people."[7] In *State and Revolution*, Lenin dealt with actual examples of revolutions, which he criticized and rejected on the ground that they lacked the support of the majority:

> If we take for examples the revolutions of the twentieth century, we shall, of course, have to recognize both Portuguese and Turkish revolutions as bourgeois. Neither is a "people's" revolution, inasmuch as the mass of the people, the enormous majority, does not make its appearance actively, independently, with its own economic and political demands in either the one or the other.[8]

In the light of such passages as we have quoted it cannot reasonably be maintained that communists, because of the nature of their doctrine and movement, are committed or inclined either to the indiscriminate use of armed revolution or to the carrying out of revolutions that represent the will only of a minority. Of course, persons who call themselves Marxist communists may do all sorts of things in violation of the principles of Marxism, just as persons who call themselves Jeffersonian democrats may violate their principles. That is a problem on all sides, and it is quite different from the problem of whether a certain doctrine or movement, *if followed*, will necessarily lead to minority revolutions or criminal aggression. The plain truth, as we have seen, is that the doctrine of Marxist communism concerning the preconditions of justifiable force, violence, armed revolution, and warfare is essentially the same as the Jeffersonian democratic doctrine expressed in our most basic ideological credo, the Declaration of Independence. It is equally plain that this truth has not yet reached the great majority of our government officials, policy makers, leaders of public opinion, and citizens. Any ignorance about large and important matters can be costly of human resources, but this particular ignorance may possibly cost mankind more than it has ever had to pay before. It could conceivably play the role of a false premise leading to an unnecessary thermonuclear conclusion, beyond possibility of correction.

A contemporary example of the utmost gravity can be seen in the Vietnamese War. Over and over again some of the most highly placed officials of the Johnson administration, such as Mr. Dean Rusk in his capacity of Secretary of State, adduced, as basic reasons for the military measures taken by that administration in southeast Asia, doctrinal statements of Chinese communist leaders expressing their readiness to take up arms in the revolutionary struggle against imperialism, their belief that this struggle would be fought out in all the leading capitalist countries to the utter defeat and destruction of capitalism, and the like—as if all this were, of course, equivalent to an admission of intent to commit criminal aggression.

But this is to forget, or to be ignorant of, precisely that which such statements are alleged to reflect: Marxist doctrine. Every Marxist understands and takes for granted that any instance of armed revolution, or warfare carried on as a result of such revolution, for example, a war of national liberation, to be acceptable must be preceded by a revolutionary situation, a situation in which the government being challenged is unable to govern in its usual way and unwilling to carry out the will and implement the rights of the majority, and in which the majority, convinced that such is the case, are ready to support forcible measures to remove that government. In the absence of any one of these conditions, "for a Marxist, there is no doubt that a revolution is impossible," as Lenin puts it. In this connection, with particular reference to the Vietnam problem, it is necessary to remember that Mao Tse-tung and the Chinese Communist party, though they have sharp differences with the Soviet leaders on various matters, do not differ on the basic principles of Leninism. There has been no repudiation, on either side, of Lenin's doctrine of the revolutionary situation.

It is also necessary to remember that there is an important difference between predicting a bloody conflict and advocating bloody conflict. Someone who says he is convinced that certain problems and situations in which he is involved are going to include physical conflict is not necessarily saying he will be the one to *initiate* the physical aspect of it, or that he prefers or desires the present conflict to become one of physical force. Not to recognize this is a failure of elementary logic. Specifically, when the Chinese communists say that they do not believe in peaceful coexistence with the United States, anyone who has an elementary knowledge of the doctrinal context within which they are speaking as communists and Marxists will understand that they are not saying they prefer, desire, or intend to initiate war. They are saying they are convinced the United States will initiate war rather than carry on peaceful competition with communism on a basis of equal rights. One cannot find in Marxist communist ideology a doctrinal preference for war, or a doctrinal justification of preventive war.

If one wishes to examine contemporary examples of ideologies that teach that war is superior to peace, that the values of war are higher than those of peace, that war is to be preferred because it alone brings out the true dignity of men and nations, one may turn to fascism and naziism. In *The Doctrine of Fascism*, an essay taken as basic in his whole movement, Mussolini wrote:

> First of all, as regards the future development of mankind —and quite apart from all present political considerations— Fascism does not, generally speaking, believe in the possibility or utility of perpetual peace. War alone keys up all human

> energies to their maximum tension, and sets the seal of nobility on . . . peoples.[9]

In Hitler's *Mein Kampf*, the Bible of naziism, the same thought is laid down early in the text: "Mankind has grown strong in eternal struggles, it will only perish through eternal peace."[10] Later, Hitler candidly remarks, ". . . might alone makes right."[11] Nothing of this kind can be found in the works of any Marxist communist authority.

The foregoing discussion points up the necessity of distinguishing among three interrlated questions: (1) whether armed warfare is preferred to peace; (2) what the conditions are under which resort to armed warfare is considered justifiable; (3) whether, in regard to any given social change, such as a transition from capitalism to socialism, armed warfare is considered empirically unavoidable or not. We have discussed the first two; the third involves what is referred to in Marxist literature as the problem of peaceful transition. If it is granted that, in accordance with Marxist doctrine, armed force would be used only against a government unwilling and unable to carry out the will of the majority, and only when the majority are ready to support forcible measures against it, the further question is: Do Marxist communists maintain that the transition from capitalism to the form of society they consider better will always involve armed force, or is there a possibility of a peaceful transition?

There can be no doubt of the fact that in our country, at the highest governmental levels, the prevailing impression, implemented in domestic legislation and foreign policy, is that Marxist communist ideology does not allow for any possibility of a peaceful transition. For example, Judge Learned Hand, in finding against the communist defendants in the key Dennis case in the U.S. Court of Appeals in 1950, made the following flat statement concerning Marxist communist doctrine: "The violent capture of all existing government is one article of the creed of that faith, which abjures the possibility of success by lawful means."[12]

This is a painfully embarrassing situation for an American to confront, because it is not difficult to ascertain that such statements are in error, and it presents him with a tragic situation, because grave issues of justice, peace, and war are involved. For example, in a well-known public speech in 1872 Marx specifically pointed out that "there are certain countries, such as the United States and England, in which the workers may hope to secure their ends by peaceful means."[13] He indicates that the basis of his judgment is the existence of dependable electoral machinery and parliamentary processes. In 1886, Engels, in his Preface to the first English translation of Marx's *Das Kapital*, emphasized Marx's view of England as a "country where the inevitable social revolution might be effected entirely by peaceful and legal means."[14]

While Lenin and Stalin in the period between World War I and World War II maintained that, since Marx's day, conditions had changed in the direction of increased power of the military, so that a peaceful transition would not have been possible in England or the United States during that later period even if the majority had wished such a transition, Lenin and Stalin never called for a violent transition in those countries. The reason, as they readily acknowledged, was that there was no evidence of a majority will for socialism. However, in the period between World War II and the Sino-Soviet rift practically all communist leaders throughout the world acknowledged that a peaceful transition was once again possible if and where the will of the majority was for a change from capitalism to socialism. The main reason given was the increased power and influence of "the camp of socialism" in world affairs. In the current *Program of the Communist Party of the Soviet Union,* it is stated:

> Socialist revolution is not necessarily connected with war. Although both world wars, which were started by the imperialists, culminated in socialist revolutions, revolutions are quite feasible without war. The great objectives of the working class can be realized without world war. Today the conditions for this are more favorable than ever . . . The working class, supported by the majority of the people . . . can . . . win a solid majority in parliament . . . and provide the necessary conditions for a peaceful socialist revolution.[15]

A review of the ideological situation as a whole against the background of the war activities, war dangers, and war tensions that are so evident and threatening in our contemporary world cannot but lead to the conclusion that those activities, dangers, and tensions are not rooted in ideological factors as such. Between Marxist communism and Jeffersonian democracy there is a common ground of ideology quite sufficient to allow peaceful coexistence and competition between them. If we fear war, it is not because of differences between these two ideologies; it is rather because of what we have failed to do educationally, morally, and politically about the common ground the two ideologies share.

NOTES

1. The two following examples, at the highest policy levels, are typical. In his Inaugural Address, January 20, 1949, President Harry Truman said: "Communism maintains that social wrongs can be corrected only by violence." Mr. John Foster Dulles, then Secretary of State, in a speech before the United Nations, October 26, 1948, as reported by the United Press, said: "There is a basic contradiction between the Charter theory of peaceful change by evolution and the Communist doctrine of violent change by revolution."

2. When President Johnson ordered American bombers across North Vietnam's borders for the first time, this was a clear and deliberate act of war on a massive scale against a small country that did not possess any significant air power. Had President Johnson followed the Constitution, he

would have laid before Congress the reasons that in his view necessitated such an action and asked for a declaration of war, as President Wilson did after the Germans sank various ships, bringing us into World War I, and as President Roosevelt did after the Japanese bombed Pearl Harbor, bringing us into World War II. The path Johnson chose, of not giving Congress a chance to debate and decide the issue of war beforehand, was chosen also by President Truman when he ordered our naval forces into action against North Korea prior to any judgment by Congress or by the United Nations. In both cases everyone was presented with a *fait accompli;* in neither case was there any general protest from Congress or the people at large. It is hard to decide whether they lacked awareness, felt hopeless, or simply did not attach any importance to the fact that this procedure meant that one man, or a very small group of men, was being allowed, unconstitutionally, to plunge the whole country into warfare that could become thermonuclear, with all that is thereby implied. What dictatorial power could exceed this? The explicit constitutional provision is in Art. 1, Sec. 8, under "Powers of Congress: 11. To declare war . . ."

3. *See* ch. xix, §§ 222–225.

4. V. I. Lenin, *The War and the Second International* (New York: International Publishers, 1932), p. 13. Original italics.

5. V. I. Lenin, *Selected Works,* Vol. VI (New York: International Publishers), p. 293. From "Can the Bolsheviks Retain State Power?" (Oct., 1917).

6. *Ibid.,* p. 29. From "A Dual Power," written Apr. 22, 1917.

7. *Ibid.,* pp. 219, 220. From "Marxism and Insurrection," original italics.

8. V. I. Lenin, *State and Revolution* (New York: International Publishers, "Little Lenin Library"), p. 34. Written in 1917.

9. The present writer tried to analyze in some detail the position of fascist and nazi ideology on the question of war and peace in *The Philosophy of Peace* (New York: Gaer, 1949; rev. ed., Liberty, 1954), ch. ii.

10. Adolf Hitler, *Mein Kampf* (New York: Houghton Mifflin, 1932), p. 175.

11. *Ibid.,* p. 949.

12. For an analysis of the reasoning involved, *see* the present writer's *The Communist Trials and the American Tradition: Expert Testimony on Force and Violence* (New York: Cameron, 1956), pp. 139 ff.

13. G. M. Stekloff, *History of the First International* (New York: International Publishers), p. 240.

14. Karl Marx, *Capital* (New York: Modern Library), p. 32.

15. *Essential Works of Marxism,* ed. Arthur Mendel (New York: Bantam, 1961), p. 401.

CHAPTER NINE

National Sovereignty and International Anarchy

Paul Arthur Schilpp

Distinguished Professor of Philosophy, Southern Illinois University

For, disguise it as one may, the doctrine of national sovereignty is simply the denial on the part of a political state of either legal or moral responsibility. . . . It is a doctrine of international anarchy . . .

JOHN DEWEY

That the relations among nations with each other today can, in truth, only be characterized as anarchical no one who knows the meaning of the word anarchy and looks out upon the world today can deny. This is merely another way of saying that the relations of nations with each other are *not* subject to law. If they were subject to law, there, first, would have to exist laws to govern such relations, and, second, some agency that could see to it that those laws could be enforced. Neither of these conditions exists today.

The United Nations is—at least so far as the control of war and peace are concerned—essentially a world debating society. This is good as far as it goes. It certainly is a great improvement over having no such public international debating at all. It is obviously far better to have nations and national governments talk with each other across the tables, even if and when such talk is highly vituperative, than to stab each other in the back (by word or deed) behind each other's back. And the World Court at The Hague, again, is good for what it is good, but it certainly is at best only *advisory* and has absolutely no way of enforcing its decrees, to say nothing about the fact that disputes can be brought before the court *only* with the consent of all involved parties. The very concept of "International Law" is, therefore, in today's world situation, either a self-contradictory or else an ironically humorous one—despite the fact that numberless courses on so-called International Law are being given in innumerable colleges and universities.[1]

If one remembers both the theoretical and the practical meanings of the concept of national sovereignty, what I stated in my opening sentence becomes self-evident. Even such a relatively small but widely used dictionary as the *American College Dictionary* says that sovereignty is the "supreme and independent power or authority in government as possessed or claimed by a state." And, inasmuch as every existing national state today lays claim to sovereignty, it follows that no national government today will accept any law as being above its own laws. Consequently, the relations of nations with each other are not—and, so long as such claim to national sovereignty is maintained, cannot be—lawful relations, that is to say, relations maintained in obedience to laws above the separate, individual nations. Consequently, all such relations can, in the nature of the case, only be anarchical. And there is no better seed bed for war than international anarchy, the absence of any and all lawful relations with and among nations. So long as each nation is a law only to itself, all decisions by the respective nations are made solely on the basis of pure national self-interest, and even so-called international treaties are observed *only* so long as they serve the national self-interest. In fact, to abide by an international treaty when the treaty is considered to be against the national interest would—

from the standpoint of the nationalist—amount almost to treason.

Practically the entire so-called civilized world reacted with shocked moral revulsion when, in 1914, Theobald von Bethmann-Hollweg, Imperial German Chancellor, justified Germany's violation of Belgian neutrality by characterizing the international guarantee of Belgian neutrality as "a scrap of paper." In reality, the world should have been grateful to him for having the courage to tell the truth; for, under existing conditions of international anarchy, made inevitable by the claim to national sovereignty, *all* international treaties are just that: *scraps of paper*, scarcely worth the paper they are written on.

If additional concrete evidence for this fact be called for, consider the "Pact of Paris," better known as the Kellogg-Briand Renunciation of War Pact. This international treaty, officially signed on behalf of the government of France by its Foreign Minister, Aristide Briand, and on behalf of the United States government by the Secretary of State, Frank B. Kellogg, as well as by the official representatives of thirteen other national governments in Paris on August 27, 1928, and later actually formally endorsed by forty-eight additional governments—that is, by no fewer than sixty-three governments in all, agreed to "renounce war as an instrument of national policy" and thus became the first formal renunciation of war treaty. Has that formal and official renunciation of war kept one of its signatories from engaging in war or from using it "as an instrument of national policy" since 1928? To ask the question is to answer it. Not a single one of the signatory nations paid the slightest attention to it and to their own formal declaration, once the respective government had decided that—to use governmental language—the only way to preserve and advance the national interest demanded the waging of, the participation in, or the preparation for war.

The Kellogg-Briand Peace Pact proved to be exactly what Von Bethmann-Hollweg had called Belgian neutrality, nothing more or less than "a scrap of paper." And, let it be emphasized once more, so long as individual nations and governments lay claim to national sovereignty, that is to say, to the principle of merely being a law unto themselves and of refusing to acknowledge any law above that of the nation, just so long the "scrap of paper" doctrine of international law and international relations is inevitable. International anarchy is the unavoidable consequence of national sovereignty, regardless of what theoretical hair-splitting political scientists and philosophers may engage in when discussing national sovereignty. And this is not theory but demonstrated fact, proved over and over again in the actual behavior and experience of nations with each other. Moreover, as the already cited illustrations show, this nullifying attitude toward international treaties is by no means the policy merely of dictatorial and imperialistic powers. Such nations as England, France, and the United States are just as guilty of it as are any—and, one should add, all—others. In brief, this attitude is universal. Nor is it likely to change as long as individual nations lay claim to this pernicious doctrine of national sovereignty.

The most tragic aspect of this failure lies, indeed, in the fact that this claim is by no means the exclusive fault of the respective formal governments themselves. Rather, it is the common populace to whom this doctrine is of all sacred cows the most sacred.[2] Just imagine what would happen to a speaker who, on the platform of the national conclave of the Daughters of (no more) American Revolutions or on the platform of the national convention of the (un-)American Legion, would dare to attack the concept of national sovereignty! I leave this to the kind reader's own (I hope, fertile) imagination. Certainly the least that would happen to him would be to be shooed off the platform as a traitor to the United States. Yet, as anyone who is acquainted with the Space Age's nuclear and cobalt capability knows, international anarchy—and a resulting nuclear confrontation—amounts to treason against mankind. It is not merely strange, it is almost unbelievable that the nationals of individual nations do not have sense enough to recognize the fact that treason to mankind is infinitely worse than treason to the nation; for, obviously, when mankind has ceased to exist, so will all individual nations have ceased to exist. But this simple fact does not seem to penetrate the thick skulls of nationalistic "patriots," who find it impossible to see beyond their own national noses.

The dogged emotional commitment to the doctrine of national sovereignty is, then—in today's Space Age—the single greatest sin against mankind.

There is thus only one way to prevent a nuclear World War III from destroying mankind, and that is to get rid of the doctrine of national sovereignty and to arrive at a position that will accept, proclaim, and abide by the sovereignty only of all mankind. Only when the relations of nations to and among each other are and can be regulated in orderly fashion by law superior to that of *any* national laws will it be possible to achieve a world of law and order, in which war as recourse to the settlement of international disputes will have been actually abolished. Immanuel Kant, the great German philosopher, saw this clearly as long as 175 years ago. But humanity, and even so-called social scientists, have been a long time catching up with him. They are far from having done so even yet.

In 1784, in his treatise *Idee zu einer allgemeinen Geschichte,* Kant wrote that the establishment of a universal rule of law

> may seem utopian, . . . [yet] it is the inevitable escape from the distress into which human beings bring each other. It

> must force the states to the resolution (however difficult a pill it may be for them to swallow) to which savage man was forced equally unwillingly, namely: to surrender his brutal freedom and to seek calm and security under a lawful constitution.[3]

And, earlier in the very same paragraph, Kant had said:

> . . . Through the wars, through the excessive and never realized preparation for them, through the need which hence every state even in the midst of peace must feel, nature drives man to make attempts, at first quite inadequate, to leave the lawless state of savages, and to enter a league of nations; where each state, even the smallest, may expect its security and its rights—not through its own power nor by its own legal judgment, but—alone from this great league of nations, *from a united power, and from a decision according to laws* arrived at by united will.[4]

These words by Kant appeared in print a year before the appearance of his second *Critique* and show rather conclusively that even then Kant was comparing the internationally lawless behavior among nations with "the lawless state of savages," which marked the common behavior of so-called primitive man. And such comparison must indeed sound appropriate to any sane person who has lived through all the various carnages of our twentieth century, even to that right now being perpetrated in Vietnam.

And nine years later, in 1793, Kant inveighed in no uncertain terms against the notion that peaceful relations among sovereign states could somehow be maintained by the establishment of the oft-praised and even today still-defended "balance of power" when he wrote:

> An enduring universal peace by way of the so-called balance of power in Europe is—like Swift's house, which, having been perfectly erected by a master-builder according to all

the laws of equilibrium, which, as soon as a sparrow came to sit on it, collapsed—a mere chimera.[5]

Two years later, in 1795, in his famous—although actually up to now totally *uninfluential*—tract, *Zum ewigen Frieden* (*On Perpetual Peace*), the great Sage of Koenigsberg returns to the same theme in these words:

> Just as we look with deep contempt upon the way primitive peoples [note!] are attached to their lawless liberty—a liberty which enables them to fight incessantly rather than subject themselves to the restraint of law established even by themselves; in short, to prefer wild freedom to a reasonable one. We regard such an attitude as raw, uncivilized, and an animalistic degradation of humanity—; so, one should think, civilized peoples (each united in a state) would hasten to get away from such a reprehensible state as soon as possible. Instead, each *state* insists upon seeing the essence of its majesty (for popular majesty is an absurd expression) in this, that it is not subject to any external coercion.[6]

What a clear description not merely of the existing international anarchy but also of the reason for such, namely, each state's seeing "the essence of its majesty," that is, of its sovereignty, in its independence from any laws beyond those of the state itself! Had Kant written almost two centuries later, he could have said the same thing, because he would have found the same situation in international relations still existing, nations and governments still flaunting their lawless sense of wild, "raw and uncivilized" majesty. The majesty of the sovereign state still is "not subject to any external coercion." As we have been witnessing in the case of Vietnam, the sovereign is not even subject to the widely expressed public opinion of the civilized part of mankind. Worse than that: even the moral revolt of public opinion of a very large percentage of our own people is practically helpless in facing this "majesty." The modern state is, in brief, a lawless state and is, therefore, anarchical.

Kant himself, in the next paragraph of his treatise, expresses surprise that the very term "law" "has not yet entirely been banned from the politics of war" as being merely "pedantic." "One cannot name the example of a single state," Kant continues, "which has ever allowed itself to desist from its [warlike] design by the arguments of even important experts."[7] How contemporary this sounds! And since, in such a lawless situation, "each nation is the judge in his own cause," even "a treaty of peace can," at best, "put an end only to a particular war, but not to the universal state of war which consists in finding ever new pretexts for starting a new one"![8]

According to Kant, there is only one possible way of getting away from this lawless state, and that is, "just as in the case of individual men, [for states] to give up their wild and lawless freedom, to accept public and enforceable laws, and, in this way, to form a (constantly growing) federation of nations (*civitas gentium*), which finally would include all nations."[9] But this, Kant adds, the nations and governments do not wish to do. The sacred cow of national sovereignty still is too sacred to be tampered with, even though not to do away with it may—in the present anarchical state and with the nuclear weapons arsenal at man's disposal—spell the possible annihilation of the human race.

What one dare not overlook in this connection is the fact that blame for this devotion to this sacred cow is by no means limited to sovereigns themselves and to those in authority in the national state. The entire population of practically every existing independent state has been indoctrinated from kindergarten through the entire public school system with the absolute sacredness of this notion of sovereign nationhood. The consequence is that this notion has become not merely a firmly entrenched idea but one that from infancy is loaded with a deep emotional commitment in comparison with which even the equally original emotional commitment to some specific—institutional—religion proves to be powerless. Is it not clear that when the precepts of the Judaic-Christian religion enjoin their devotees with the command, "Thou shalt not kill," but the letter of the nation's president invites the citizen to join armed forces dedicated to the principle of learning to kill in the most expeditious way possible, there is scarcely one young citizen in a hundred who does not choose to obey his president's invitation rather than the precepts of his—professed—religion?

It should be clear, therefore, that a deep emotional commitment such as this, imbibed in infancy and sedulously reinforced by all kinds of institutions throughout most of life, is something not easily eradicated or even changed. When, more than a half-century ago, the great American philosopher William James called for "A Moral Equivalent to War," he was indeed calling Americans' attention to a great need. But, even fifty years later, men still seem not yet to have found that equivalent. And, so long as neither the religious nor the educational institutions of any country are willing to attack this basic national idol of national sovereignty for what it is, I do not see how it would be possible to find such an equivalent. If (and so long as) national sovereignty is the most sacred of all of the individual citizen's idols, getting rid of the existing international anarchy would seem to be nothing more than a futile and hopeless dream. And, so long as this is the case, men must face the possibility of mankind's annihilation.

Kant, in the same paragraphs cited above, calls upon men to use their intelligence and reason, instead of merely their emotional commitments, to do whatever is necessary to construct and create such a federation of states, to which each national state would surrender a goodly portion of its "lawless freedom" in order thereby to bring into existence a world federation that could produce, enforce, and maintain peace among all the nations of the world. Certainly this is a well intentioned appeal, and one that one can only applaud. Unfortunately, it is precisely in the areas of men's deepest emotional commitments that we are least amenable to appeals to our rational intelligence.

In other words: How do you change men's basic and deepest emotional commitments? The person who, on the widest possible human application, is able to come up with a viable, satisfactory answer to this question will not merely be one of the greatest benefactors of mankind. He may quite literally be humanity's savior. Thus far, it seems, such a person has not yet appeared. Buddha tried his hand at it, and so did Socrates and Jesus. So have, in more recent times, Gandhi, Schweitzer, Kagawa, and Martin Luther King. But, up to now at least, not one of these has found sufficient universal acceptance to rid the world of the bugaboo of national sovereignty. Men by the millions *profess* allegiance to the universal principles of human brotherhood lived and advocated by those avatars of history. But, most unfortunately, when men—at least for the most part—have to choose between allegiance to such humanity-wide commitment, on the one hand, and allegiance to the national state, on the other, the overwhelming majority still choose the national state. And, thus, not only is the commitment to national sovereignty, sacred or not, still with us, but so is its resulting international anarchy—and, in the nuclear and Space Age, with that the threat of annihilation.

Let him who has ears hear!

NOTES

1. This is, of course, by no means the only instance of universities offering courses in nonexistent subjects.

2. The sacredness of the cow in India may, indeed, in such an underfed and overpopulated country, be a most expensive drag on the national economy, but it does not at least present a dangerous attack on the very lives and

existence of India's neighbors. In contrast, the sacred cow of national sovereignty constitutes precisely such an attack, not merely on the existence of neighboring states, but today on that of the entire human race.

3. *Immanuel Kants Werke*, Cassirer Edition, Vol. IV, p. 159; English translation by present writer.

4. *Ibid.*, p. 159. Trans. and italics by present writer.

5. In Kant's essay, "Über den Gemeinspruch: Das mag in der Theorie richtig sein, taugt aber nicht für die Praxis," *Werke, op. cit.*, Vol. VI, p. 397.

6. *Zum ewigen Frieden, Werke, op. cit.*, Vol. VI, p. 439.

7. *Ibid.*, p. 440.

8. *Ibid.*, p. 441.

9. *Ibid.*, p. 441.

CHAPTER TEN

War as a Problem of Government

Carl J. Friedrich

Eaton Professor of the Science of Government, Harvard University

The discussion of war, like that of all topics in the field of social studies, can be carried on within different frames of reference. A good part of the most intensive work on the subject has been in moral terms, but these are often mixed up with utilitarian and historical, as well as legal, considerations. When I say, War as a problem of government, I wish to stress the nonmoral side of war. I want to ask: What has been the function of war in the governing of men, and how has it been controlled through such governing? I want to treat as marginal to my inquiry the moral issues of the "just" war and individual personal responsibility in making or participating in war, basic though they are in the history of political philosophy.[1] I also wish to leave aside the question of whether war is a procreator of virtue, as has so often been claimed for it. Force and violence are intrinsic to human relationships. There has never been a political order without war, and the problem has always been how to keep it within bounds.[2]

Natural law doctrines have linked war to the right of self-defense. Rights apart, self-defense has been and remains a primary objective of any political order. To be sure, in dealing with the basic drives leading toward war, defense and self-preservation, though often overshadowed by the search for food, procreation, territory, adventure, and domination—to use the terminology of the leading work on war[3]—have played a decisive role. In modern times they have been envisaged by various writers as drives, the political, the economic, the cultural, and the religious motives.[4] But actually war, in the sense of organized, sanguinary fighting on a substantial scale, has resulted from these other drives or motives only because one political community was prepared to defend its food, women, territory, and independence against another that attempted to deprive it of these possessions. It may be true that the most gentle cannot live in peace if it does not please his bad neighbor,[5] but this is only so because even the most gentle will defend himself against an aggressor. Thus all other drives or motives may, in the political perspective, ultimately be subsumed under defense.

This view is substantiated by what is known about war in primitive societies. Much of the research of anthropologists, concerned as it often is with a particular tribe, seems to suggest that the aggressor's outlook is prevalent among primitives. But when the detailed motivations are analyzed, the general prevalence of defensive motivation becomes visible. By this statement I do not wish to deny that there are considerable differences between primitive peoples on this score; there are certainly belligerent and peaceful ones.[6]

What about the distinction between war and peace? Is it an absolute one, as most of the moralists assume? The inclination to define war in contrast to peace goes back to eighteenth-century rationalism and romanticism. We are not ready to return to the old Christian notion that the contrast is between just wars and unjust wars, and that the task is to recognize war as an inescapable sanction for the purpose of maintaining justice and the moral order. But we are ready to recognize that war is endemic in human society and that therefore the task is to organize the world community under a world government, thereby regularizing the use of physical violence and anticipating war in the form of specific small-scale punishment, as is done under the criminal law. The distinction has been challenged from time to time. Heraclitus apodictically declared that *polemos pater panton,* which is traditionally translated as the proposition that war is the father of all. Perhaps the translation is mistaken and all Heraclitus wanted to assert was that "all is struggle." Vauvenargues, in his *Maxims,* asserted that "all in the universe is done by force," and that this was the most general, inexorable, and unalterable law of nature. If this is so, then armed conflict is only a special instance of a universal propensity of all life, and "peace" is nothing but an interstice, a kind of truce between recurrent outbreaks of sanguinary conflict. The military theorist Karl von Clausewitz, following Hegel, appears to have thought so.

> There is a recurrent failure to realize that the fabric of history is woven upon *one* loom. The theory which makes an absolute distinction between war and peace is false. War is an overt expression of covert tensions and conflicts which exist in every stable and peaceful social situation. In war, things that have been hidden become revealed.[7]

This failure leads to erroneous theories concerning the nature and origins of war; particular causes springing from particular social structures have again and again been universalized. And yet, Clausewitz's own most famous proposition, namely, that war is the continuation of politics by different means, is itself false or, at least, easily subject to misunderstanding. In a very real sense, war is not the *continuation* of politics but rather its *abandonment* in favor of violence. It would indeed be more correct to say that diplomacy (politics) is the continuation of war by other means. It is when men despair of finding political solutions that they take to arms. This aspect is particularly patent in civil war situations. Clausewitz himself seems to have been quite aware of it. In what might be called the most mature form of his theory,[8] he put it this way:

> War is nothing else than the continuation of political transactions intermingled with different means. . . . these political transactions are not stopped by the war itself, are not changed into something totally different but substantially continue, whatever the means applied may be. . . . How could it be otherwise? Do the political relations between different peoples and governments ever cease when the exchange of diplomatic notes has ceased? Is not war only a different method of expressing their thoughts, different from writing and language? War admittedly has its own grammar, but not its own logic.[9]

This notion of war as an expression of the thoughts of a people is fairly clearly Hegelian—as indeed may be expected of an adherent of Hegel's view—and it is a view diametrically opposed to the approach that will be set forth in the pages that follow.

Definitions of war, like definitions of other social phenomena, may stress ends (teleological definitions), or they may stress causes (scientific definitions), and they may concern themselves with the question as to who are the participants, or what are the methods employed, or, finally, what are the moral and other effects of war. Such definitions have been given in bewildering variety, and there is little value in a complete survey. A definition will usually be designed to serve the particular purpose of those making it.

The realist, functional view of war—functional, that is, in relation to government—sees war as the extreme form of social conflict: large, organized groups engaged in more or less systematic killing for the attainment of believed-in group ends. Thus war is closely related to the task of government: to manipulate power for the purpose of realizing communal purposes and to attenuate, reduce, and if possible eliminate communal conflict and the tensions that such conflicts entail. Ever since men have speculated on the problem of government, this end has been recognized in one form or another. It was, however, abandoned in the more radical forms of nineteenth-century liberalism epitomized in the statement: "That government is best which governs least." This outlook was part of the generally optimistic assessment of human nature and the readiness of human beings to cooperate rather than to compete. Liberalism shared this estimate of man's natural inclination with anarchism and utopian socialism; even in Marxism it survives in the vision of a world without war after the overthrow of capitalism. All this is so familiar that one hesitates even to recall it, and yet it is part of the setting for our topic: war as a problem of government, for liberalism, anarchism, and socialism-communism are all convinced that war is rather the result of government, is a consequence of the evils of the "monopoly of the means of physical coercion"—as the classic characterization of the state has it. It has to be borne in mind that this anarchic approach grew from a belief in the preestablished harmony of interests (and related doctrines) and in, therefore, the automatic disappearance of social conflict once the coercive elements in society, property, and the state were eliminated. If government, in this perspective, appeared as the main cause of social conflict and hence of war, the anarchist demand for the abolition of the state was the logical, if radical, consequence.

If, then, theories of war lead into theories of human nature, they raise also, on account of the ubiquity of the phenomenon with which they deal, the general problem of society and history. It is a striking fact that the most celebrated writings on war and its elimination are linked to distinct philosophies of history. Indeed, in some ways philosophies of history and theories of war are two sides of the same coin. Kant, more hopeful than Rousseau in believing that war may be eliminated, less hopeful in arguing that only effective government can provide the means for coping with the bellicose propensities in man, is willing in his general view of history to attribute to war a providential function. War now appears as the unfortunate, but necessary, instrumentality of progress toward a universal order of peace under law. Not only in his famous *On Eternal Peace,*[10] but in his sketch of a philosophy of history, *Idea for a General History with Cosmopolitan Intent,* he sets forth the view that there can be no progress without conflict. "The means which nature employs to bring about the development of all its potentialities in the *antagonism* of these potentialities in society—because in the end this antagonism becomes the cause of a social order according to law."[11] Still, war remains morally objectionable, and Kant considers, as everyone knows, that the command "there shall not be war" is a corollary of the categorical imperative. The inherent contradiction between these two positions Kant resolves, of course, by his dualism of the worlds of "is" and "ought," each operating according to its own laws. Although morally absolutely wrong, war can nonetheless be seen as a means of that "natural" progress toward the eventual state of a world federation when mankind will be united under law.

> The wars are therefore so many attempts to bring about new relations between states and to form new bodies by dividing the old ones which in turn cannot maintain themselves and hence will suffer similar revolutions; until, finally, partly as a result of the best possible arrangement of the constitution

> internally, partly as a result of a common agreement and legislation externally, a state [of affairs] is reached which, like a commonwealth, can maintain itself automatically.

When mankind reaches this stage, progress will be possible without any conflict of arms, just as it has been possible within states, because world government will provide the means of attenuating, reducing, and, it is to be hoped, transcending the conflicts and tensions that the antagonism of men engenders. In short, Kant is clear on one decisive point: the importance of government for resolving such conflicts as inevitably arise. He is Hobbesian in believing that there can be no political order without government, but he is Lockeian in stressing that such government must be constitutional, and indeed federal, if it is not to issue in a universal despotism. What this means, incidentally, is that the problems of civil war and revolution are transferred from the parochial to the world scene.

It is obvious that these thoughts have become part of the reality in which we live. They are manifest in much of the words and deeds of the United Nations, as they were in those of the League of Nations before the United Nations. The failure of the organizations to live up to the constitutional requirement of the Kantian analysis has plagued them and continues to do so. These bitter disappointments do not warrant us in abandoning the thoughts underlying them. Even the notion that such an organization as the United Nations occasions wars rather than elimiates them is not really sufficient reason for denying the truth of the analysis upon which they are built; for coercion has always been part of government, and the armed resistance of robbers and revolutionaries does not prove the function of government unnecessary: quite the contrary. Modern weapons development has in fact reinforced the Kantian analysis by adding prudential to moral arguments in support of the proposition that "there shall not be war."

Before we proceed with the general analysis, it may be well to sketch in the Hegelian and Marxian version of these ideas. Just as in Rousseau and Kant, so also in Hegel and Marx the conception of war is intimately related to their philosophy of history and their theory of society. It is quite obvious that this must be so, but it has not always been recognized. Hegel, in abandoning Kant's critical rationalism and making reason absolute once more, sees it as the motive force of all history.[12] Personifying it as the World Spirit, Hegel relates the progressive stages in mankind's evolution to roles that, successively, peoples are called upon to play upon the stage of world history. War becomes a testing ground for reason and acquires an intrinsic value that Kant had denied it. There was no room in such a conception for an eventual universal order of peace under law. If world history is the world court, then the victor, rather than the "moral law within," becomes the incarnation of reason. In a sense this is a secular form of the Christian tradition of the just war. As St. Augustine had put it in the *De Civitate Dei:* "They who have waged war in obedience to the divine command, or in conformity with His laws have represented in their persons the public justice or the wisdom of government, and in this capacity have put to death wicked men; such persons have by no means violated the commandment: 'Thou shalt not kill.' "[13] It is significant that the wisdom of government turns up in this key passage, which presumes a world order in which certain rulers are called upon to enforce what is right against the wrongdoers. Such a moralistic conception seems far removed from the Hegelian historical vision, and yet it really is not, when the theological overtones of the notion of a World Spirit are borne in mind, along with Hegel's explicitly stated purpose (at the end of his *Philosophy of History*) that what he intended was to provide a "theodicy."

I am ready to assert, in spite of Marx's sharp denunciation of religion as the "opium of the people," that the Marxian view of war and history is in fact another form of the same basic doctrine expounded by Hegel. One must not allow oneself to be misled by Marx's bitter criticisms of war between nations, which he saw as manifestations of bourgeois imperialism; for he called upon the proletariat to wage ceaselessly another war, namely, the war against capitalism and its social and governmental institutions. Class warfare is considered good because it is functionally related to the overthrow of a bad, and the institution of a good, society and government. Like the war to establish the Christian order and government, such a war is eminently just and desirable. When Reinhold Niebuhr so poignantly recalled the biblical tradition of the notion of the "children of light and the children of darkness," he provided a telling formula for all such theories of war in terms of human destiny and its fulfillment. The ideological conflict between the U.S.S.R. and China is cast in these terms, and I for one am inclined to think that the Chinese have the better of the argument, in spite of the primitiveness of their Marxian understanding. These brief hints may serve to bring out the idea that in seeing history as a succession of class wars directed toward the achievement of an ever juster social order, Marx went far beyond the supposed "materialism" of what he thought of as a historical dialectic; for his sanction of class war by the proletariat is a particular notion of social justice.[14]

What is common to these historicist-moralist views of war is that they treat war as inevitable, at least in the past. Kant, to be sure, saw a possibility for escaping this inevitability in the future, but as for the past, he wrote at the beginning of his essay on history: "Whatever one may think, metaphysically, concerning the freedom of the will, the human actions through which this will appears are, like all other natural phenomena, determined by the general laws of nature." War and violence are, in his view, part of this order of nature. Although much popular thinking proceeds on the assumption that wars are caused by the arbitrary decision of wicked persons, the prevailing notion among the philosophically inclined has in modern times been that impersonal "factors," "forces," and "trends" are playing a decisive role. The issue is, of course, an open and perennial one, and the activities of men such as Hitler have revived a notion that underlay the official doctrine about World Wars I and II, namely, that particular men were responsible for the outbreak of the war, that its origin must primarily be sought in the guilt of men and nations.

The opposing view has been the mainstay of Tolstoy's masterpiece, *War and Peace*. Indeed, Tolstoy wearies the reader a bit by his insistence upon this theme. He returns to it repeatedly.[15] He makes Napoleon appear ridiculous because he imagines himself as making a decision to go to war (and to direct battles). Wars arise out of the womb of history, the "series of shifting events." Indeed, Tolstoy proclaims rulers and generals as "history's slaves." It may therefore be justifiable to quote at some length the memorable reflections of the great Russian on this point. When discussing the outbreak of . ıe War of 1812, he asks:

> What produced this extraordinary occurrence? What were its causes? The historians tell us with naive assurance that its causes were the wrongs inflicted on the Duke of Oldenburg, the non-observance of the Continental System, the ambition of Napoleon, the firmness of Alexander, the mistakes of the diplomats, and so forth and so on. . . . To us, their descendants who are not historians and who can therefore regard the event with unclouded common sense, an incalculable number of causes present themselves. The deeper we delve in search of these causes, the more of them we find; and each separate cause, or whole series of causes, appears to us equally valid in itself and equally false by its insignificance compared to the

> magnitude of the events, and by its importance to occasion the event. To us the wish or objection of this or that French corporal to serve a second term appears as much a cause as Napoleon's refusal to withdraw his troops beyond the Vistula and to restore the Duchy of Oldenburg; for had he not wished to serve, and had a second, a third and a thousandth corporal and private also refused, there would have been so many less men in Napoleon's army and the war could not have occurred. . . . And there was no one cause for that occurrence, but *it had to occur because it had to*. Millions of men, renouncing their human feelings and reason, had to go from West to East to slay their fellows . . . The actions of Napoleon and Alexander . . . were as little voluntary as the action of any soldier who was drawn into the campaign by lot or by conscription . . . It was necessary that millions of men in whose hands lay the real power . . . should consent to carry out the will of these weak individuals.[16]

In writing thus, Tolstoy expressed a very deep conviction of modern thought. He also laid the foundation for his appeal to the individual to take things into his own hands and refuse to fight. War, seen as a natural catastrophe resulting from myriad causes, cannot be brought under control by rational direction from the top. This essentially anarchist view that Tolstoy does not hesitate to call "fatalistic" underlies a good deal of the agitation against the war in Vietnam, both in the United States and abroad, and it is part of the dialectic of such an approach that the very same men who refuse to fight in that war are prepared to fight for racial equality within the country. All such views are semi-religious and even mystical, in the sense that they deny direct control. War is for such a conviction not a problem of government but a matter of conscience and individual responsibility.

Diametrically opposed to such a moralizing approach to war, but equally remote from considering it a problem of government, is William James's famous notion that a "moral equivalent of war" must be found.[17] Let me recall that he starts his discussion with some moving pages in which he extols the virtue of the soldier, culminating in the sentences:

> Militarism is the great preserver of our ideals of hardihood, and human life with no use for hardihood would be contemptible. . . . The war party is assuredly right in affirming and reaffirming that the martial virtues, although originally gained by the race through war, are absolute and permanent human goods.

James then proceeds to ask: How can we produce conditions that will produce the same sort of human being without war? H. G. Wells sounded a similar call when he wrote: "When the contemporary man steps . . . into the barrack yard, he steps to a higher social plane, into an atmosphere of service and cooperation and infinitely more honorable emulations."[18] William James would have agreed and then would have asked: How can we secure this kind of attitude without war? And his own answer was that this can best be done by setting before a pacified mankind some goals involving considerable risk and personal sacrifice. In fact, William James in his answer wrote the program for the Youth Corps: "If there were, instead of military conscription, a conscription of the whole youthful population to form for a certain number of years a part of an Army of enlisted against *Nature* . . . the military ideals of hardihood and discipline would be wrought into the growing fibre of the people." What I miss here is a recognition that such service ought to be voluntary, as indeed military service has been under conditions of freedom. But there is another point to be noted here in passing. It would seem that working people in farm and factory are confronted with hardihood and discipline anyhow. James was a little astigmatic in seeing only the educational needs of the middle class. Why then not simply provide for a year in factory, mine, or farm as part of a civic education? Such notions are familiar from the totalitarian regimes of our time. Could they be adapted to a free society? Must we not in any case beware of the romanticizing of hardihood, valor, gallantry, and sacrificial devotion? Are any of these fine qualities likely to develop when they do not spring from free choice? It does not seem a matter of providing for a "moral equivalent" of war, since war is neither moral nor immoral but an aspect of human society springing from conflict of interest, temperament, and conviction and the willingness to use force in making them prevail. There has always been so much misery connected with war that its limitation and elimination are clearly expedient.

The etiology of war is therefore, to say it once again, as multiform and complex as are conflicts between human beings. Hence war's prevention and even its limitation can only be expected from a multipurpose agency, namely, government. But before I turn to this matter, a word may be permitted on a psychic aspect: the question of "inherent" combativeness or bellicosity or aggression in men. The claim that war results from "inherent" aggressive propensities has been based on both biological and psychological grounds. Recently, basing his work on comparative biology, Konrad Lorenz made a profound impression with his rangy recital of evidence of the ubiquity of aggression in the animal world. But he is at the same time convinced that such aggression can be controlled. "I do not mind admitting that, unlike Faust, I think I have something to teach mankind that may help it to change for the better."[19] The preventive measures that he argues for are not new; he even speaks of them as banal. They are self-understanding, including the understanding of sublimation, the promotion of individual friendship between members of different nations, and most importantly the "channeling of enthusiasm" by "finding causes worth serving"—in other words, William James's moral equivalent of war. In short, the crucial role of effective government is here, as so often, omitted.

Psychological investigations have shown that a tendency toward aggression is generated by frustration.[20] In particular, the different schools of psychoanalysis have contributed a good deal of insight into the processes by which such frustration and the consequent aggression are engendered. Wars, and other forms of lethal conflict and violence between men, arise *inter alia* between men who are inadequately employed in creative effort. Different psychological schools give different reasons for this phenomenon and the resulting frustration, but there is a general inclination to speak of the damming up of creative impulses, from the crudest sexual to the most sublimated spiritual ones. A large part of such damming up occurs because of social conventions, beginning with parental controls in early childhood. It is, in the light of all this evidence, not a question of artificially seeking a "moral equivalent" for war but, quite the contrary, of providing sufficient outlets for the creative urges of men.[21] Then they will not have to engage in aggression as a release for their desperately frustrated energies.

These new insights have a definite bearing, not only on the problem of international wars, but also on the genesis of civil wars. Need it be added that the range of possibilities for manipulating life in the light of these understandings is definitely limited and that no great optimism is warranted on this score? However, it is becoming increasingly clear that the major reasons for such frustration are to be found in three directions: an overly restrictive sex ethic, making for repression and consequent tension, an unduly limited production and distribution of economic goods, making for too low a standard of living and unemployment, and an inordinately restricted participation in political decision-making, causing a sense of excessive dependency and leading to rebellion.

Sex ethics are rapidly evolving toward a more permissive and relaxed attitude, especially in the West, where formerly ascetic beliefs were particularly severe. The subject has been explored in some detail by Herbert Marcuse. He has argued that a release of erotic drives is vital for mankind's pacification.[22] But the other two factors are primarily a matter of government. Here, too, considerable changes have taken place, with a consequent marked reduction in general bellicosity. Unemployment has been disappearing in Europe, while the standard of living has been rising, and the democratization has been moving ahead in various nations. Obviously, these trends cannot be argued here, nor is it necessary, since most of the facts are well known. It is also well known that the changes that have occurred are largely the result of joint, and more particularly of governmental, effort and of the internal evolution of government. However, counter-trends have to some extent nullified the pacifying effects. It is often said at present in the United States that "for every ounce of governmental help we get, we lose an ounce of personal freedom." Aid programs have occasioned similar reactions on the international scene. Accepting assistance means subjection to him who renders aid. What is more, the rapid increase in the size and complexity of governmental operations has enhanced the sense of helplessness. Modern novelists, especially Kafka, have offered dramatic portrayals of these frustrations in a bureaucratized mass society. The more comprehensive the operations, the more difficult it becomes to maintain the cooperative pattern. To be sure, the so-called interest and pressure groups provide new channels for more effective participation, but only if their internal structure does not become hierarchical and autocratic, as it is apt to do. The several basic rights guaranteeing the several freedoms and protecting minorities are therefore, in a sense, means of reducing the likelihood of war, by toning down aggressive propensities.[23]

In a culture that is literate and accustomed to written legal documentation, such procedural restrictions of government are explicitly recognized, that is, "constitutionally guaranteed." This "internal pacification" is lacking in the totalitarian regimes that, contrary to their publicly confessed concern for peace, engender constant frustration and resulting belligerence by their failure to protect men against government and other power-wielders. "Internal pacification" is also proving difficult in the newly emergent states, many of which are more or less devoid of constitutional traditions and the convictions, religious and other, upon which it rests. The readiness to extend constitutionalism, especially in its subtlest form—British parliamentarism—to these nations has led to breakdowns of government and recurrent coups d'état and revolutionary upheavals.[24] In short, war and warlike conflict have been on the increase. The inclusion of regimes that have not been adequately "internally pacified" in the United Nations has made its machinery more and more unwieldy and has rendered it ineffective as a peace-keeping and even as a war-reducing instrumentality. These experiences in turn have induced a widespread resignation as to the possibilities of controlling war. Far-reaching proposals for the "reform" of U.N. machinery have remained largely academic, and the noninclusion of Communist China and Germany has excluded two of the great powers the problems of which are especially apt to produce the danger of war.

In spite of these disappointments, the basic premise of the approach to war remains true, namely, that there is only one possible solution to the problem of preventing war: the establishment of a workable government. This argument has recently been given a seemingly novel form by certain writers who talk about integration and system.[25] On closer inspection, it becomes clear that they are in fact talking about government. "The indispensable political system, especially in the form of a central government," is posited as decisive—and rightly so, since all integration presupposes power, and indeed structured power, that is to say, rule or government. On all levels of community, local, national, regional, or global, peace can only be maintained by organizing the community for dealing with the conflicts that arise. No preestablished harmony or other illusions absolve men from the need to provide machinery for arguing out their differences and arriving at equitable compromises. As far as the world community is concerned, the situation is roughly the same as it is for regional and national communities: one has to have machinery for arriving at the required decisions (especially decisions concerning rules of behavior) and for enforcing these decisions against all challengers. It is almost impossible to set up machinery of the latter type that is effective against the more powerful states, unless they have had a decisive share in arriving at the decisions in the first place.[26]

In practical terms, such an undertaking consists of two parts: (1) building a union government sufficiently worldwide to enable it to cope with world economic problems effectively and to promote "development," and (2) giving such a union government sufficient armed strength to make attack upon the peoples living under it unpromising and to enforce its rules and decisions. If such a government were created, and if it were willing to accept any nation that might be prepared to join it as a member, the prospects of controlling war would be as great as the scope of the organization's sway. It is urgent not to deceive oneself into thinking that the United Nations is providing such a government or is likely to develop into one in the near future.[27]

I am well aware that many practical men look upon

statements such as the preceding ones as rank utopianism. But in the light of experience and sound political theory, it is the practitioners who are the utopians, expecting from an organization more than it can provide. The United Nations is not without its uses: on a number of occasions it has served to attenuate the tensions and has thereby contributed to the maintenance of peace. But it does not fulfill the essential requirements of a government capable of preventing war, that is, large-scale, organized killing for the believed-in group ends. The very nature of national governments forces them into belligerent posture in the defense of their supposed interests as long as there is no workable process other than armed conflict for advocating and defending these interests.

The slogan of "peaceful change" while often abused nonetheless has real meaning. The failure of the League of Nations to provide for such peaceful change was probably the prime reason for its demise. The balance of power in and around the League did not and could not provide the needed decisions, and yet only balance of power politics is available in loose confederations.[28] The history of the U.N. organization to date confirms this insight. But not only the need for balance but also the lack of homogeneity is fatal, as was pointed out above.

At this point, it becomes clear that civil war must always be included in any realistic study of war. A great deal of confusion has resulted from a preoccupation with wars between the particular groups called nations that have dominated the modern world. Characteristically, neither Rousseau nor Kant nor the builders of the League of Nations who followed in their footsteps saw this problem clearly. Yet, in a very real sense, the conquest of power by the Fascists in Italy and the Hitlerites in Germany was the beginning of a worldwide civil war, just as the conquest of power by Huey Long in Louisiana might have been the beginning of a civil war in the United States. But so wedded were most of us to the idea that "war" is wars between national states that the real nature of the fascist challenge was misunderstood. The appeal of Italians and Germans asking for aid against the fascist revolutionaries was ridiculed, or at least neglected.

A clear grasp of the threat of civil war is particularly important at this time because schemes for securing the world against war through international organization are likely to lead to disaster if the nature and conditions of civil war are overlooked. A survey of civil wars in the past shows that they are likely to arise over class divisions of an economic nature or over issues of basic conviction, more especially religion. Civil wars are most likely when there is no outside enemy to take advantage of the turmoil in the nation, as during the English Civil War and the American Civil War, for example. This, of course, would be the case under a world government. Civil wars are also made more probable if the class or religious divisions are localized in definite geographical areas, which can thus become the center of opposing forces (Thirty Years War, American Civil War). This condition also is likely to prevail under a world government, with its far-flung territories. A civil war may be defined, then, as a resort to arms by a party or group within one body politic for the purpose of forcing the opposing party to accept the will of the warring party. The distinction between civil and foreign war is only a special case of the general phenomenon of in-group conflict that anthropologists have found to be ever recurrent in primitive societies along with out-group conflict.

The conclusion of these brief reflections is a depressing one; for the prospects of eliminating war are dim indeed. If the requirement of homogeneity is met, the union is too limited in scope to accomplish more than a firm alliance (and it must not be a holy alliance, at that). If the requirement of worldwide scope is fulfilled, the union is too heterogeneous and contains too many autocracies to be workable. Both horns of the dilemma therefore fall short of the goal of maintaining peace. The "posture of gladiators" Hobbes spoke of in discussing the relations between sovereign states in the seventeenth century is still very much apropos. So is Kant's insistence that the posture impedes human potentialities. The fear of total destruction, reinforced by the direct danger for rulers themselves to be killed in a nuclear holocaust, has limited warfare to varieties of agonistic fighting in which victory remains elusive and stalemate is the probable outcome. But who knows how long this kind of tournament will last? Will we have to conclude with Paul Valéry's pessimistic assessment: "Rien dans l'histoire n'est pour enseigner aux humains la possibilité de vivre en paix. L'enseignement contraire s'en dégage,—et se fait croire."[29]

NOTES

1. These moral issues are taken up in other chapters of this volume.

2. Cf. my article "Political Pathology," in *Political Quarterly* (London) (Jan., 1966). Pitirim Sorokin, in his book *The Crisis of Our Age* (1941), measured the frequency and intensity of wars in history and found that considered from the standpoint of duration, size of armies, and casualties, there were 967 important wars in the history of Greece, Rome, and the Western countries from 500 B.C. to 1925 A.D. He adds: "If to the European wars of 1900 to 1925 we add all the subsequent wars up to the present time, the figures will eclipse even those for the third century B.C. [an extremely warlike century]" and predicts that the twentieth century will probably prove to be "the bloodiest and most belligerent" of all the twenty-five centuries. His fulsome statistics (pp. 212–217) are a good indicator of the ubiquity of international violence.

3. Quincy Wright, *et al.*, *A Study of War*, 2 Vols. (1943), pp. 74 ff. and 131 ff. Besides the five drives mentioned in the text above, independence and society (meaning social solidarity) are discussed as basic; the maintenance of independence and social solidarity are, however, aspects of defense. Wright's

magistral treatment offers the most exhaustive survey of human experience with war. Cf., in addition, Raymond Aron, *Paix et Guerre entre les Nations* (1962), which restricts itself to modern national wars.

4. Wright, *op. cit.*, pp. 273 ff. Cf. also Samuel Huntington, *The Soldier and the State* (1957), *passim.*

5. "Es kann der Frömmste nicht im Frieden bleiben, wenn es dem bösen Nachbarn nicht gefällt." Schiller, *Wilhelm Tell*, IV, 3.

6. *See* for an elaboration of this aspect of the matter my *Man and His Government* (1962), ch. xxiii, and the literature given there.

7. Karl von Clausewitz, *Hinterlassene Werke über Krieg und Kriegführung, 1832–1834.* I cite the edition of 1857; *see* Vol. I, p. xviii; cf. also Vol. III, p. 121, and for commentary Hans Rothfels, *Karl von Clausewitz: Politik und Krieg* (1920), and the same, "Clausewitz," in *Makers of Modern Strategy*, ed. E. M. Earle (1943), pp. 93–113.

8. Rothfels, *op. cit.* (1943), pp. 105–106.

9. Clausewitz, *op. cit.*, Vol. VIII, ch. vi, §B.

10. *Zum ewigen Frieden* (1795), Cassirer Edition, Vol. VI, pp. 425 ff. Cf. also my study *Inevitable Peace* (1948), ch. i, and the essay in *Annales de la Philosophie Politique*, Vol. IV (1962), ch. vii.

11. *Idee zu einer allgemeinen Geschichte in weltbürgerlicher Absicht* (1784), Cassirer Edition, Vol. IV, pp. 151 ff., esp. p. 159.

12. The role of reason in Hegel's philosophy is not easy to assess and has become the subject of extended controversy in recent years, but this much can be asserted.

13. *De Civitate Dei*, Bk. I, 21. Cf. also most recently the article by Richard S. Hartigan, "Augustine on War and Killing," *Journal of the History of Ideas*, XXVII (1966), 195 ff, and Herbert A. Deane, *The Political and Social Ideas of St. Augustine* (1963), *passim.*

14. It has been remarked, and rightly, that "the Marxian theory, attributing imperialist war to the steady pressure for colonial, commercial, and financial expansion by the capitalists, because of the declining internal market and the increase of productive capacity, has not been generally sustained by detailed historical studies." Wright, *op. cit.*, pp. 284–285. Surely the wars of this century, great and small, have only very partially been so motivated.

15. Sir Isaiah Berlin, *The Hedgehog and the Fox* (1953). Cf. also his *Historical Inevitability* (1954), *passim.*

16. *War and Peace,* Bk. IX, ch. i.

17. William James, *A Moral Equivalent of War* (1910). *See also* Eugen Rosenstock-Huessy, *Soziologie*, Bd. I (1956), "Die Übermacht Räume," pp. 84 ff. and 232 ff.

18. Mr. Justice Holmes's views on war may be compared to this as they

are discussed by Edmund Wilson, *Patriotic Gore* (1962), "Justice Oliver Wendell Holmes," pp. 743 ff.

19. Konrad Lorenz, *On Aggression* (1963), p. 275.

20. Gardner Murphy (ed. & coauthor), *Human Nature and Enduring Peace* (1945)—a very broad survey.

21. Lucy P. Mair, *Primitive Government* (1962); Jomo Kenyatta, *Facing Mount Kenya* (1938, 1953); E. E. Evans-Pritchard, *Social Anthropology* (1951); and M. G. Smith, *Government in Zazzau: 1800–1950* (1960)—to mention only a few representative studies.

22. Herbert Marcuse, *Eros and Civilization* (1955).

23. Cf. my "Rights, Liberties, Freedoms: A Reappraisal" in *American Political Science Review*, LVII (1963), 841 ff, and the literature cited there.

24. Cf. my *Transcendent Justice—The Religious Dimensions of Constitutionalism* (1964), and a paper contributed to Herbert Spiro (ed.), *Patterns of African Development* (1967), entitled "Some Reflections on Constitutionalism for Emergent Political Orders."

25. Karl Deutsch, *Nationalism and Social Communication* (1953), pp. 34 ff. Cf. also his *The Nerves of Government* (1963).

26. Cf. Walter Schiffer, *The Legal Community of Mankind* (1954); Arthur Freund, *Of Human Sovereignty* (1964); Lincoln P. Bloomfield, *The United Nations and U. S. Foreign Policy* (1960).

27. R. Barry Farrell (ed.), *Approaches to Comparative and International Politics* (1966), esp. Pt. II, and the works cited in previous note.

28. These problems were explored in *Foreign Policy in the Making* (1938). Cf. also Jiri Liska, *International Equilibrium: A Theoretical Essay on the Politics and Organization of Security* (1957).

29. "Nothing in history teaches men the possibility of living in peace. It is the contrary lesson which emerges from it and is believed." Paul Valéry, *Mauvaises Pensées, Oeuvres*, ed. Hytier (1960), Vol. II, p. 903.

IV

The Unjustifiability of War

CHAPTER ELEVEN

The Categorical Imperative and the Cold War

Barrows Dunham

Lecturer in Philosophy,
Beaver College

I

Americans, despite what their government causes them to do, are a "moral" people and feel it necessary to judge policies by standards of right and wrong. No doubt there are many scoundrels among them and hypocrites yet more numerous. Nevertheless, it is the fact that Americans in the mass will not support a program they believe to be cut off from morality or violative of it.

The present protest against our war in Vietnam has exactly, and chiefly, this ground. There is little self-interest in the protest, and no class interest at all. The leaders of labor are more reactionary than the reactionaries, whilst the protesters come from among the well-to-do or the utterly impoverished.

Parents no doubt worry for their sons, and the sons for themselves. But the parents would give their sons, and the sons their lives, if the war could be shown to be in any way "rigtheous." It cannot. Hence the moral revulsion.

I think it cannot often have happened in history that a large and skilled and intelligent population has been asked to do what it morally abhorred, and consequently has morally abhorred what it was asked to do. Morality, to be itself, must resist seduction by false morality. Europeans of the nineteenth century were far too gullible about "the white man's burden." Germans of more recent time received superiority-nonsense with a stupid, illicit, and murderous joy. But Americans are not doing either of these things—or, at worst, only some of them are.

I am trying to assert facts only, apart from national prejudice or pride. Probably the idea of "benevolent" exploitation (the white man's burden) is gone beyond recall. So also the idea of "superior" peoples. These notions, so far as they survive, survive in the duller and dimmer minds. Accordingly, when Americans arrived at dominance in the world (so it is described to us at any rate), there were some gross absurdities no longer fit to be believed. But I have the idea that even if such absurdities had lingered, there are certain things in our tradition that would have blocked them.

One of these things, I dare say, is the doctrine of equality, born of the eighteenth-century Enlightenment and laid down by our founders. One prospers under this concept as under the sun. But I am concerned with another—older—force in our tradition: a force not immediately social, one only secondarily so. This force, a moral force, was in the Puritans and, before them, in the Pilgrims, the saints of the *Mayflower* passage. It is Calvinist and Augustinian and, long, long before, an insight of the poets who wrote the book of Genesis. What interested these poets—and, after them, Augustine and Calvin and the rest of us—was not the question how our species came physiologically and socially to be what it is, but how it happens that we don't do what we very well know we ought to do, and instead do what we very well know we ought not to do.

This question, cast like a dart, a nuclear weapon, across our enterprises, does not ask what will be the effects of our actions or whether those effects are desirable. It asks only:

Are the actions right? If they are wrong, no consequences, however benign, will quite redeem them, and if they are right, the consequences don't need to be benign, though probably they will be. Thus far, the most resolute and most successful rendering of this doctrine into philosophy is the ethics of Immanuel Kant.

If I judge correctly, American youth of the present day are, most remarkably, practicing Kantians. The fact—if it is a fact—has not been easy for me to discern. Intellectually, I belong to the 1930's, and I tend to look first for social causes and social solutions. It is a habit as ingrained as the rule never to cross a picket line. Old horses obey old signals; new signals confuse them.

What I find is that the youth will listen to social explanations with some respect, as to ideas received and not irrelevant. But these social explanations don't touch the main problem as the main problem touches the youth. The old views, just because they are old, have something reactionary about them, however militantly radical they once were and can still be made to sound.

Our youth (the liveliest part of them, at any rate) are pure in heart to an extent that optimism itself can scarcely conceive. We older folk have been so, but thirty years ago our concern for the right social relations led us to look chiefly at ends. What our youth now believe, however, I think can be expressed in one signal negative: that, although some ends may justify some means, no end justifies villainy. Accordingly, they will not sacrifice or even risk their integrity for any purpose whatever. The imperative they accept is categorical only; they will accept nothing merely pragmatic or hypothetical. Thus they are Kantians, true moral descendants of the *Mayflower* saints.

The saints intended to build, and did in fact begin building, a society that gave room for personal righteousness. A thousand things have intervened since: lures, lies, lusts, hates, and modes of violence. Rogues have seized our riches and now reach out for the riches of the world. Lying is organized, deft, and technological. We have rulers who apparently suppose that anything can be done by death or the threat of death.

Yet here are our young folk who say that all of this is quite wrong, and who in their growing power show that it may also be ineffectual. "It's worse than a crime; it's a mistake," said Talleyrand once, a man most cynical yet wise. This saying may well be the epitaph of American capitalism.

II

I think that no sophisticated observer of politics, particularly international politics, supposes that the announced moral purposes are likely to be a clear and candid expression of the actual purposes. Rather, he recognizes a state of affairs (the words are now Kant's, translated) "where everybody chatters of sympathy and goodwill, but also takes every chance to deceive and plunder or otherwise to violate the rights of man."[1] Or we may take a passage yet more specific, written when Kant was meditating on "radical evil" (as he called it) in human nature:

> . . . the international situation, where civilized nations stand towards each other in the relation obtaining in the barbarous state of nature (a state of continuous readiness for war), a state, moreover, from which they have taken fixedly into their heads never to depart. We then become aware of the fundamental principles of the great societies called *states*—principles which flatly contradict their public pronouncements but can never be laid aside, and which no philosopher has yet been able to bring into agreement with morality.[2]

The chief purpose of the Cold War—perhaps the only

purpose—has been to establish and maintain an American empire, extremely profitable to American business, an empire with no fixed boundaries, so that it might one day embrace perhaps the entire globe. The Cold War was begun hard on the heels of World War II and had therefore to be made acceptable to various war-weary populations. This was done by calling the war "cold." We were to think that, though some of our sons might die here and there in the new war, we ourselves would grow rich in a kind of peace.

Propaganda seeks, for it feeds upon, simplicity. Few things are simpler than the number 2. It would be interesting to know with what secret laughter and at the same time secret anxiety the hardened, bitter diplomats of the West watched that strange, wholly American phenomenon, the late John Foster Dulles. The anxiety, if there were any, would have had to do with his professed willingness to kill everybody (going "to the brink" requires that willingness). The laughter, if there were any, would have had to do with his Manichean idea (quite heretical, by the way, in Christian doctrine) that there are just two powers in the world, one of them good enough to be called Good, and the other evil enough to be called Evil. In the Secretary's view, Good was capitalism in its perfected American form. Evil, as we have been tediously reminded, was (is) communism—but in what form? For the forms of it proliferated, to the astonishment not least of Communists themselves, until a man of the West, of the United States, found that he could not oppose Evil without accepting, if not help, then at least forbearance from some part of Evil itself. The reappraisal was indeed agonizing.

However deep this perplexity, there has been no trouble indicating what portion of Evil is presently to be opposed. If any population anywhere in the world undertakes to possess itself of its own natural resources and the fruits of its own labor, *that* is communism, *that* is Evil, and American policy (which is not necessarily the policy of Americans) will try to prevent it. Prevention, which, it now appears, is no longer more than attempted prevention, will scorch babies with napalm and shatter their mothers with that "mother of the thousand pellets," a form of grapeshot technologically "advanced"—our scientists are no laggards.

What the shattered mothers wanted for the scorched babies—and the fathers too, since they have fought for it—was, and is, a prosperous future, in which the infant talent and intelligence and (at the last) wisdom might flower and make a new world. Since, however, these new worlds, most attractive to human hope, cannot be made without loss of profit to businessmen far away (and yet so near), they are made, and can as it seems only be made, at the cost of burns and scars and agony and death. The new worlds are worth the cost, and even the attempt at them is worthwhile, though it fail; for the law and inward nature of business are to get cheap and sell dear, whence it follows that the wealth of a few is founded upon the poverty of many.

"In the realm of ends," wrote Immanuel Kant, "everything has either a PRICE or a DIGNITY."[3] Kant, I suppose, never wrote anything insignificant, but he liked occasionally to capitalize every letter in words he thought to be big. The collision of PRICE with DIGNITY will settle for us the ethics of the Cold War. Let us hear Kant further:

> Whatever has a price can be replaced by something else as its equivalent. But what is raised above all price and therefore admits of no equivalent, has a dignity.
>
> That which relates to general human inclinations and needs has a *commercial price;* what applies, even without presupposing a need, to a certain taste . . . has an *emotional price;* but that which constitutes the condition under which alone

something can be an end in itself, has not a mere relative value, that is a price, but an intrinsic value, that is *dignity*.

And where does this dignity, this intrinsic value, lie? In people, in human beings, in everybody on earth. It lies even in the men stricken with what Kant called "radical evil"—which is not at all an evil of being radical, but the root-evil of being unable to make decisions on any other ground than self-interest.[4] These men, too, are worthy of fair treatment, even though most of what we do in their regard is to protect ourselves from their rapacity.

Where among these categories businessmen would be, and their politicians, and the anarchic criminals who imitate both, Kant does not specifically say, and we can only guess. I think we have seen, and do still see, more than a few whose behavior is best explained by the hypothesis of radical evil. The rest of us (and, as it seems, they too) belong to the "kingdom of ends." We are, what it is most natural for people to be, "ends in ourselves," that is to say, members of the one class of beings in the world who are worth doing things for. And the rule of our conduct is this: "Act so that in your own person as well as in the person of every other you are treating mankind also as an end, never merely as a means."[5]

I suppose that Kant called mankind a "kingdom of ends" in order to express its importance. The feudal metaphor came readily, although he himself held republican and anti-monarchical views.[6] Indeed, in the early 1790's, he was sympathetic to French Jacobins, and, because of this, his name adorned the police register at Koenigsberg. "Kingdom" can have meant only importance, for in every other respect the kingdom was not a kingdom at all, nor a hierarchy of any sort, nor even a republic. It was, and is, a pure democracy: the only pure democracy, perhaps, that human intellect has ever conceived.

In this democratic "kingdom" equality is absolute. Every human being is worth doing things for, just because and only because he is human. And insofar as men are human, none of them is more worth doing things for than any other. Our humanity confers upon us a common, equal, and indestructible worth, whence it follows that we can be fairly judged according as we have respected that worth in others and in ourselves.

It is therefore clear that in the acts and policies and even the words of those who govern the "free world" (can a free world indeed have a government?) nothing of the Kantian ethic will be found. The whole purpose of those acts and policies and words is to make profit and privilege prevail by free scorchings and abundant death. But the essence of profit and privilege lies in treating very many people, not as ends at all, but as means merely. The great moral rule that Kant perceived in 1785 condemned all the social systems, up to and including his own, and equally condemned the capitalist system he saw in its first dawning. It remains to be seen whether the socialist system, which accepts his ethic, will in fact live up to it.

When one reads and (as one should) rereads the *Grundlegung*, one gets a marvelous sense of liberation. All the compromises are swept aside, all the maneuverings and enticements, everything in which (as Kant said) *das liebe Selbst immer hervorsticht*.[7] We are thrown back upon, turned toward, what alone can be the ground of ethics: an attentive regard for the multitudes of men. None of us has any ground (whatever the factual possibility) to profit from them or exploit them, still less to scar them and kill them in order to profit and exploit. Accordingly, the late Secretary, a failed Presbyterian, had his ethics exactly wrong.

Morally, all this might seem enough. But what seems

enough morally, or seems in any way moral, has very little influence upon makers of policy in the "free world." Morality is the thing the "free world" is freest from. It exists as a façade. What the makers of policy in the "free world" need to be told is not that we all see that the façade is only a façade but that the building will collapse. Then and only then—though perhaps not even then—will they desist.

It happens that Kant has also told them this. The late Secretary might have read the passage in his student days at Princeton. Kant had, more than most other thinkers, a flair for ultimates. Ultimates are, of course, hard to come by, and it is possible that Kant, who was reasonably sure of them, was also reasonably mistaken. I wouldn't want to be the man who said so. The masters, in whatever art or science, have an alarming talent for being right.

I have been reproducing the Kantian argument in reverse, for greatest effect. The rule (sometimes known as the Second Maxim)—that we are to treat people never as means only but always as worth doing things for—is, as Kant gives it, a derivative rule. Perhaps it is the rule he was after in the long run, but it isn't the rule he asserted as categorical. He was at great pains to remove from consideration anything that might involve an "if." There remains something a little hypothetical about the Second Maxim: it seems as though one can still say, "People are worth doing things for *if* they do indeed have that much intrinsic value."

Kant wanted to find what it was you could morally assert without any "if" whatever. And this is what he found: "Act only on that maxim which will enable you at the same time to will that it be a universal law."[8] Breaches of this rule he found to be of two sorts: either the act, if supposed to be universally done, would contradict itself, or the willing of the act (the decision to do the act) would contradict willing and decision. That is to say, there are some acts (such as lying) that in time defeat themselves, and there are decisions (such as passivity, the refusal to develop one's talents) that contradict the motives they rise from.

What the rule, the celebrated Categorical Imperative, says or seems to say is that self-defeating behavior, of whatever sort, is senseless ("contrary to reason" would have been Kant's phrase). No man of brains would do anything of the sort. For who, except a fool, would labor to effect what will defeat itself in the attempt?

Very well. In 1785 Kant produced four examples (not altogether clear) of the working of this principle—classroom examples they were, constructions no doubt drawn from his lectures. But since the bombs fell on Hiroshima and Nagasaki, we have seen the Categorical Imperative in its full power. The rulers of America boast that they can destroy mankind twenty times over and allow that the Soviet Union can destroy mankind at least once. If mankind be destroyed once, I don't see what is gained by destroying it twenty times.

However this may be—the arithmetic seems silly—the destruction of mankind once or twenty times would be an event in which not only this or that purpose had been defeated but all human purposes whatever. If the capitalists engage in nuclear warfare to "defend" capitalism, or if the socialists engage in nuclear warfare to "defend" socialism, there will in the result be neither capitalism nor socialism, because we shall all be dead.

Nuclear warfare—and, possibly, short of it, any prolonged warfare of attrition (is *this* the true Cold War?)—will be a last and ultimate breach of the Categorical Imperative. Kant could not, of course, foresee this, but his genius was such that he could apprehend and state the rule without awareness of the supreme demonstration.

How the thing will turn out I do not know. I believe it quite possible that our rulers, confidently breasting the

Categorical Imperative on a tide of self-interest, may in the end destroy us all. They have never said that they would not. The survivors of all this, if there are any, will of course know what did happen and will also know, by having survived, that Kant understood what is essentially the case.

And I have the idea that, if this survival comes to pass, the grand effect will be owing to our young people, the new Kantians and Pilgrim saints; for it will have been they who spoke not of advantage or result but of righteousness in the act itself.

NOTES

1. *The Fundamental Principles of the Metaphysic of Morals*, trans. Otto Manthey-Zorn (New York: Appleton-Century, 1938), p. 41. Original text of the *Grundlegung* in the Cassirer Edition, Vol. IV (Berlin: 1922), p. 281.

2. *Religion Within the Limits of Reason Alone*, trans. Theodore M. Greene & Hoyt H. Hudson (Chicago: Open Court Publishing, 1934), p. 29. Original text in Cassirer, *op. cit.*, Vol. VI, p. 173.

3. Manthey-Zorn, *op. cit.*, p. 53; Cassirer, *op. cit.*, Vol. IV, p. 293.

4. Greene-Hudson, *op. cit.*, pp. 24–25; Cassirer, *op. cit.*, Vol. VI, pp. 168–169.

5. Manthey-Zorn, *op. cit.*, p. 47; Cassirer, *op. cit.*, Vol. IV, p. 287.

6. *See* Karl Vorländer, *Immanuel Kant, der Mann und das Werk* (Leipzig: Felix Meiner, 1924), Vol. II, pp. 219–222.

7. "The 'dear self' everywhere comes to light." Manthey-Zorn, *op. cit.*, p. 23; Cassirer, *op. cit.*, Vol. IV, p. 264.

8. Manthey-Zorn, *op. cit.*, p. 38; Cassirer, *op. cit.*, Vol. IV, p. 279.

CHAPTER TWELVE

Can War Be Rationally Justified?

A. C. Genova

Professor of Philosophy,
Wichita State University

One has fears for philosophy sometimes. Several commentators have characterized the contemporary lovers of wisdom as being more inbred and clannish than ever, making their living by such esoteric practices as linguistic analysis, phenomenological reduction, and what have you—all the while leaving significant questions of social policy, ethical norms, and even the meaning of life to others. Some of us in the philosophic camp are inclined to think that the political scientists, sociologists, psychologists, anthropologists, and the like have made a bad job of it also, and, indeed, the critics often judge the specialized sciences to be equally remote, comparably abstract, and at least as inclined to avoid value judgments.

Yet it is probable that if the philosophic voice dared to recommend a "philosophic resolution to war," we could rest assured that our naive but cooperative Muse, like Sheridan's "old weather-beaten she-dragon," would be charged with a malapropism. After all, wars are settled by political or military means; philosophers should stick to philosophic problems. To be sure, waving the flag of philosophy on the battlefield would be incongruous, although I suggest that philosophy can provide red flags to help us avoid the battlefield altogether.

I

The problem of war, like any other problem about what we ought to do, is concerned with the possible implementation of a practical policy. A positive policy of war, like other practical policies, can be construed as a formulated disposition to initiate the activity of war under certain generally definable conditions. An *activity* can be analyzed in terms of (1) *the context* to which it applies, (2) *the end or goal* to which it is directed, and (3) *the intelligible norms or rules* that regulate the actions which realize the relevant end. In one important sense, activities are independent of empirical considerations. What I mean is that the intelligible canons governing an activity serve as a set of systematic norms for action, and in respect to the meaning, validity, and relevance of these norms, the appropriateness of the prescribed lines of action is independent of the actual *facts* of human behavior. When we actually identify a specific case of activity (that is, determine whether a piece of behavior involves an agent engaged in an activity), part of the required data will be an empirical description of the relevant observable *behavior*. In this empirical context, the activity can be viewed restrictively as a patterned sequence of observable and measurable events admitting of scientific explanation (an explanation, incidentally, that is itself the result of an activity, namely, an explanation in accordance with the standards of some specific, empirical science). Just as it follows that there are no activities without in some sense presupposing rules of action directed to a purpose, it is usually assumed that there are no natural events without natural laws of their occasion that result in predictable effects.

A related way of contrasting activities and the sequences of events that constitute the content of their empirical descriptions is to take note of the inherent *intentionality* exhibited in the structure of an activity. Activities, like thoughts, are always *about* something—or more correctly, rule-directed behavior refers to *contexts or objects* to which it applies and to *ends* that it is designed to actualize in accordance with *norms* that it obeys. In short, activities are *situational, purposive,* and *rule-directed.* Indeed, the primary reason that the function of thought admits an interpretation as intentional, in contrast to "things," is that thought itself is a kind of cognitive activity directed to its proper end.

Of course, factual considerations do affect the *application* of intelligible norms. For example, the collective thought of an unruly mob would hardly conform to logical rules, but this has nothing to do with whether or not the rules are valid principles for the activity of logical thought. Again, all sorts of empirically determinable psychological or physiological states might make an intelligent performance in a chess game impossible, but this does not affect how the game ought to be played relative to the formal rules of chess and the theory of chess strategy. In effect, empirical considerations can contribute significant information about the circumstances that are conducive or detrimental to the successful performance of activities, but they do not determine the kind or relevance of norms in respect to the ends of the activities.

Now, the problem of war primarily concerns the possibility of a rational justification for a policy of war, and in light of the above discussion, there are five consequences we need to set forth.

1. If war is construed as an activity, then the problem

cannot be expressed simply as "To war or not to war." Such a formulation is abstract at best and absurd at worst, for we have seen that the appropriate formulation of an activity must have reference to *the context, the end,* and *the regulative maxims* of the activity. Clarification of these internal elements is a necessary condition for understanding the activity in question.

2. Without at least some informal understanding of the relevant norms and purposes of an activity, an agent cannot (except perhaps incidentally) be engaged in *that* activity at all (although he may be engaged in a different activity such as following orders issued by a superior); he would merely be going through the motions. This implies neither that an active agent actually must be able to state accurately these criteria when asked, nor that the concepts involved have some kind of residence in a "mind" somewhere and somehow backing up his overt action. In most circumstances, we have no great difficulty distinguishing between cases in which the relevant behavior is due strictly to non-intellectual considerations, cases in which the agent is indeed engaged in an activity but not the one we are considering, and cases in which the agent is engaged at some measurable level in the specified activity. At any rate, in respect to the issue of war, it should be clear that not all persons implemented or involved in a practical policy of war need be actively engaged in the activity of war to the same degree—or, perhaps, to any significant degree at all.

3. We must clarify the ambiguity of characterizing activities and practical policies as "rational." We want to distinguish (1) rational as opposed to empirical, (2) rational as opposed to irrational or incoherent, and (3) rational as opposed to unjustified or unwarranted. In sense (1), all activities are rational because they involve functions of intelligence that regulate purposive behavior, and as such they cannot be reduced to the content of their correspond-

ing empirical descriptions. In sense (2), some activities are rational, those that exhibit an internal consistency or coherence that is revealed in the philosophical analysis of their formative elements. For this internal rationality of an activity, the regulative norms must be compatible with each other, applicable to the appropriate context, and relevant to the purpose of the activity, while the end of the activity, if it is a complex end, cannot contain incompatible elements. An example of such internal irrationality would be discovering that two of the rules of chess were incompatible, or that an application of some combination of the rules made it impossible for the game ever to terminate in the allowable ways set forth in the rules. In sense (3), we can tentatively assume that some coherent activities are rational in that they admit of an external justification or vindication in respect to prior ends or fundamental philosophical assumptions. In other words, given a possible activity that is rational in sense (2), we can ask if it is *rationally justified.* Or in an even stronger sense, if it is the *most rational* of available alternatives. To give a rational justification for an activity is to establish it as an acceptable or obligatory line of action in the light of certain presuppositions, values, or assumptions that are not constitutive elements of the activity itself.

Now there are many kinds and levels of rational justifications of practical policies of action. Sometimes these justifications occur at the philosophical level, but their more common occurrence is in the ongoing context of sociopolitical argument. Three rather common forms of such argument have reference respectively to *fact, legal precedent,* and *traditional ethical values.* For example, in terms that emphasize factual considerations one might argue that a particular policy of war as applicable to a particular situation is right or wrong because such a policy is or is not feasible or practical. The appeal here is to factual circumstances that can be empirically determined. Legal considerations predominate when it is argued that the war policy is right or wrong because it is required by or violates certain international laws or preestablished conventions. The appeal here is to legal precedent, common law, or traditions, and the argument has a deductive character. Finally, it might be argued that regardless of legal or factual considerations, a particular policy of war is right or wrong because it is or is not justifiable in terms of certain ethical prescriptions. Here the appeal would be to moral considerations that normally override legal precedent or practical feasibility.

Factual, legal, and ethical evaluations of practical policies often conflict, and such conflict demands some basis on which the relative priority of these alternative claims can be examined. Scientific evidence, legal scholarship, and ethical persuasion play their role in bolstering these competing alternatives, but ultimately the interrelation between facts, values, and laws, along with the identification of any primary principles that ground these alternative approaches, constitutes philosophic problems. But, as with all philosophic problems, a historical survey of the variety of philosophic positions may very well leave one thinking that just about any practical policy of action has been or will be justified by some philosophic system or other, and that any objective attempt to discover a philosophic resolution to such sociopolitical problems would be futile. Thus, the practical application of philosophic thought becomes ambiguous and somewhat suspect because philosophy is embarrassed by its own riches. On the one hand, our argument implies that it must be philosophy that ultimately establishes the fundamental principles that rationally justify sociopolitical arguments concerning practical policies; on the other hand, the diversity of philosophic positions apparently leaves us with insurmountable difficulties with nowhere else to go. Who can blame the philosopher's critics?

4. Since empirical descriptions are not directly relevant to the analysis, definition, and evaluation of activities, the problem concerning the rational justification of a policy of war (like any other activity) is not one for empirical science as such, but necessarily one for philosophic analysis. The analysis, clarification, and evaluation of activity (including the activity of physical science) is a philosophic task. Thus, the question of war is, in the final analysis, a philosophic concern. For our purposes, the critical question is: Can we, through an analysis of the nature of war as an *activity*, avoid the approaches that justify or reject the practice of war by a process of deduction from metaphysical or ethical presuppositions external to the activity of war itself? In short, we want to explore the possibility of reaching a reasonable conclusion from the standpoint of a philosophic analysis of activity, and not from presuppositions (though such presuppositions may or may not be true) concerning God, the purpose of the universe, the purpose of man, inalienable rights, or particular ethical values.

5. A final consequence concerns a possible misunderstanding about the kind of relevance philosophy has for the problem of war. In one sense, "philosophic war" has been waged continuously since the beginning of the systematic presentation of ideas, and this might suggest that the philosophers should settle their own intellectual disputes before they worry about the military kind. But the usage of "war" as it occurs in "philosophic war" is clearly a metaphor. After all, "Sticks and stones will break my bones but names will never harm me." Also, those who confuse ideology with philosophy often see systems of philosophic ideas as causes of war and envision the role of philosophy in terms of the vivid ideologies that so often accompany warfare. But ideology is a vulgarization of certain philosophic ideas.

It arises from political motivation, not from philosophic inquiry. Typically, ideologies result from antecedent political decisions and commitments that then become associated with the rough outlines (liberally adjusted) of a philosophic system, thus providing a kind of pseudo-intellectual support for a particular brand of political action. Ideologies are usually constructed by an intellectual élite, but they are designed for popular consumption as quasi-justifications for policy. Ideologies thereby become the ad hoc hypotheses of political action.

Clearly, the relevance of philosophy to the problem of war does not stem from the fact that philosophers have had the most experience at internecine warfare or are the vehicles for political ideology, but from either the relevance of philosophic systems that entail conclusions concerning the practice of war or the analysis, clarification, and criticism of *the concept of the activity of war*. In our discussion, we will restrict our analysis to the second of these dimensions and emphasize two basic questions: (1) whether war is an internally rational (coherent) activity, and (2) whether a policy of war can be rationally justified. Let us first turn to a typical argument for the justification of the practice of war.

II

War is somewhat paradoxical. What could conceivably be the point of engaging in mortal physical combat when the matter of dispute could just as easily be settled by agreeing, say, to abide by the results of a chess tournament duly monitored and competently judged by experts? After all, chess is somewhat analogous to war, and such a civilized surrogate for aggression would avoid the loss of life and property invariably shared by the parties of war.

The inadequacy of any such simple solution to the problem of war becomes obvious when we learn about notions such as "self-preservation," "moral principles," "just wars," "holy wars," and all the other highly sophisticated concepts that history provides so generously for the justification of aggression. We come to realize that certain ideals and values are far too important to be left to the contingencies of a chess tournament and the idiosyncracies of representative chess players. But there is more to it than that. Not only do the issues at stake exhibit an importance out of proportion to the relatively trivial recourse to chess as their resolution, but there is no essential, normative relation between the activity of chess and the issues of war. The use of a chess tournament to resolve the issues of war is as incoherent as playing chess to solve a mathematical problem, or engaging in physical combat to settle a legal question. The internal rationality (coherence) of an activity requires that the regulative norms be essentially relevant to and derivative from the nature of the goal to be achieved. The fact that one side would win the chess tournament would merely necessitate that we recognize the winner as superior in chess, but not as being correct about the issues at stake. Anything similar to the chess solution is incoherent because it merely replaces the problem at hand with another task and then treats the original problem as solved. So a coherent activity constitutes a *normative* solution to problems or ends. But then the question arises: Isn't the activity of war, like chess, similarly irrelevant as a means to the resolution of the typical problems that engender wars—problems such as those concerning geographical borders, political differences, and economic conflicts?

Now those who argue for the legitimacy of warfare would probably agree that it would be absurd to settle disputes by immediately resorting to violence. The move here might be to say that a resort to warfare is still justifiable as a *final* resort, an unfortunate but necessary alternative when fundamental values are at stake. Hence, the exponents of rational war might very well agree that any immediate resort to war would be irrational and irrelevant but still want to maintain that it *becomes* the rational line of action when the issues at stake are critical, for warfare is the only available alternative. Indeed, negotiation and compromise, by their very nature, are strictly rational methods of solving such serious disputes, for these alternatives involve discussion, argument, and compromise *about* the issues themselves. But again, if negotiation fails or is impossible, war becomes a justifiable and presumably rational alternative. Thus, if war *is* the only remaining alternative, it might be argued that to refuse to engage in war would be tantamount to being irrational and probably immoral.

Generally, this argument contains a distinction between a justifiable and an unjustifiable war. The policy of war is justifiable if it concerns matters of self-interest or principle that are fundamental values of an individual or a social system, and if all other relevant alternatives are unavailable. War is viewed here as a last resort analogous to the way some people view child-spanking. Stating it negatively, the practice of war is unjustifiable when the issues in contention are minor or secondary (that is, when a resolution either way is compatible with the fundamental values of both sides), or if the issues are sufficiently critical when other relevant alternatives such as negotiation or compromise over the issues have not been exhausted.

But there remains a serious ambiguity. On the one hand, the above argument apparently admits that warfare would be an irrational (incoherent and unjustifiable) means to resolve everyday economic, geographical, social, or political issues; on the other hand, if these concrete problems are actually the manifestations of a conflict concerning fundamental values and all other alternatives fail, then a policy of war becomes both internally coherent and externally justifiable through an appeal to those ultimate values. Granted that an activity can be *justified* by an appeal to prior ends, how can an incoherent activity become *coherent* by an appeal to prior ends? If, in our normative sense, violence is an incoherent means in respect to the resolution of problems of chess, mathematics, economics, geography, law, and politics, then why would it not be likewise incoherent in respect to the rational achievement of the higher ends—whatever they may be? The fact that these higher ends are the most important ends and that all other alternatives so far fail is irrelevant to the question of whether the activities that realize these ends are coherent. The conditions for the coherence of an activity refer to the internal structure of the activity. They have to do with the normative and logical relations between *the regulative canons* of the activity, *the context,* and *the end* (remote or proximate, ultimate or subsidiary) of the activity; they do not depend upon the relative importance of the end or upon the empirical fact that all other ways of achieving the goal have failed. If this is true, the argument in question does not establish the possible *coherence* of warfare. And if warfare is rationally incoherent, then it is highly doubtful that anyone would contend that it is nevertheless rationally justifiable. Such an argument would be self-contradictory, unless its advocates were prepared to claim that rational coherence is not a necessary condition for the practical possibility of an activity. But perhaps there is another way of arguing for the coherence and justifiability of the activity of war.

It might be argued that up to this point we have been treating war only as a *means* to other ends (like the resolution of a border dispute, a problem of international law, an economic conflict, a religious issue, etc.), but we have ignored the fact that the activity of war, like all other activities, has a proximate end of its own. By the *proximate* end of an activity, I mean the end that is universally present in any performance of the activity—the end that essentially determines the standards of the activity in any of its instances. By a *remote* end, I mean one which would further modify the standards of an activity in an essential way if the active agent admits the priority of the remote end over the proximate end. The proximate end of war is something such as conquest or military victory over the enemy, and in *this* respect, it might be maintained that the activity of war expresses a coherent use of intelligence if it could somehow be justified in its own right—as a worthwhile end in itself. War, like any other activity, generates certain norms of conduct that constitute the strategy or tactics that will lead to military victory. Consequently, war (abstracted from any reference to external ends) appears to be a coherent activity after all. Of course, it would remain true that even if war *is* an internally rational activity in this sense, yet when it is employed as a means to a further or higher end, for example, when military victory is in turn viewed as a means to resolving problems concerning geographical borders, economic conflicts, or even moral issues of fundamental importance, then in respect to these primary ends war remains incoherent. The critical question, then, is concerned with whether or not the practical policy of war admits of something like self-justification—or, perhaps less elliptically, whether warfare involves intrinsic benefits that can be justified without an appeal to values that supersede the proximate end of warfare. But perhaps we have been overstating our case, and our opponents are not yet convinced that warfare would be an incoherent resort in respect to any external or remote ends.

Let us take an example. The lumberjack is engaged in an activity resulting in the procuring of raw lumber. This activity in turn may very well be construed as a means to other activities, such as the preparation of the raw lumber for use in making musical instruments. The latter activity might in turn be viewed as a means to the activity of violin-making, which is directed to the production of a certain kind and quality of violin. The latter in turn might function as a means for the violinist to produce a certain kind of music. The violinist then becomes an element in the resources the conductor employs in the activity of conducting an orchestra. And so on. Now this hypothetical means-ends schema interrelates a series of activities in a hierarchy of relevance, each activity having its own proximate end with its corresponding relevant norms, and each activity also having its relation to an ascending order of remote ends, which also thereby become relevant to the norms of the original activity. This is so because the regulative norms of any lower-level activity are always partly determined by all the ends in the relevant series. For example, the lumberjack, besides his immediate activity of cutting down trees, is also providing lumber for the woodworking industry and will be influenced by the purposes of this industry in his selection of trees to be cut while the norms of the violin-maker's art will be partly conditioned by the requirements set forth by violinists.

But how would the activity of war ever have an analogous relevance to remote ends of any kind? What conceivable relevance or essential application would physical violence have to an economic conflict, a border dispute, or an issue of international law? The resolution of each of these problems may indeed presuppose a descending order of other activities that are required as sources for the materials, contexts, and means by which economic, geographical, or legal disputes are settled, but how could war have this kind of normative relevance to anything other than its proximate end of conquest, victory, destruction, or whatever?

One might attempt to avoid the above questions by making a distinction between a normative and a descriptive end. Normative ends are those that require a solution in a particular way that is relevant to the nature of the problem at hand, while descriptive ends are ends that contain the proviso that the goal is to be realized regardless of the means—at all costs, as it were. If the latter is the kind of end we hold, then war as a means to its resolution is a coherent means, regardless of whether one interprets the end as the proximate end or some remote end of war. But this argument also fails when the apparent distinction between descriptive and normative ends is subjected to analysis. What does it mean to postulate an end with the added proviso of "at all cost" or "regardless of the means"? It is simply tantamount to assuming that *any* means (including war) is an allowable alternative. But the latter is precisely part of what it *means* to say that the means is irrational, that it is not essentially relevant to the nature of the end. Such an unqualified interpretation of ends merely presupposes the activity of war as a possible route to their realization, and, thus, the very question at issue is begged.

Let us briefly summarize our inquiry as it now stands. We have been examining the *practical possibility of war*, that is, *whether there are conditions under which the activity of war is a rational alternative for action.* Practical possibility would require both internal rationality (coherence) and external rationality (justification). But if an activity is incoherent, it is practically impossible and therefore cannot be a genuine candidate for rational justification. Again, if the activity cannot be rationally justified, then regardless of whether the activity is in some sense coherent, it would still lack practical possibility. In respect to the activity of war, our argument at this point is as follows: War must be a coherent or incoherent activity. If it is incoherent, then it cannot be rationally justified; if it is believed to be coherent, then it is either functioning as a means to some higher end, or it is functioning only in respect to its own proximate end.

If it is a means, then since there is no conceivable end to which the activity of war relates with any essential relevance, it is in respect to any higher end incoherent and therefore unjustifiable. But if the proximate end of war is somehow interpreted as an intrinsic end (worthwhile in its own right), then if it is to be rationally justified, there must be some statable principles from which this justification follows. So this argument still allows the possibility that unilateral aggression in respect to its own proximate end might be coherent and can also possibly be justified—an alternative we will consider shortly.

The phrase "unilateral aggression" in the last sentence is the cue for another critical distinction—the absence of which may have already taxed the patience of the reader. This is the distinction between so-called wars of self-defense and wars of aggression, the latter being the unilateral initiation of offensive action against an opponent, and the former being merely of the preventive nature. How does this distinction affect the conclusions reached so far? Would not a war of self-defense provide a counter-example to our view that warfare is always incoherent (and therefore unjustified) when grounded upon an appeal to higher ends such as self-preservation?

Consider the crucial difference between these two modes of conflict. The defensive mode is always *limited* by the conditions of overt aggression. It is justified only to the degree and to the extent that it is necessary for the very existence of the defender or his way of life. In this context, the aggressor is analogous to a physical object following a line of force that must be diverted if destruction is to be avoided. The agents of self-defense are not motivated toward aggression or warfare; they merely act in accordance with norms that regulate preventive measures that will deter physical or perhaps psychological warfare. Thus, we ward off diseases, wild animals, and national catastrophes as best we can, and similarly with human aggressors. Strictly speaking then, in spite of the fact that the term "war" is applied to both aggressive activity and the activity of self-defense, an analysis of the respective activities will reveal that the two are contrary in most respects.

Unfortunately, this rather obvious distinction becomes cloudy in practice because it very often is the case that the parties engaged in war both claim self-defense as a justification. It might be argued that the fact that a given side initiated the war is not a sufficient condition to identify the aggressor, because it might be claimed that striking first was the only feasible way to protect themselves against the imminent aggression of their neighbors. But even if it *were* impossible to determine who in fact was the aggressor, if both sides claim self-defense as their justification, then at least we can say that self-defense is here recognized as the relevant criterion that vindicates a resort to violence and thereby excludes such violence from the category of aggressive war, thus indirectly supporting our argument that if an instance of violence is a case of self-defense, then it is "war" only in an incidental sense. Strictly, a "war of self-defense" implies a contradiction in terms.

III

In the light of our discussion, one very prominent alternative still remains open, namely, the possibility of a coherent policy of war employed not as a means to some other end but as an end in itself. It might be argued that violence and war are essentially connected with certain values that are worthwhile as such. For example, warlike activity may constitute part of the character of the "superman" to which the human race must evolve. Or perhaps the expression of physical power over others is an essential element of happiness. It is not always clear whether this kind of argument is maintaining that the inherent, proximate end of war itself constitutes the value in question, or whether war (in spite of our argument) is still being viewed as a justifiable means to certain higher ends such as an improvement of the human race or happiness. But taken either way, the question now is whether the proximate end of war or any other end that is claimed to justify war can be rationally justified. Another kind of argument might claim that violence is an expression of some kind of natural psychological instinct (death wish, suicidal instinct, etc.), or that order and revolution are natural stages in some kind of historical and inevitable dialectic leading to an ideal social goal. Now theories that try to establish that the activity of war is an essential characteristic of the nature of man because it has in fact a psychological, physiological, historical, or metaphysical basis in the scheme of things are all irrelevant to the question whether war is a coherent activity that is rationally justifiable. Such factual or metaphysical claims about the nature of man or the universe have their place of course, but even if one of these theories is true in some philosophically relevant sense, our present problem concerns the *normative question of whether or not war*—regardless of whether or not it does occur, will occur, or never occurs—*is rationally justified.* A simple analogy will help express our point. It is conceivable that for all sorts of physical, psychological, historical, and metaphysical reasons human beings have always cheated and will always cheat in computing their golf scores, but this has nothing to do with the norms of the game of golf or its rational justification.

Are there *any* activities that have *practical necessity,* that must be categorically presupposed for the practical possibility of any activity whatever? If there are, then if a given activity encompasses an end (proximate or remote) that is incompatible with the categorical end of this practically necessary activity, it would follow that the given activity cannot, in principle, be rationally justified. We maintain that *inquiry is a practically necessary activity*. All activities, by their very nature, presuppose inquiry because all activities presuppose knowledge of their respective norms, materials, contexts, and proximate ends. But knowledge results from inquiry. Moreover, all activity presupposes inquiry pursued for its own sake, not merely inquiry for some end other than inquiry. This is true because inquiry pursued for the sake of another end itself presupposes inquiry in its pure form. Let us take an illustration. To argue that it is true that the end of inquiry is not simply knowledge, but is, for example, wealth, power, fame, or pleasure, entails that *this* conclusion was reached independently of these various motives, but for the purpose of truth. In short, the very point of making a truth claim is that the truth value does not depend on irrelevant or accidental (though practically possible) ends such as wealth or power, but upon objective criteria with which everyone would agree if they understood the maxims of inquiry and had the appropriate data. Consequently, inquiry pursued for its own sake is presupposed for inquiry directed to any other end. And *all other activities*, since they presuppose knowledge for their implementation, *presuppose inquiry*. Consequently, inquiry provides a condition for the practice of all practically possible activities and also entails an end to which the ends of all practically possible activities must conform. The crux of the matter is that if there is to be any kind of rational activity at all, then inquiry must be presupposed as a categorical activity that conditions the possibility of all other practically possible activities. Thus, inquiry (and philosophy as the most fundamental mode of inquiry), as an intellectual excellence, is a categorical precondition of rational action because it provides the fundamental criteria for the use of intelligence in action.[1]

Now what precisely is it that differentiates war from other activities? If war constitutes a genuine activity, it apparently is a very unique one; for unlike all practically possible programs of action war is peculiar in that it *sets no limits* for the realization of its end. War is a parasitic activity because it makes use of the materials, results, techniques, and knowledge of any other activity in order to accomplish its purpose without making any rational contributions to the realization of any other practically possible ends. All other activities (including philosophy itself) are at the arbitrary disposal of war, to be used at any time or in any way depending upon their probable success in achieving the end of war. The violinist *needs* the violin if he is to be a violinist; the accountant *needs* certain principles of mathematics if he is to do his work. But what do we need for the conduct of war? Everything and nothing in particular. War requires a *carte blanche* in respect to all other available activities and their products, because war amounts to a policy of getting one's way at all costs, no matter what the consequences are for your opponent or the ends of any other activity. Again, who *needs* war? When we explicate the proximate end of any rational activity other than war, we find that the nature of the end or problem to be resolved is an essential source for the generation of the regulative norms that guide conduct, but the alternative of war is never a relevant technique, never a line of action prescribed by the essential norms. Anything that *makes sense* can be accomplished without resorting to war because anything that makes sense involves normative limitations and bounds and implies certain general principles that regulate behavior—principles that cannot be discarded or replaced simply because one is confronted with difficulties or the factual possibility of failure. True, subsidiary rules or modes of strategy that are optional and changeable are usually associated with most activities, but there are also the general norms that constitute the "rules of the game," and to violate these would be analogous to terminating a chess game by moving the rook diagonally, or reaching a solution to a mathematical problem by flipping a coin.

War as an activity can claim some semblance of internal coherence only if warfare is conducted for its own sake or for some other end that is construed as containing an unlimited prerogative allowing any means whatever for its actualization. In these terms, wars, like any other activities, can be conducted stupidly or intelligently, where the latter means that any and all available means are skillfully employed to accomplish the unlimited end. Stated this way, the argument seems to support the view that as long as war is conducted as an end in itself or as a means to a higher justifying end, which includes the "at all cost" parameter, then war is a rational activity. However, it should already be obvious that this strategy will work only if we ignore inquiry as a categorical activity.

Let us complete our argument. Taken in abstraction from any practically possible system of ends (that is, war viewed as an end in itself or as justified by another similarly unlimited end), the activity of war presents the appearance of internal coherence and external justification. In the final analysis, *any* mode of behavior directed to getting one's way about anything while reserving the right to achieve this end by any means that will succeed is a mode or instance of warfare—an attitude that would allow any degree of violence to persons and their property without their consent. So the end of war necessarily allows the violation and destruction of all rational standards, only employing such standards as temporary and contingent techniques to bring about an ultimate condition in which rational limits, reasonable considerations, the canons of truth, and so on have no essential place and no necessary bearing on human problems—where the general notion of law has no relevance. Thus, the unlimited end of war is necessarily incompatible with the categorical limitations imposed on all activity by the demands of fact and logic. War is self-contradictory because insofar as it is an activity at all, then like all other activities (as we have seen), it must presuppose the activity and objective value of inquiry for its own sake, while striving for an end that is incompatible with inquiry and would permit the ultimate negation of inquiry itself. In our normative sense of practical possibility, war has no rational justification and therefore is not a practical possibility. Abstracted from the rational requirements of any practically possible system of ends, war achieves a kind of philosophic whitewash. In a paradoxical way, war would be a rational activity only if performed in complete isolation, as a loner among activities. But, of course, that would be absurd because without the rest of the world of actions and agents (and the knowledge resulting from inquiry) there would be no activity of war and no objects to war against. Thus, the fulfillment of the very condition logically required, as it were, to protect and defend the alternative of war from the assault of reason totally disqualifies the activity of war as a practical possibility. Consequently, from the point of view of a philosophic analysis of the structure of activity, war is at best a pseudo-activity, incoherent in relation to any practically possible system of ends and lacking rational justification.

We may delude ourselves into thinking that there is something called limited war. But this is a fatuous rationalization that has been shown time and time again to hold no water. So-called limited wars do, of course, occur, but they are necessarily tentative arrangements that depend upon the prospect of successful warfare without the necessity for unlimited action. International law, treaties, moral principles, traditions—all become secondary when the prospect of failure confronts a program of war. Limited wars are conducted because (1) more extreme means are not necessary, (2) there is fear of the consequences of all-out war, or (3) the aggressors do not want to destroy certain potential gains of conquest. Moreover, a program of war always applies to a particular context, for example, a particular nation, a definable group, or even an individual person. Within its context, limited war is actually unlimited in respect to its proximate end. To say "limited war," merely means that it is not an all-inclusive war, not a war on everything. In this sense, all wars are limited wars. The limitation refers to the *scope* of the activity of war, not to the quality of its performance or its degree of irrationality. In short, temporary restrictions relating to the means of war are themselves calculated risks designed for ultimate victory at all costs.

IV

The relation between philosophy and war presents a final paradox. If our characterization of rational activity is correct as far as it goes, then philosophy is both a necessary condition for war and the anathema of war. Inquiry (and therefore philosophy as the primary form of inquiry) necessarily conditions the *ends, norms,* and *contexts* of all other activities, but it is itself unconditioned by any activity. War conditions no activity whatsoever, and though dependent upon the potential support of all activities, it attempts to proceed as an unconditioned activity. Philosophy has its unconditioned character because as the foundation of all inquiry, it is the primary ground for intelligent practice. But war achieves an unconditional character, only at the expense of everything else, by its refusal to cooperate with the community of intelligent life or respect the integrity and autonomy of the specifiable modes of rational action.

Science and scholarship, along with the plethora of arts and skills that make up the domain of rational action, are necessary for the successful implementation of a practical policy of war. Yet philosophic insight, since it in turn is logically presupposed for a genuine understanding of the application of reason to problems and ends, would be the most valuable instrument of all for the waging of war. Consequently, the most effective practitioners of war would be philosophers, not simply in their capacity *as* philosophers, but in their capacity as warriors implementing knowledge for the successful prosecution of war. These philosopher-warriors would be a formidable foe indeed—so much so that they would, in principle, be invincible and guaranteed of success. For what could possibly deter our philosopher-warrior? Only the self-imposed obligations arising from his cognizance of the rational conditions of practical action and his awareness of the self-contradictory character of his actions. Hence, to the extent that he *understands* the meaning of rational activity, he will necessarily recognize that the imperatives of truth are unquestionable and undebatable; that his involvement in any coherent activity at all presupposes the categorical canons of inquiry; that in spite of his sterling credentials for the prosecution of warfare, the end of war is a practical impossibility; and, finally, that to question the imperatives of inquiry, the obligation to seek truth, is itself to request a true answer to this question, and thereby to assume the standards of truth and the categorical canons of inquiry in spite of himself. The paradox of war is that the very requirements necessary to guarantee its successful practice contain the ground for its impossibility as a rational alternative.

But, of course, the *fact* of war remains with us. What are we to do about it? Recourse to such formal measures as universal education, social reorganization, political improvement, and moral persuasion will not in itself be sufficient.

To be sure, a calculated, efficient implementation of these measures may serve as a basis for habituating or indoctrinating many to a precarious (because equally reversible) mode of peaceful behavior. This probably would be better than nothing, and yet the problem of war cannot be resolved through a slumbering conformity to the dictates of social pacification. The crucial importance of such formal measures—especially the right kind of education—rests in the fact that they can provide the occasion, leisure, and opportunity for genuine reflection and understanding. If such a program is to be relevant, it must contain the ingredients of tolerance and liberality that will allow and stimulate men to think for themselves, discover anew the irrationality of war, and develop a rational character which is critical of any kind of indoctrination. What is needed is not peace, but a rational peace.

NOTE

1. For a more detailed discussion of the activity of inquiry, the reader is referred to the author's "Inquiry as a Transcendental Activity" in *Inquiry*, X, (1967), 1–20.

V

The Alternative to War

CHAPTER THIRTEEN

The Biology of War and the Law of Peace

Lydio Machado Bandeira de Mello

Professor of Law,
University of Minas Gerais, Brazil

I

Living creatures are not purely and simply the products of a supposed evolution of mineral matter. Stones left to themselves were not transformed into plants and animals. Everything indicates that life is a force of a special nature that took an insignificant portion of our planet by assault and that now fights energetically to maintain the beachhead that it managed to establish and implant on earth. In vain, astonishingly greater and more powerful physicochemical forces converge against life and bring dangers without number and tremendous disasters down upon living things. Life lavishly reproduces seeds and multiplies the number of creatures born so that though the seeds and living things perish in heaps, multitudes will escape, multitudes will survive, multitudes will dwell, extending themselves over the surface of the earth and within the waters of the seas.

If life were the natural result of the dumb work of blind forces, it would be born from them just as light is born of a flame, without encountering resistance, opposition, attack, or devastation. Life would emerge from lifeless nature with the serenity of an aurora predestined to illuminate and warm the entire universe.

But life is an intruder, an unexpected assailant, a *conquistador* of the physical universe. And, therefore, *the dawning and emergence of life is an act of war,* and the maintenance of life a combat without truce against brute forces.

As I explained in my *A Origem dos Sexos (The Origin of sex),* life is an activity over and above the physical universe, or, what comes to the same thing, an activity opposed to the universe. Life is a victory against the physical world in which the vital force wrested away from inert matter and brute forces a body that incessantly renews itself and yet tends to revert to the inertness and brutishness from which it arose.

Death is the reaction of the physical universe; it is the return of the body to the pure and simple rule of physics and chemistry. Where there are only the laws of physics and chemistry, there is death.

In man, life is the beginning of liberty, because it has the power of setting itself in motion and of producing changes in the motions it encounters. Life is the power to create and sustain a body to serve as instrument to a being essentially free: the soul. By means of the body, the soul acts upon the universe. Giving forms to inert and plastic matter and governing the lifeless forces, the soul acts to bring the physical universe gradually, by fits and starts, under the dominion of man. Consequently, on one small surface of the planet, life must concentrate on an activity to overcome the opposition of the whole universe and introduce spontaneity and creativity where only mechanical causality existed.

This is the reason that nature creates gametes (reproductive units, either masculine or feminine) in astronomical numbers so that at least some are fertilized, despite enormous external resistance and aggression. The number of grains of pollen, of spermatozoa, and of ova spent by nature for the purpose of producing each existing individual is prodigious. Only one dandelion flower produces some two hundred forty-three thousand pollen grains, and just one peony flower about three million, six hundred fifty-four thousand (according to Harssall). From these hundreds of thousands, often only one or two plants are born. Frequently, none at all.

According to Waldeyer, the ovaries of a newly born girl contain one hundred thousand gametes. Of these, the more perfect proceed to eliminate the imperfect, so that in the ovaries of a girl of fourteen months, the number of ova is lowered to 48,808. Hansemann found 46,174 ova in the ovaries of a girl of two years; 26,656 in another of eight years; 20,862 in yet another of ten years; and never more than 7,000 in a young woman of eighteen years.

And what of men? In each ejaculation of sperm there are about three hundred million spermatozoa! Two or three emissions of sperm from just one man could fecundate all the sexually mature women now living in the world. Yet most of the time not even one human being is engendered.

Here, unexpectedly, we catch a glimpse of what I call the biological paradox: *Nature, in order to make possible and sustain life, had to establish death!* To defeat the aggressive and monstrous hostility of the physical universe by means of numbers, nature created germinal elements, or gametes (ova, pollen grains, spores, spermatozoa), in such quantity that they have to struggle against one another. The number of individuals engendered in this way is so vast that the species are forced to decimate one another so that only a small number, comparatively speaking, in each species reach the fullness of their development.

From this comes the true *law of the struggle for life,* or law of the struggle between species, that I formulate in the following fashion: In order to conquer the material universe and take its place in it, life created germinal elements in such large numbers that even after excessive quantities have perished, destroyed by the physical environment, they persevere in superabundance. There then arises a new limited struggle of the species, a struggle of selection and equilibrium (but more of the latter than of the former), between the surviving germinal elements and between the individuals and species engendered by them.

The struggle for life—for the survival of life—is of such imperious nature that *to live is to kill.* Not a plant or animal lives and preserves itself without other plants' and animals' being prevented from birth or being destroyed. *To permit, maintain, and preserve each life, the sacrifice of millions of lives is necessary.*

And how insignificant in volume is the total mass of living substance in comparison with the total mass of lifeless, useless, and hostile matter! If we brought together and heaped up all the plants and animals on the solid surface of the world, they would not suffice to make a solid block of ten meters mean height. In other words, they would not amount to a global covering of two meters thickness. What does two meters thickness represent in comparison with the six million meters of terrestrial radius? By an effort of imagination, let us reduce the earth to a sphere of one meter radius. In it, the piled up living things would have a height of .000,000,333 of a meter. They would appear as fine dust of a microbial aspect. What assurance or prospects for survival can such a pinch of living stuff have on top of such a vast mass of brute matter?

But the destiny of the earth shares the fate of the sun. Without the sun, the earth perhaps would not exist. And without the activity of the sun, life on earth would be impossible. But that further augments the precariousness of living matter. The mass of living bodies would appear wretchedly insignificant amidst the mass of lifeless matter and frightfully unprotected when confronted by the total sum of the blind and brute energy in the solar system. A tremor, a pronounced cooling, a great warming, a cataclysm of widespread violence, in either the earth or the sun, would be enough to cause the soil of this planet to disintegrate or burst into flames in a matter of minutes. Not a living thing would endure, not a vestige would remain of the passage of life in the solar system.

The maintenance of life is a prodigious phenomenon. And thus the ensemble of living things has to make unbelievable sacrifices in order to maintain and extend the beachhead that life established in its disembarkation on earth.

There is only one thing that can assure the survival of living things: their union and the sacrifice of some to benefit all in a universal cooperation. This implies for men a duty that they neither have clearly understood nor yet fulfilled: *the respect for life in all of its forms;* the duty of not killing an animal or plant uselessly or for the production of superfluous and harmful things. *A living thing is only to be killed*—and here I employ legal language—*on condition of necessity* (for example, in order to eat so as to survive), *or of legitimate defense* (for example, combat against species inimical to the human race).

Directly or indirectly the conservation of each species affects every other species. In the animal and vegetable kingdoms, the species nourish themselves at the expense of one another. Yet the healthier and more vigorous a species shows itself, the more probability the ensemble of living things has of surviving in the ceaseless struggle against brute matter.

II

In the preceding section we dealt with the fact that nature lavishly multiplies the reproductive elements of each species with an aggressive excessiveness so that—in spite of all the attacks and mischances—a small number of individuals capable of preserving and extending the species will be born. What would happen, though, if the environment were not hostile to the reproductive elements?

More individuals in each species would be born. There would not be sufficient place for them in the matter that has to be assimilated to nourish and constitute them. From this comes *the necessity of a second conflict,* no longer between living things and lifeless ones but this time *between the species.* This second conflict is called by naturalists beginning with Darwin "the struggle for Life." And they give to it, along with Darwin, an incorrect explanation.

The species do not struggle against one another for the purpose of disputing biological supremacy. If the struggle had as end the survival of the strongest, the earth would now be populated by super-iguanodonts, super-ichthyosaurs, and other armored and titanic monsters. At the least, the waters of the oceans would have to be full of whales and sharks, the skies crisscrossed by eagles and condors, the land overpopulated by tigers, lions, crocodiles, and elephants. Ferocity would be the supreme law. The Will to Power, in the Nietzscheian sense, hardheartedness, or extreme egoism would be the golden rule of human conduct. Yet what do we see? The rapid and progressive elimination of the strongest, the wildest, the most violent, the most ferocious, to such a point that I, for one, have never seen an eagle in spite of the skies' being free for domination by more robust birds of prey over other winged creatures. Everywhere the biblical prophecy is realized: Blessed are the meek, for they shall inherit the earth.

In his book *Mutual Aid, A Factor of Evolution,* Peter Kropotkin understood well the central thesis that I formulate thus: *those species that learn the advantages of mutual aid and of cooperation are the only ones to have a serene prospect of unlimited survival.*

What the Darwinians call the "law of the struggle for Life," I call the law of the *struggle for establishment of a numerical equilibrium between species* (or law of the numerical limitation of the individuals of each species). I maintain that each species has one or more species that combat it in order that the number of its individuals will not become prejudicial to the ensemble of living things. And in my *The Origin of Sex,* I justify this theory thus:

The species devour one another because if they did not do so, they would not be able to survive. Let us suppose for a moment that one species did not devour another, that the animals, like the plants, performed organic syntheses exclusively with mineral nutrients extracted in the very same way from the bowels of the earth. The earth would be turned into the bodies of plants and animals at the end of a brief number of years and generations.

Hence we have the law, among others, denominated *law of the nutritive chain between animals and plants.*

Herbivorous animals are specialists: each species of herbivore has, customarily, one or two species of plants as its exclusive nutriment. J. H. Fabre in his *Souvenirs entomologiques* demonstrates this for the world of insects. Each herbivorous insect feeds only on a determined plant, of which it is the born parasite. This exclusive feeding reaches the point where a louse on a rosebush, or elder bush, or spindle tree, or apple tree, dies of starvation when transported to a pear tree or peach tree, although these half-dozen plants all belong to the family *Rosaceae.* Where there is cabbage, there is, for certain, the white butterfly. Similarly each lepidopteron has its own plant the leaves of which nourish the myriad bands of its voracious and insatiable larva. Transplant a vegetable to where its parasite has not been transported and it will spread out in every direction, sometimes astonishingly.

III

War is not an anomaly, an abnormal or sporadic phenomenon in the evolution of the human race. Yet the aggressive and bellicose temperament is not an unfortunate natural endowment of men.

In the first place, nature established a natural struggle between the species, which does not have for object selection of the fittest, as Darwin thought, but rather limitation of the number of individuals of each species, as I tried to make clear in Section II. A glimpse of some interior stretch of ocean, photographed, say, in the manner Walt Disney brought to his nature films, would startle us: billions of animals move about night and day there, a whirlpool of living bodies, of variegated forms, armed with serrated teeth, tentacles speckled with suckers, claws that slash, equipped with illuminating apparatus. Their lives unfold in movements of attack and defense, in acts of destruction and of flight. For them existence is a struggle without truce, without remorse, in which to lose one's strength, to commit a mistake, to miss one's aim, to block one's escape, almost always means death.

In the second place, nature is not content with the type of struggle, solitary and limited, that we call *individual combat;* for example, the violent and irresistible attack of *one* tiger on *one* gazelle, the clamorous struggle between *one* lion and *one* bull, the hunt of *one* bird-catching spider for *one* hornet. *Nature formed and armed animals for collective combat and equipped and trained natural armies for predatory wars.*

Property is the principal efficient cause of war. Why? Because hunting and war are *natural forms* for the acquisition of property.

This observation led Aristotle in his *Politics* to an abominable doctrine. According to Aristotle, the strongest and more intelligent have the right to subdue the more backward by war.

Aristotle arrived at this absurdity by defining the family as a twofold combination, that is, a binary union, "that of the man and the woman; that of the master and the slave." For him the family at the start of its formation is a society formed by one man, one woman, and one or more slaves. The latter can only be obtained by means of predatory war. And Aristotle justifies this: It is necessary to unite first of all men and women in couples, with a view to generation.

> And there also has to be, by nature's intention, and for the preservation of the species, a being fit to command and another being fit to obey. The authority and the power of the master fall naturally to the one whose intelligence is capable of foresight. The one who only possesses brute force was made for carrying out orders and ought naturally to obey and serve.[1]

"The slave is owned by the master in an absolute manner." Now men do not become slaves except by being conquered by other people by means of war. Nonetheless, Aristotle concludes:

> The art of war is in a certain fashion a natural means of acquisition, being part of the art of hunting, in which ferocious animals are combated and war waged against brutish men, who refuse to submit and yet are destined to serve because they are dull-witted. In this way their nature is declared to us and makes known that such war is just.[2]

Now every predatory animal is subject to fall victim to crimes and wars, to robbery, plunder, and conquest. For that reason, nature never ceases to give it deadly arms. However, by creating the arms, nature created, or favored, war, that is, the fight of masses against masses, collective struggle with arms. From this comes robbery, pillage, and battles throughout the whole reach of the animal kingdom.

I divide the proprietary animals into two groups:

1. *Animals owners of collective goods, independent of a fixed territory:* bees, wasps, and hornets. Each swarm of bees possesses a dwelling place, the beehive, and a deposit of provisions for the future, the honeycomb. But the hive or the hornet's nest is constructed anywhere, in trees or even on the façades of buildings. Among these arthropods there are no natural armies or soldiers. Each worker is born armed with a venomous sting destined to wound pillagers seriously. These hymenopters are prepared exclusively to defend themselves against assaults, pilferage, and robbery. They never set about wars of conquest.

2. *Animals that become owners of a portion of territory:* the ants and termites. These hexapods can be dislodged from the territory that they inhabit, and they are obliged to defend it in order to avoid perishing, dispersed by conquerors. For that reason each ant hill and each termitary has soldiers produced and armed by nature itself, natural armies organized and disciplined by her, subject to a characteristic military comportment and skillful whether in a war of conquest or of defense. Of course, there are specialized libraries devoted to this subject, but one might consult with profit the résumé made by a non-naturalist, a dilettante named Maurice Maeterlinck, in *The Life of the Ant.*

IV

Study of human conflict reveals that there is a *natural propensity* of peoples for war, just as there is a *natural propensity* of species for struggle, and just as there is a *natural propensity* of individuals for crime. Crime and war are species that belong to the same genus: conflict. They result, almost always, from a conflict of interest. We can, then, define wars and crimes of aggression as *the attempt to resolve conflicts of interest by force*. And when there is such at attempt, there is a substitution of violence for reason, of the dispute by arms for a dispute by means of reasoning. Obligatory rules of conduct (and when needed of performance) imposed by force are established. A rational employ of the force of all against the irrational use of force made by some is undertaken.

The nations must learn to combat war with the very form and methods with which individuals learned to combat crime.

Individuals learned to combat crime by means of the contractual creation of Law in general and of Penal Law in particular, and by the contractual creation of the State, destined above all to impose obedience to the Law, by force if necessary. The nations will have to combat war by means of the creation of a supranational or World Law in general, of a supranational or World Penal Law in particular, and by the creation of a supranational or World State—and not merely a simple League or Federation of Nations. In other words, they will have to create a World Law that will rule over or discipline the nations just as national law (whether that of Brazil, the United States, England, etc.) rules over individuals, and they will have to create a World State that will exist for the present-day states or nations just as each actual state exists for the individuals who live together in the national territory.

But why did I say "to combat" crime and war, instead of "to eliminate" or "to destroy" crime and war? Because crime and war being natural phenomena—phenomena arising from natural propensities and causes—it will be possible to *diminish* enormously the number of crimes and the number of wars, but it will be impossible to *extinguish* either of the two: *there will always be crimes and wars that Law and the State will not succeed in eliminating.*

Man set himself as an absolute within nature, put down on earth not as a product or manifestation of matter but like a lord resolved to govern it. And for that reason nature disdained him, not taking much account of him, leaving him deserted. He was not given the tranquil hardiness of the elephant or the aggressive might of the lion. He was not armed with razor-sharp talons or sickle-shaped and pointed claws or muscles of wonderful strength. He was deprived even of the defensive means that are afforded to the other animals: swiftness in running, agility in flight, the power of mimicry. And to crown this defenselessness, he is divested of the instincts with which individuals of the other species find direction and organize things. While an ant hill or a termitary, for example, has a perfect order, founded in a system of organizing instincts, men are abandoned to a total ignorance and to a vast and generalized disorder in which cruel passions arise, fighting against one another. And they will only cease to arise at the expense of one's own efforts when egoism and the caprice of disoriented desires give way to the authority of reason.

Hence, it is necessary *that we replace the natural order*—offspring of an instinct that does not exist for us—*by a social order created by us* to allow us to harmonize as much as possible our egoism and make compatible our liberty.

The science and art of establishing and maintaining human social order and, consequently, domestic peace or public tranquillity is that which is called Law.

There is reason for calling the human social order the legal order: *the harmony of the liberty of individuals, by virtue of which the conduct of each is not an obstacle to the rational conduct of others.*

Who established the *national social order?* The people by a Social Contract, tacit or explicit. Nowadays, this Social

Contract is celebrated by means of representatives, or legislators, chosen for that purpose in periodic elections that are free and direct.

This legal order is expressed by the formulation of rules of conduct, or norms of social existence, the observation of which is obligatory. Each one of these rules or group of rules that pertains to the same matter, to the same set of relationships, receives the name of law. The ensemble of laws in force for each people constitutes its positive national Law. There are therefore, as many bodies of positive law as there are countries on the terrestrial globe.

It is apparent, however, that the positive law is not automatically put into action by itself. A law, in order to be in force, in order to have efficacity, in order to be obeyed even by rebels and recalcitrants, has to have its execution demanded and imposed by human volition served by force.

This makes it necessary to divide the individuals of each nation into two groups: those who govern, the holders of public power; and those who are governed, the total mass of people, the ensemble of citizens. When a people performs this division, it creates the State. This gives us the descriptive definition of the State: *The State is a fraction of the population of the earth confined to a territory exclusively theirs and divided into governors and governed, into authority and citizen, that is, into givers and receivers of orders.*

And in what does *public power*—authority or political power—consist? Principally in the power to define, establish, and maintain the State's legal order. It is the power to legislate, that is, to establish the positive Law, and to impose on each and every citizen respect for the established legal order.

To this legal power, the original essence of government, the modern states add the power to promote the public good and to command and direct the execution of public services that are necessary or useful to the nation, the power of administration.

In summary: the State, in my view, is a creation of Law destined precisely to maintain the national social order also created by Law. Law creates the order and creates the organs entrusted with achieving it and protecting it. The ensemble of these organs, in their original simplicity and purity, is the State—the healthy State, without excessive growths and without degeneration.

The principal law of a State, fundamental and ruling over all the others, is its constitution. And after that comes its penal code.

What is the constitution? It is the law that establishes the system of government chosen by a people, that creates the organs of government, fixes their duties, and declares those rights of the citizen that are natural and therefore inviolable. It is, in brief, *the law that defines the legal order preferred by the majority of the nation.*

And why does the penal code have its place after the constitution? Because the principal function of the penal laws is to defend the legal order established by the constitution. *It is to put force, in a disciplined fashion, at the service of Law.* That is why before written constitutions there already existed written and well-deduced penal laws.

And what are the principal organs entrusted with the maintenance of the legal order? The police, whose mission is essentially the preventive function of averting crime, and the organs of judicial power.

What is the means by which the State disposes to give active and effective voice to laws? Force guided by reason, *force disciplined by laws.*

And what is the force that the State can and ought to lay hold of? It is unique: collective force, the public force. However, since in present-day nations there is a division of labor by the citizens, a distribution of functions, and since collective life is increasingly complex, the states call on or accept only a certain number of citizens to compose the organs of force that are placed at the service of Law. And with them the states also compose and organize the army and the security police (understood by the latter is a police force for maintenance and defense of the legal and social order; it can be divided into civil and military).

The police is the principal organ on which the public or political power can count for the preservation of order and of social tranquillity. A government without physical force in a state containing imperfect citizens, egoists, and recalcitrants cannot maintain itself or even govern. For this reason, many people confuse the word "police" with the word "politics." There is no science and art of governing, *politics,* without there also being a science and art of preventing harm and favoring good, *police practice* (which is related to Von Liszt's "criminal politics").

I define the security police as the state organ that has the mission of preventing harm and—note this addition—of favoring good. As Bluntschli said:

> It is a political and magistral power [a power to discipline and educate the people] which watches over the daily needs of security and of public good, and which orders or prohibits that which is necessary or indispensable to its maintenance. Its care embraces the whole public order. It bears the security for every inch of the State's territory, combats all the dangers that menace society, even those of natural forces (fire, plague, flood). And it protects the liberty of conscience against all the oppressions of spiritual or sectarian authorities.

With these ground points, one can come to the central thesis of this chapter: *How can wars be avoided?* By organizing the national states into a World State that will be to them exactly as each national state is to the individuals that compose it.

V

The organization of the World State has to begin as did the first North American constitutions:

1. *By a clear and complete declaration of human rights,* to be guaranteed and declared inviolable by the constitutions of all the member states, that is, by *all* the nations of the earth without any exception permitted.

2. By a clear and positive delimitation of the *purpose* of this World State, namely, *the establishment of a world legal order,* of rules of conduct to be observed by the governments of all the nations. This legal order will have for its object: (1) *the maintenance of peace between nations,* and within each nation, and the maintenance of peace between individuals; (2) *such social assistance* as will make possible *for each and every human being* the genuine, effective, and peaceful enjoyment of the fundamental goods of life.

A World Constitution must come after this basic declaration, establishing a universal government that will not have the right to interfere in the internal affairs of the various countries or to employ force against them except to (1) prevent acts of aggression or of war by one country against another country, (2) prevent or curb the practice of any of the crimes against humanity, particularly genocide, persecution by religion, persecution against religion, forced migration, slavery, (3) prevent or curb the deliberate practice of crimes against the permanent human rights in the basic declaration to which we can refer and which must be incorporated in the constitutions, and (4) aid a country should grave internal disorders appear capable of throwing the country into chaos, or in the event of a national calamity.

Law pure and simple (the rules of social conduct necessary to have order and peace between individuals and between nations) is worth nothing if it is not supported by force. Only well-disciplined force is capable of enforcing obedience to the laws by disobedient troublemakers and despotic individuals.

Moreover, as a complement to the World Constitution and as legal guarantee of the Universal Declaration of Human Rights, there must be established a World Penal Code, completed by a World Code of Penal Process and by the organization of a Court of World Justice, the task of which would be to watch over the application of supranational laws.

To these measures must be added the following:

1. A relative or limited disarmament of each nation. Each state must possess and maintain an army and a police force adequate strictly for the protection and defense of its domestic order. It must not be, however, an army or an armament sufficient for a victorious war of foreign aggression.

2. Destruction and prohibition of the manufacture of all weapons applicable to the indiscriminate extermination of large groups of unarmed people.

3. The creation of a powerful World Army capable of suppressing, in a lightning war, any caprice of aggression or disorder that drives and flings one country against another.

It would be easy for me to outline in a complete fashion the structure or organization and the operation of this World State. I refrain from doing it, however, largely because this solution, in the actual state of evolution of the world, still seems to me utopian.

Yet the measures that I suggest appear more complete and more feasible than the solution proposed by Kant in his monograph on *Perpetual Peace*. I think it is impossible for all the countries to accept the liberal republican form of government. And even if they did accept it, there would be major and more powerful republics and minor and less powerful ones. And it is human nature, so burdened with natural miseries, that the strong exercise their superiority over the weak. Only with a Universal Justice and an invincible World Police Force will it be possible to keep the nations in order, within humanity, just as a national justice and public force are capable of keeping individuals in order, and in peace, within each national collectivity.

NOTES

1. Aristotle, *Politics,* Bk. I, ch. ii, 1252[a] 25–35.
2. *Ibid.,* Bk. I, ch. viii, 1256[b] 21–26.

CHAPTER FOURTEEN

Peace: The Hindu View

Swami Nikhilananda
Founder,
Ramakrishna-Vivekananda Center, New York

The world malady is spiritual. Political friction, moral unrest, and economic confusion are but the outer symptoms of a deep-seated illness. Man is not at peace with himself, with nature, with other human beings, or with God. He has separated himself from universal life. He is like a bone dislocated from its socket, like a wheel separated from its axle. This is the cause of friction in human relationships, of pain and suffering. But the bone can be put back into its socket, and the wheel can be joined with its axle. The separate life can be made one with the universal life. The great prophets and saints have shown the way and prescribed disciplines that may vary according to the time and temperament of the people but will ultimately lead to the same goal.

In their search for peace, East and West use different approaches. The countries of the East, especially those influenced by Hinduism and Buddhism, seek inner peace through control of physical desires. Individuals practice spiritual disciplines in order to create serenity of mind. The West stressses peace in the outer world, through elimination of the causes of friction and war. Both methods have merit, though neither has been able to banish war. Perhaps a combination of both methods would be more effective in creating a climate of peace and reducing the possibilities of war.

The attainment of peace, individual and collective, is the teaching of Hinduism, especially of nondualistic Vedanta. Vedanta is not based on any particular dogma or creed but on the inner experience shared by men and women irrespective of caste, creed, or sect. It is the essence of the Vedas, the ultimate authority of Hindu religion and philosophy. Its four cardinal points are the divinity of man, the oneness of existence, the nonduality of the godhead, and the harmony of religions. The supreme Reality is one without a second; it is therefore free from quarrel and contradiction and conducive to the welfare of all. This Reality pervades the whole creation and transcends it. As the power behind the universe, it is called Brahman, and as the power behind man, Atman, or the true soul. According to Vedanta, Brahman and Atman, as realized in deep meditation, are identical. This is declared through the four Vedic statements: "I am Brahman," "That Thou art," "This Self is Brahman," "Brahman is Consciousness"—formulations that are supported by the Scriptures, reasoning, and personal experience.

The divinity of the soul is the spiritual basis of freedom and democracy. Every soul is potentially divine. The purpose of life is to manifest this divinity. One can achieve awareness of this divinity through either worship or ritual, through philosophical discrimination between the real and the unreal and the renunciation of the unreal, through selfless work, or through psychic control. Thus alone does one become free. Scriptures, temples, and rituals are of secondary importance. There are, as it were, two souls. One is identified with the body, the senses, the mind, and the ego. It is the doer of action and the seeker of fruits of action.

Birth and death, heaven or hell, rebirth, happiness or misery, exaltation or depression apply to the lower soul, which is embodied and known as the apparent soul. But the real soul, called the Supreme Soul, is the detached witness of action and its result. It is ever free, ever pure, and ever illumined. It is birthless, deathless, immortal, without beginning or end, all-peace and all-bliss. What causes this free soul to act like a bound soul? In association with *maya,* a sort of metaphysical ignorance, it appears to be subject to birth and death and to experience the fruit of action. This maya, the cause of our experiencing multiplicity, is inscrutable to the finite mind, which itself is the product of maya. Maya is a power inherent in Brahman, with whose help the Absolute appears to create, preserve, and destroy. It cannot be called real because maya disappears when one attains to the knowledge of Brahman, nor is it unreal or nonexistent, like the son of a barren woman, because the tangible universe cannot come out of nonexistence. It consists of three *gunas* or qualities, as a twisted rope consists of three strands. Maya hides the reality and projects the diverse objects of the phenomenal world. On account of maya we see the mirage in the desert or dream in sleep. Maya makes us accept the apparent as the real though it cannot affect the true nature of Reality. The water of the mirage cannot soak one grain of sand in the desert. Illusory dream cannot affect the true nature of man.

Let us briefly discuss the three gunas that influence our thought and actions. According to Vedanta, the tangible man consists of Self or Spirit and nonself. He is a mixture of Deity and dust. The nonself or the physical part of man includes the body, the sense organs, and the mind. The Self when identified with the nonself, on account of maya, becomes embodied. The embodied soul is under the control of the three gunas, called *sattva, rajas,* and *tamas.* Sattva is the spiritual element in man, luminous, stainless, and healthful. It makes one happy and creates attachment to happiness. But sattva is also a sort of chain that entangles a man in the world. Rajas is the essence of passion and the cause of thirst and attachment. It binds fast the embodied soul by attachment to action. Tamas is born of ignorance. It deludes all embodied creatures; it binds fast by inadvertence, indolence, and sleep. The three gunas are present in all embodied beings in varying degrees. Sattva sometimes asserts itself by prevailing over rajas and tamas; rajas asserts itself by prevailing over sattva and tamas; tamas asserts itself by prevailing over sattva and rajas. When the light of knowledge shines through all the gateways of the body, then sattva has prevailed. Greed, activity, enterprise, unrest, and longing arise when rajas prevails. Darkness, indolence, inadvertence, delusion arise when tamas prevails. From sattva springs knowledge, from rajas greed, and from tamas inadvertence, delusion, and ignorance.

The three gunas influence our faith, worship, food, charity—everything in the realms of the organic, inorganic, and psychic. For instance, the food that promotes longevity, vitality, strength, health, pleasure, appetite, that is succulent, oleaginous, substantial, and agreeable is of the nature of sattva and is favored by people endowed with sattva. Food that is excessively bitter, sour, salty, hot, acrid, dry, and burning is characteristic of rajas and is liked by people endowed with rajas. It causes pain, grief, and disease. And food that is ill cooked, tasteless, putrid, stale, unclean, and left over is characteristic of tamas and is favored by people endowed with tamas.

It will be seen from the foregoing that an excess of rajas is the root cause of ambition, lust for power, and greed, culminating in war. A man endowed with an excess of rajas shows ostentation, arrogance, self-conceit, anger, rudeness, and ignorance. In the Bhagavad-Gita such a man is called demoniac. He knows not what to do and what to refrain from doing. Purity is not in him, nor good conduct, nor truth. He says: "The world is devoid of truth, without a moral basis, and without a God. It is brought about by the union of male and female, and lust alone is the cause: what else?" Holding such a view, these lost souls of little understanding and fierce deeds rise as the enemies of the world for its destruction. Giving themselves up to insatiable desires, full of hypocrisy, pride, and arrogance, they hold delusory views and act with impure resolve. Beset with innumerable cares, which will end only with death, looking on the gratification of desire as their highest goal and feeling sure that this is all, bound by a hundred ties of hope, given up wholly to lust and wrath, they strive, by unjust means, to amass wealth for the satisfaction of their passions. Such a person says, "This I have gained today, and that longing I will fulfill. This wealth is mine, and that also shall be mine in future. That enemy I have slain, and others, too, I will slay. I am the lord of all; I enjoy; I am prosperous, mighty, and happy; I am rich; I am of high birth. Who else is equal to me? I will give, I will rejoice." Deluded by many fancies, entangled in the meshes of delusion, addicted to the gratification of lust, he becomes the victim of excruciating pain. The Bhagavad-Gita gives a vivid description of ruthless dictators and warmongers.

Tamas can be controlled through rajas, and rajas through sattva. A man established in sattva ultimately realizes self-knowledge and goes beyond the three gunas. Such an illumined soul is not always absorbed in meditation. He devotes himself, in the normal state, to the service of others. He utilizes the three gunas to serve a divine purpose. He may engage in business and industry, participate in a just war, and perform various civic duties, always conscious that the Self is separated from the nonself. He does not hate light, activity, and delusion when they are present, or long for them when they are absent. He sits like one unconcerned, unmoved by the gunas, remains firm and never wavers, knowing that the gunas alone are active. He always dwells in the Self and regards alike pleasure and pain, looks on a clod, a stone, and a piece of gold as of equal worth, remains the same amidst agreeable and disagreeable things, and sees no difference between praise and blame. He is the same in honor and dishonor, the same to friend and foe. He has renounced all undertakings prompted by his ego. The virtues of sattva have to be acquired by special spiritual disciplines prior to the attainment of Self-knowledge. The aspirant for Self-knowledge should therefore cultivate these virtues, as they are the means of attaining it. But on the birth of Self-knowledge, when the aspirant has become a *Jivanmukta,* liberated while still living in the body, all the virtues form part and parcel of his nature and serve as marks of liberation, which he can perceive for himself. In the Hindu tradition there are instances of a hunter, a housewife, and an emperor who, endowed with Self-knowledge, pursued their respective vocations. Arjuna, the chief warrior of the Bhagavad-Gita, saw the most exalted vision of the godhead on the battlefield, where the basest passions of men are let loose.

According to Hinduism, the world will never be completely free from strife and war because all embodied beings contain elements of the three gunas. Even the gods fight among themselves. The Creator God begot two sons, a god and a demon, who since their birth have engaged in fighting. Perhaps a little bloodletting is necessary to perpetuate the creation, but the more people endowed with sattva guide society, the less chance there is of the world's engaging in widespread wars.

Complete peace is possible only for the individual who can give assurance of fearlessness to all because he sees all beings as manifestations of himself.

Realization of oneness of existence or the solidarity of

men is the metaphysical foundation of peace. The mystics perceive that spirit alone pervades the universe. The Upanishads say that all that exists is Brahman. They see the universe as a spiritual entity. Multiplicity of names and forms is seen only in the relative world projected by maya. When truth is known, multiplicity disappears. The illumined soul sees the oneness of existence in the deepest meditation; when his mind comes down to the relative world, he sees unity in diversity. He sees the creation as a tree made of wax —the stem, branches, twigs, leaves, flowers, and fruits all made of the same stuff. Or he regards the creation as a vast ocean, the waves, bubbles, and foam all made of the water of the ocean. As long as one takes separation to be real, one cannot altogether get rid of fear. We read in the Vedas: "Fear arises from the consciousness of the second." Love and charity can be shown only by those who see the oneness of existence. One of the great commandments of Christ is "Love thy neighbor as thyself"—for your neighbor is no other than yourself. Vedanta speaks of all living beings as our neighbors.

This idea of oneness flashes sometimes in the minds of poets and artists. Hemingway surveying a battlefield in the Spanish Republican War exclaimed: "I see the same soul being killed over and over again, and finally I realize I am that soul." St. Francis, knowing this oneness of existence, established the relationship of love and kinship with birds, beasts, and the celestial orbs. In our own day Ramakrishna, prophet of modern India, demonstrated the oneness of existence in different ways. One day two boatmen on the Ganges outside his room were fighting with wooden poles. He did not see the fight but the marks of the blows were impressed on his back and Ramakrishna felt great pain. On another occasion, while suffering from the intense pain of throat cancer, he could not swallow even liquid food. At the earnest request of a disciple, he prayed to God to make it possible for him to partake of a little nourishment. The Divinity sharply reminded him: "Are you not eating through millions of mouths?" On a third occasion, he was lying on his bed when he cried out in great agony. His attendant rushed to his room and saw red blisters on his chest. When he could not determine the cause, Ramakrishna told him to look outside. A man was walking on the tender grass, and the blisters appeared on Ramakrishna's chest. Thus Sri Ramakrishna demonstrated oneness of mankind, oneness of life, and even oneness with the apparently insensible grass. The ideal of human solidarity should be stressed from pulpits, classrooms, and political forums. The divinity of the soul bids us show respect to all human beings in spite of differences in color, creed, sex, and economic or social position. The divinity of soul is the spiritual foundation of the freedom and democracy so much prized in the West.

The nonduality of the godhead and the harmony of religions are the two other cardinal points of nondualistic Vedanta. The Rig-Veda declares: "Reality is one, though people call It by various names." As has been explained earlier, the Ultimate Reality is called Brahman or the Spirit, which is devoid of name, form, or attributes. In the relative universe its highest manifestation is the Personal God, who is worshiped under different names and forms by Hindus, Jews, Christians, and Moslems. A passage in one of the Hindu Scriptures says: "Though without parts or attributes, Brahman assumes forms for the welfare of spiritual seekers." The finite mind cannot conceive of the Infinite. But the Personal God leads devotees to the realization of the impersonal Spirit. Christ taught that in His Father's Kingdom there are many mansions. It is good to be born in a church, but one should not die in a church. Religions, as human institutions, cannot be absolutely perfect, as God is perfect. Religion is not God, but it shows the way to God. The teachings of any organized religion deviate somewhat from those of its founder. It is said that Satan was once asked how he would tempt a possessor of pure truth, and he answered that he would tempt him to organize it. No clock ever gives perfect time; it has to be corrected occasionally according to the sun. Correction in religion is made by saints who directly commune with God, and not by theologians who only interpret the Scriptures according to their limited understanding.

The purpose of religion is to awaken a yearning or aspiration in the minds of the devotees which ultimately leads to the realization of Spirit. Lecomte du Noüy once remarked:

> Independent of any rite or any church, there has always existed a religious spirit, a desire to believe, a desire to adore without any restriction, a desire to humiliate oneself in total veneration, a desire to elevate oneself by approaching a conceivable but inaccessible ideal. It is this desire which is of divine origin, because it is universal and identical in all men.

Archbishop Temple of Canterbury said: "It is a mistake to suppose that God is only or chiefly concerned with religion." He notices the fall of a sparrow even as He watches the unfoldment of the spiritual consciousness of a saint. He hears the footstep of an ant.

Hinduism, both at its source and during the period of its subsequent development, exhibits a remarkable spirit of catholicity. We read in one of the Upanishads:

> May He, the one without a second, who, though formless, produces by means of His manifold powers various forms without any purpose of His own, may He from whom the universe comes into being at the beginning of creation and to whom it returns in the end—endow us with holy thoughts.

Again: "As flowing rivers disappear in the sea, losing their names and forms, so a wise man, freed from names and forms, attains Brahman, who is greater than the great." One cannot distinguish a Hindu from a Moslem, a Christian from a Jew, when they are absorbed in the Infinite Spirit. One sees differences on a lower level, but from the summit all distinctions disappear.

That all paths lead to the same goal is emphasized in the following hymn:

> Different are the paths laid down in the Vedas, in Samkha, in Yoga, and in the Saiva and the Vaishnava scriptures. Of these some people regard one and some another as the best. Devotees follow these diverse paths, straight or crooked, according to their different tendencies. Yet, O Lord, Thou alone art the ultimate goal of all men, as the ocean is the goal of all rivers.

Divine Incarnation is accepted by Christianity and Hinduism. But unlike the former, Hinduism provides for more than one Incarnation. The Bhagavad-Gita says that whenever righteousness declines and unrighteousness prevails, the Pure Spirit assumes a human form to restore spiritual values. Subtle spiritual truths are expressed through a God-man in order that they may be grasped by the average man of the world. The eternal voice—to use an illustration given by Arnold Toynbee—tunes itself to its present audience's receiving set, otherwise it cannot be picked up. All Incarnations commune with the same Supreme Spirit and teach by Its command. The teaching is the same in its essence, but the language in which it is presented varies according to the people's taste and temperament. A good Vedantist respects not only the Incarnations mentioned in the Hindu Scriptures but also those of the non-Hindu traditions.

The harmony of religions found its most vivid expression through the spiritual experiences of Ramakrishna. He practiced all the dualistic and nondualistic disciplines of Hinduism and ultimately arrived at the same state of God-consciousness. He pursued the teachings of Christ and Mohammed and attained the same spiritual goal. One noticeable feature of his spiritual practices was that when he followed a particular faith, he became completely absorbed in it and forgot all else. For instance, while pursuing Islamic disciplines, he ate, dressed, and acted like a Moslem, removed the pictures of the Hindu deities from his room and stopped going to the Hindu temples. Thus he taught from actual experience and not from mere book knowledge that all religions are but different paths to the same goal. He also taught that a devotee of any faith need not give up his own rituals and beliefs, for he will surely realize truth with their help if he is sincere, earnest, and steadfast.

On one occasion, addressing some members of a religious sect who believed only in a formless God, Ramakrishna said:

> We are calling on the same God. Jealousy and malice need not be. Some say that God is formless, and some that God has forms. I say, let one man meditate on God with form, if he believes in form, and let another, if he does not believe in any form, meditate on the formless Deity. What I mean to say is that dogmatism is not good. It is not good to feel that my religion is alone true and all other religions are false. The correct attitude is this: my religion is right, but I do not know whether other religions are right or wrong, true or false. I say this because one cannot know the true nature of God unless one realizes Him. Suppose there are errors in the religion one has accepted; if one is sincere and earnest then God Himself will correct those errors. If there are errors in other religions, that is none of your business. God, to whom the world belongs, takes care of that.

The harmony of religions as taught by Ramakrishna fulfills a pressing need of the times. Owing to science and technology the world has shrunk, as it were, and human beings have come closer together. Since religion is a vital force in men's lives, how can there be peace in the world unless religions show mutual respect and work for the common good of humanity? In the past, religions have produced both good and bad results. On the one hand, they have contributed greatly toward peace and progress, building hospitals and charitable institutions, inspiring art and literature, and conferring many other blessings upon humanity; on the other hand, in the name of religion people have waged war, persecuted their fellow beings, and destroyed great monuments of civilization. Indeed, religious intolerance has made many turn away from religion and seek solace in an ethical life, philanthropic activities, or the study of science and the humanities. Nevertheless, it is not the teachings of the prophets that are responsible for hatred and cruelty; it is the human bigotry and narrowness.

Different religions emphasize different facets of the Supreme Reality. Islam, perhaps more than any other religion, stands for brotherhood among its own devotees. Moslems recognize no social distinctions. Before God all Moslems are equal. The Christians' central idea is "Watch and pray, for the Kingdom of Heaven is near at hand"—which means, "Purify your minds and be ready for the coming of the Lord." One cannot but admire the love of God that innumerable Christians show through love of man, to whose service they devote their time, energy, and material resources. The idea of "sharing" is perhaps the most striking idea of Christianity in practice. Judaism has clung to the idea of God's power and justice, and the Jewish people with dauntless patience have faced ordeals and sufferings through which they have passed for two thousand years without losing faith in God's power and justice. Buddhism teaches how to attain peace through renunciation and service. In these days of selfishness and competition it lifts up one's heart to see Buddhist monks serving people with great love and compassion, as taught by their prophet. Hinduism makes the realization of God, who is both within and without, the central fact of life. Thousands of Hindus are willing, even today, to renounce everything—including the world itself—to experience the reality of God. Thus the various religions are like vessels of different shapes; people can fill all of them with water. The water takes the form of the jars; it is the same authentic water of the lake. And after all the vessels have been filled, the lake still appears to contain the same amount of water. None can exhaust the infinite power, beauty, love, and goodness of God.

There are a surprising number of similarities in the essentials of all the great religions, whether evolved in the desert of Arabia or on the fertile banks of the Indus and the Ganges. They all declare the existence of the soul, which does not die with the destruction of the body, and the reality of God, who is above nature and is without beginning or end. They assume the original perfection of the soul, and they also hold that men, by their own actions, have made themselves imperfect. And they all agree that every soul will regain its perfection through knowing God. The Golden Rule is both implicit and explicit in all religions. All consciously or unconsciously exalt God's holy name, and it is the intention of all to show the way out of the prisonhouse of the world. All exhort their followers to practice such spiritual disciplines as faith, prayer, self-control, and contemplation. Implicit in the teachings of all prophets is the idea that the human mind can, at certain moments, transcend limitations of the senses and reasoning based upon sense data and come face to face with Truth.

Where do religions disagree? All organized religions prescribe rituals, mythology, doctrines, and disciplines, which constitute their philosophy and are suited to different stages of religious life. Mythology, philosophy made concrete, seeks to explain philosophy by means of legendary lives of men or supernatural beings. Rituals are still more concrete; they use bells, music, flowers, lights, images, and other objects. Disciplines and doctrines vary with different religions. All three—rituals, mythologies, and philosophy—are necessary factors in religious growth. Like husks, they protect the kernel of reality. The essential part of a seed is the kernel, but without the husk it cannot germinate. When the sprout appears, the nonessentials drop away. The Vedas say that to one who has realized the ultimate Reality the Vedas cease to be the Vedas. It is obvious that there cannot be a universal mythology, ritual, or philosophy acceptable to all seekers of truth. Religious quarrels arise when a particular religion claims that its ritual, mythology, and philosophy *alone* are valid and that those of others are pure superstitions. Religious fanatics quarrel about nonessentials, fighting, as it were, over empty baskets when the contents have slipped into the ditch. Yet these nonessentials are necessary and must remain until men are firmly grounded in the supreme Truth which transcends ritual, mythology, and philosophy, and which is experienced in a man's heart in the depth of meditation.

Yet a universal religion is the dream of people who want to eliminate religious friction. What is a universal religion? Where will one find it? Attempts have been made in the past to create one. Bigots of various religions have hoped to make their faith a universal religion. They have tried to impose it upon others, not only by force of character, but more often by bribery, persuasion, the sword, or a combination of all these. Their efforts failed. Then people tried to formulate a universal religion on an eclectic basis, synthesizing nonconflicting ethical and other elements from different faiths and eliminating those that give rise to friction. This intellectual method met with no better success, because religion is not a product of the intellect.

It is rooted in the direct experience of God by prophets and seers. Devoid of any such root, an eclectic religion, which may look appealing, is like a bouquet of different colored flowers plucked from different plants. It quickly withers because it is without root.

The universal religion already exists, however. It need only be discovered. We do not see it because we emphasize rituals, mythology, doctrine, and dogmas and ignore the basic truth. It is like universal brotherhood. We do not easily recognize the brotherhood of man because of our emphasis on racial and national characteristics. If we rise above them, we can see our brothers everywhere. One may not be able to lay one's finger on it, yet it exists all the same.

Universal religion cannot be formulated, it can only be experienced. It is the consciousness of God that is the ultimate goal of all faiths, whether primitive, ethical, philosophical, or highly mystical. Reality is the thread that runs through the pearls, as in a necklace. Each religion is one of the pearls. Every soul, every religion, consciously or unconsciously, is struggling upward toward freedom and God. The Bible, the Vedas, the Koran—all are so many pages in the Scriptures of the universal religion, and an infinite number of pages remain yet to be unfolded. The universal religion has no location in time or space. Its area is infinite, like the God it preaches. Krishna, Buddha, Christ, and Moses all have honored places in it. With its catholicity, the universal religion embraces in its infinite arms savages and civilized people, saints and sinners, philosophers and lovers of God, active men and contemplatives. There is no room in it for persecution or intolerance. Recognizing the potential divinity of all, it devotes its entire energy to bringing out men's spiritual natures.

How to promote the universal religion? Let us recognize the fact that religions are complementary and not competitive. Saints and mystics have flourished in all religions; some such men have not belonged to any organized church. Even science and art have produced people with a universal outlook. Let us discard the idea of toleration, which carries with it a sense of superiority. Let us think of other religions in terms of respect and positive acceptance. A believer in universal religion feels equally at home in a mosque, a church, a synagogue, or a temple. He salutes all the prophets of the past, bows down before all godlike persons who are working today for the uplift of humanity, and holds himself in readiness to show reverence to all prophets of the future. Let us encourage every man to dive deep into the mysteries of his own faith, and, provided he is sincere and earnest, he will one day discover for himself the universal religion.

We see the distance between different religions because we have moved away from God. We live in a circle. The many radii are the different religions, and the center of the circle is God. As all radii meet at the center, all religions meet in God. In order to promote religious harmony, let us deepen our religious consciousness. Let us come nearer to God by following our respective faiths and not by jumping from one faith to another. If Hindus, Moslems, Jews, and Christians emphasize more the spirit of their Scriptures and not the letter, religious quarrels will soon end. Our religious edifice should keep all its windows open so as to permit fresh air to come in, but we must not allow the wind to sweep the edifice off its foundation. A Christian, as Toynbee said, can believe in his own religion without having to feel that it is the sole repository of truth. He can love it without having to feel that it is the sole means of salvation. He can take Buddha's words to heart without being disloyal to Christ. But he cannot harden his heart against Krishna without hardening it against Christ. In order to promote the universal religion, we must not destroy other faiths. When a so-called civilized religion destroys, in the name of enlightenment, the beliefs and practices of primitive people, it destroys something of their soul; for religion is a part of the soul. There must not be any proselytization. By our own ardor and sincerity we may try to deepen people's faith in their own religions. Take a man where he stands and give him a lift. We must recognize the natural necessity of variation. Truth can be expressed in a hundred thousand ways, and each of these ways is true as far as it goes.

The preachers of religion have a tremendous responsibility in the promotion of world peace through the harmony of religions. It is to them that people look for guidance. How uplifting and impressive it will be when every church observes the holy days of other faiths, when a minister, for the scriptural reading, selects a passage from Scriptures other than his own and tries to prove a point in his sermon by quoting from the words of a prophet other than his own! People will then realize that religious experiences are universal phenomena and not the exclusive property of any one faith.

As first mentioned, humanity is stricken with a spiritual malady. For its remedy a drastic change in our thinking is imperative. Human nature must be transformed. But this transformation will come neither through psychotherapy, nor through science and technology, nor through psychedelic drugs, nor through military and economic pacts. It is the contribution of religion that in a large measure can bring about the change. The major faiths of the world owe it to humanity to rise to the occasion.

In this fateful hour it is the duty of religions to act as pointers to the goal of freedom and peace. Let them preach not destruction but fulfillment, not condemnation but acceptance, not dissension but harmony. Thus they will give tired humanity a song to sing to lift up its depressed spirit.

CHAPTER FIFTEEN

God and War

C. A. Qadir

Iqbal Professor of Philosophy, University of the Panjab, Pakistan

I

The Holy Koran records an important dialogue that took place between God and the angels at the creation of Adam. When God created Adam, the angels felt apprehensive, for they could not understand how a creature endowed with capacities for good as well as bad could restrain himself from causing what they termed "disturbance" or "disorder." In Chapter 2, verse 31, of the Holy Koran it is stated:

> And when thy Lord said to the angels: "I am about to place a vicegerent in the earth," they said: "Wilt Thou place therein such as will cause disorder in it, and shed blood? and we glorify Thee with Thy praise and extol Thy holiness." He answered: "I know what you know not."

The dialogue quoted above is important in more ways than one. It not only reveals the fear that humanity all along the ages has felt about its own purpose and destiny, it also limits the area of nondivine knowledge and cuts at the roots of pessimism. God's answer may be regarded as diplomatic, for God neither affirmed nor rejected the statement of the angels. He simply says, "You do not know what

I know." It could mean that God knew that there lay something in the nature of man that would cause disorder, and yet God was aware of the fact that it was something not entirely despicable or damnable. In one sense, God agreed with the angels that human beings would cause upheavals and disaster, but in another sense, one much more significant for the destiny and survival of mankind, God disagreed with the angels, for He did not share their pessimism.

The question raised by the angels was also raised by Voltaire, in *Candide*. "Do you think," asks Candide of Martin as they approached the coast of France, "that men have always massacred each other, as they do today, that they have always been false, cozening, faithless, thieving, weak, inconstant, mean-spirited, envious, greedy, drunken, miserly, ambitious, bloody, slanderous, debauched, fanatic, hypocritical and stupid?" Martin replies with a further question, "Do you think that hawks have always eaten pigeons when they could find them?" "Of course I do," Candide answers. To this Martin responds, "Well, if hawks have always had the same character why should you suppose that men have changed theirs?"[1] In *Candide*, Voltaire makes fun of Leibnizian optimism and offers a rollicking commentary on the difficulties of medieval theology. But it seems to me that in criticizing the unbridled optimism that Leibniz, or, for that matter, Browning, would like people to accept as an article of faith, Voltaire struck a note of pessimism, for he maintained that since rapacity is a part of human nature, it is difficult to find in human beings anything other than vice in all its worst forms.

God's answer is different. He does not say with Martin that men will always be vicious as hawks have always eaten pigeons. He is not skeptical about the destiny of the human race despite the fact that He knows that there is ingrained in the nature of man elements that are likely to cause disorder. This attitude is fundamentally different from that of Jean-Paul Sartre, who in his *Being and Nothing: An Essay in Phenomenological Ontology* observes, in his philosophy of other men, "My original fall is the existence of other people; original sin is my entry into a world in which there are other people."[2] Sartre feels that inclosed as we are within our own existence, we cannot understand others any more than we can make ourselves understood by them. Hence arise misunderstandings, clashes, conflicts, and wars. For Sartre, "Hell is other people," but for those who do not subscribe to Sartrean philosophy, paradise may be other people, though as a matter of fact "other people" may be both hell and paradise, depending upon the attitude one has regarding the nature of human relations and their working. God's answer is not in the line of Sartre's thinking. He does not say that the presence of other people necessarily leads to hellish conditions.

Sartre is an atheistic existentialist. He borrows uncritically a lot from other thinkers, in spite of the fact that he believes other people to be hell, and assumes quite a lot just as uncritically. I do not propose to examine his credentials, but I would like to look closely at his theory of human relations as embodied in his view of "other people." Sartre supposes that the existence of other people constitutes a threat because other people have consciousness, projects, and viewpoints as I do. This differentiates them from inanimate objects the presence of which, in my world, is an indifferent or neutral factor to be exploited by me in the furtherance of my plans and ambitions. But the case with human beings is different. They have their own plans. They can exploit me as well as I can exploit them. Multiplicity of purposes leads to dissensions. Sartre does not think that multiplicity of viewpoints, plans, or purposes can ever lead to a unity that transcends differences and welds together the discordant notes into a harmony.

To illustrate his point of view, Sartre says that if I am in a park, looking down an avenue of chestnut trees, when all of a sudden a stroller enters the field, stops, and looks at the view, immediately my world begins to disintegrate and its elements start organizing themselves about the newcomer. All things "turn towards the other a face that eludes me." But Sartre the nihilist says, not only does my world disintegrate on the entry of a stroller, but my self, that is to say, my being, also evaporates. The stroller judges me, not according to my projects, but on the basis of my physical appearance or my past, thus reducing me in Sartrean jargon to a thing-in-itself, an *en soi*. Moreover, since I cannot defend myself, I become what the stroller likes me to become. Like the Gorgon he has the power of turning me into a stone. I therefore find myself included among things to be exploited by him in the advancement of his own interests. This causes in me a sense of shame, the sense of

> being an object, that is of recognizing myself in this degraded state, dependent and fixed as I am for another person. Shame is the sense of original fall, not from the fact that I have committed this or that sin, but simply from the fact that I have "fallen" into the world, into the midst of things, and that I need the mediation of another human being in order to be what I am.[3]

From this, Sartre draws a frightful conclusion. He says that human societies must ever remain in a state of tension. "The essence of relationships between conscious minds is not *Mitsein*, 'being with,' as certain philosophers have recently claimed." It is a conflict. Thus existence, which is the supreme good if there is only one consciousness, becomes evil by the existence of other people. Sartre's pessimism reaches its height when he says that in relation to other human beings I become superfluous, just as other people become superfluous in relation to me.

Sartre supplies an argument to confirm the angels' fears, but that is not God's thinking.

Unfortunately, I belong to the group of philosophers Sartre dislikes. I believe that conscious beings, instead of living in a state of perpetual conflict, can have the relationship of "being with." Sartre has no doubt offered a brilliant analysis of the human situation as it exists today in the war-torn and war-afflicted world, but it does not take us very far. There is no gainsaying the fact that in the context of the present-day international situation one would find nothing but exploitation, depersonalization, and dehumanization. There is brutality, injustice, and enslavement on a scale unimaginable before. But that is not the whole story. There are no doubt thick clouds lowering over the world, but there can be a silver lining only waiting for an appropriate moment to make its presence felt. The difficulty with Sartre is that he feels that everybody is looking at everybody else with the eye of an enemy. This may be so in Europe, which is split into two warring groups: one constituted by the Anglo-American allies, and the other by the Communists and their sympathizers. They have a lot of science and technology to their credit, they have conquered outer space and the heavenly bodies. But what they have failed to learn is the art of living together, that is to say, of good-neighborliness or of "being with." If you feel, like Sartre, that other people are bent on disintegrating you and your world, conflicts inevitably result. If, however, one is prepared to accommodate the other and willing to recognize his place along with one's own, there can be a synthesis in which conflicts are overcome. What is urgently required is not more of science or technology, for already there are more atom bombs and hydrogen bombs than the world needs to destroy itself. With the present stock of deadly weapons—and they are daily on the increase—not only can this poor earth of ours be wiped out instantaneously but perhaps the entire universe, even those far-flung areas of lifeless matter which offended neither the Americans nor the Communists.

I believe, with the much maligned Hegel, that synthesis can emerge out of two opposing positions. In Hegelian terminology, a thesis opposed by an antithesis can generate a synthesis, which extracts the truth embodied in both and then assimilates it in itself. Hegel looked to logical contradictions or, better still, to contraries in his metaphysics, though in applying the same technique to history he did not ignore the social disharmonies that were reconciled in a higher unity, thus serving the role of synthesis. He cited in his philosophy of history a number of social movements that bred their opposites and disappeared along with them in subsequent movements of higher nature that assimilated, as it were, the truth of both. Hegel believed that the evolutionary process, through thesis, antithesis, and synthesis, ended in the Absolute, that stage when all contradictions would have been overcome. Hegel seems to be unduly optimistic, and there is no need to go along with him to that length. Nevertheless, there is profound truth in what he says. If we ignore the metaphysical trappings of his theory, what Hegel says has a great meaning for the world of today. Both thesis and antithesis, that is to say, both the warring groups, have some truth on their side. What is needed is to extract that truth and to emphasize it. If a person feels that the whole truth lies on his side and that the other party has nothing but falsehood, there can be no "synthesis," no reconciliation or understanding.

That dialectical evolution does not necessarily lead to conflict, that it may instead be an occasion for "being with," has been ably defended by the late Professor M. M. Sharif, in his theory of Dialectical Monadism.[4] It is restated by him in his Introduction to *A History of Muslim Philosophy*,[5] where he says:

> Our recognition of final cause as the determinant of the course of history leads us to the formulation of a new hypothesis. According to this hypothesis human beings and their ideals are logical contraries or discrepants in so far as the former are real and the latter ideal. . . . Hegelean ideas and Marxist reals are not of opposite nature. They are in conflict in their function. They are mutually warring ideas or warring reals and are separated by hostility and hatred. The incompatibles of our hypothesis are so in their nature, but not in their function and are bound by love and affection and though rational discrepants, are volitionally and emotionally in harmony.

Further he says:

> This hypothesis is not linear, because it envisages society as a vast number of interacting individuals and intermingling and interacting classes, societies, cultures and humanity as a whole, moving towards infinite ideals, now rising, now falling, but on the whole developing by their realization, like the clouds constantly rising from the foothills of a mountain range, now mingling, now separating, now flying over the peaks, now sinking into the valleys, and yet ascending from hill to hill in search of the highest peak.

II

It is unalloyed pessimism to suppose that the two world wars have killed God. In recent years, there has emerged a curious phenomenon in the theology of Christianity and Judaism. Quite a sizable minority of Christian theologians and Jewish religious thinkers have come to believe, on the basis of moral and spiritual bankruptcy caused by global wars, that God is dead. It would be interesting to note that during World War II, the anti-nazi Lutheran martyr Dietrich Bonhoeffer wrote prophetically to a friend from his

Berlin cell, "We are proceeding towards a time of no religion at all. For many that time has arrived." Paul Ramsey, a Princeton theologian, observes "that ours is the first attempt to build a culture upon the premiss that God is dead." Simone de Beauvoir writes, "It was easier for me to think of a world without a creator than of a creator loaded with all the contradictions of the world." Similarly, Richard L. Rubenstein, a Jewish theologian at the University of Pittsburgh, cannot believe in the God of the Hebrew Bible since that God "used Hitler as the rod of His wrath to send His people to death camps." He further says, "I find myself utterly incapable of believing this. Even the existentialist leap of faith cannot resurrect this dead God after Auschwitz." In his *After Auschwitz,* he observes that Hitler's holocaust was a proof that the "transcendent theistic God of Jewish patriarchal monotheism was no more."

As observed already, to declare God as a major casualty of the two world wars is not only grounded in insufficient data; it is also a misinterpretation of historical events. None can deny the evils of wars. But can one deny the good that wars bring about, though inadvertently and indirectly? World War I brought into prominence two forms of dictatorship, to wit, fascism and naziism, and World War II caused their downfall and rid the world of their baneful effects. It is true that these wars abolished one form of dictatorship only to leave the way clear for the growth of another. In both capitalist and communist countries there are political setups that rival the worst dictatorships of the past and outstrip them in some aspects. But let us not forget that it was these wars that freed the Asiatic and the African nations from the clutches of the Westerners who, on the plea of civilizing the black races, or what they euphemistically called the "white man's burden," exploited them and became a means of their cultural alienation and economic insufficiency. These wars have not only turned first-class powers into second-class powers—nay, into back numbers—and passed leadership on to those who were nonentities before the wars were fought, but they have also granted freedom—political, economic, and cultural—to a great many underprivileged and backward people. The political map of the world has entirely changed as a result of the two world wars, and it is further changing as a result of wars now being fought. To many tottering cultures wars have given a parting kick, and to many budding cultures they have given a fillip. They have enabled the major civilizations of the world to rub shoulders and made possible the evolution of a world philosophy, a world culture, and a world religion. Gone are the days when Thales was regarded as the first philosopher of the world and the European philosophy the only philosophy of the world. Gone also are the days when European culture was considered the only rational and sensible culture that the world ever produced. And gone are the days when Asiatics could boast of their spiritualism and condemn the rest of the world as materialistic. The world wars have given a terrible shaking to our patterns of thinking and modes of living.

Perhaps this was one of the reasons that God did not agree with the angels when they felt apprehensive at the creation of Adam. Just as earthquakes brought land from the depths of oceans, so do wars create politically independent units. But wars are not an unmixed blessing. It therefore seems to me that Nietzsche was wrong when he extolled war and eulogized hero morality, which is nothing but warfare morality.

Two things stand out in connection with Nietzsche: he was the child of Darwin and a killer of God. When Zarathustra came down from his meditative mountain to preach, the crowd turned their faces aside and began watching a ropewalker's performances. The ropewalker falls and dies. Zarathustra takes him upon his shoulders and says, "Because thou hast made danger thy calling, therefore shall I bury thee with my own hands." "Live dangerously," Zarathustra preaches. "Erect your cities beside Vesuvius. Send out your ships to unexplored seas. Live in a state of war." As Zarathustra came down from the mountain, he met an old hermit who talks to him about God. "But when Zarathustra was alone, he spake thus with his heart: 'Can it actually be possible? This old saint in the forest hath not yet heard aught of God being dead.' " For, says Nietzsche, the old gods came to an end long ago. And verily it was a good and joyful end of gods. They did not die lingering in the twilight but laughed themselves to death. That occurred when one of them said, "There is but one God." On hearing this all gods laughed and cried, "Is godliness not just that there are gods, but no god."

God died at the hands of Nietzsche, but it was the God of Christianity—the Christianity that prevailed in Europe when Nietzsche lived—who died and was buried, unsung, unwept, and uncared for. Such a God died leaving no heir to his kingdom, with no chance of a successor, for gods had outlived their utility. Their place was to be taken by human beings who believed not in a miserable struggle for existence but in Will to Life, which expresses itself in a Will to War, a Will to Power, a Will to Overpower.

Nietzsche criticized Christianity because it had, through St. Paul, accepted a doctrine of salvation by means of faith alone and thus had paved the way for the full growth of priesthood and church. It also emphasized for the same reason the role of life after death at the expense of the present one. Another very grave charge brought by Nietzsche against Christianity was that the type of men developed by it were essentially of the type of slaves. In *Will to Power*, Nietzsche says:

> What is it we combat in Christianity? That it aims at destroying the strong, at breaking their spirit, at exploiting their moments of weariness and debility, at converting their

> proud assurance into anxiety and conscience-trouble; that it knows how to poison the noblest instincts and to infect them with disease, until their strength, their will to power, turns inwards, against themselves—until the strong perish through their excessive self-contempt and self-immolation.

Nietzsche wanted the gods to die in order that a new type of humanity called Supermen could rise on their dead bodies. The new species should have nothing to do with the slave morality advocated by Christianity. Their morality would be that of the master or conqueror. Discussing the characteristics of the Superman in *Zarathustra,* Nietzsche mentions three "evil" things, voluptuousness, passion for power, and selfishness, as hallmarks of this new species. Voluptuousness, he regards as a concern for earthly existence; passion for power signifies a life of suffering and hardiness; selfishness indicates a supreme interest in one's own well-being.

Nietzsche's Superman rises not through the exercise of what Spinoza called the "monkish virtues,"—humility, pity, compassion, charity, etc.—but through the practice of valor, indomitable courage, and will to power. If occasion demands the use of ruthlessness, cunning, and chicanery, the Superman will not hesitate, for his one ambition in life is to rise, regardless of the means he is required to adopt.

The Europe of today is inhabited by Nietzschian Supermen, for all European nations, big or small, are burning with the desire to dominate with the help of forces that science has placed at their disposal. Accordingly, there is a mad race for superiority in arms through superiority in science and technology. Consequently, science instead of being a handmaid, to serve the interests of man, has become a master, dictating how human relationships are to be regulated and organized. The birth of nuclear science and the invention of nuclear weapons created problems of immense significance for the welfare and the survival of mankind. A machine is never an innocent contrivance. Its powers to do evil are immense. And once it has come into being, no power on earth can prevent its potentialities from appearing in one form rather than another. Atom bombs may not be used, but the very fact that a few nations have a monopoly in this respect creates an atmosphere of mistrust and suspicion that vitiates the even tenor of international understanding. And then there is a mad race. Every nation, irrespective of its financial capabilities and commitments, launches a program of scientific research to create in the shortest time an atom bomb of superior quality, the quality being judged in terms of its destructive capability. At first, this race was confined to the white races, but now it seems to have engulfed the nonwhites also. The underdeveloped nations, the economies of which are reeling under the weight of international loans, while their developmental programs require that the entire economic machinery be geared in their direction, have started thinking that in this war-torn world it is impossible to survive without a stockpile of nuclear weapons. And the consequences are fraught with dangers. With atom bombs all around the world, it would be a hard exercise of faith to feel optimistic about the future of mankind. At least this is the thinking of a great many intellectuals including Bertrand Russell, who instituted an international court of justice to impeach modern war criminals—among whom he included the President of the United States.

What is called "selfishness" by Nietzsche is now termed in diplomatic language "enlightened self-interest." In the Security Council as well as the General Assembly of the United Nations what moves a member to vote or to abstain is not consideration of justice or fair play; it is, on the other hand, his country's interest that prompts him to vote.

What serves his country the best, directly or indirectly, is very often the criterion for international decisions. It is very rarely the case that a voice is raised in the name of justice. The thing that weighs and decides is self-interest, which in plain language would be nothing but egoism. When Spinoza held that man is egoistic individually and collectively, his theory met with a storm of opposition. But there is no gainsaying the fact that at most levels of life what sways an average person is not benevolence but self-interest—pursued unconsciously at the instinctive level and pursued consciously at the rational level. But Spinoza's egoism had an element of justice that is sadly lacking in the international behavior of the modern states: each member state appeals in the name of justice when its own security is in jeopardy, though the same state in its dealings with others is guided by considerations of "enlightened self-interest." This contradiction between what we desire and what we practice is a great handicap in the development of common understanding.

What Nietzsche has called "voluptuousness" is scientism or, in diplomatic parlance, the economic and technical development programs of a country. There is nothing wrong in the development of technical and economic resources. Their development, however, becomes evil when they are released for diabolical purposes and made an instrument for the mental and cultural subjugation of the less fortunately placed nations. When science is taken as an end, it becomes a powerful weapon to destroy what has been prized by mankind from times immemorial. The Communists are often charged with scientism, as if they have made science an end rather than as a means, but the non-Communists have no better record. Both groups use science as an end and in the process have found themselves entangled in such problems as have defied the best intellects of the world.

III

Nietzsche's thinking is not God's thinking, not because he rejected God, but because he rejected the basic requirements of human life. Mohammad Iqbal, a poet philosopher of the India-Pakistan subcontinent, observes in *The Reconstruction of Religious Thought in Islam*[6] that modern man finds himself in a predicament as a result of his philosophies of criticism and scientific specialism. He is living in open conflict with himself, and in the domain of economic and political life he is living in open conflict with others. He is trying to overcome this conflict through the instrumentality of rationalism and atheistic socialism. But these instruments are of no avail, according to Iqbal.

> It is only by rising to a fresh vision of his origin and future, his whence and whither, that man will eventually triumph over a society motivated by an inhuman competition and a civilisation which had lost its spiritual unity by its inner conflict of religious and political values.

In his writings, especially the *Israr-i-Khudi* (*The Secrets of the Self*), Iqbal seems to have been much impressed by the ideas of Nietzsche. Not only does his Perfectman bear a close resemblance to Nietzsche's Superman, but also in his denunciation of reason as a final arbiter of truth, in his exaltation of feelings, in his reassertion of individual values, and in his emphasis on freedom, Iqbal comes very close to Nietzsche and in some respects indicates his indebtedness to him. But despite this close affinity, Iqbal has his own interpretation of the human situation and consequently has his own suggestions. Iqbal was sorry for Nietzsche, because Nietzsche failed to evaluate his spiritual experiences correctly and his philosophic thought put him on the wrong path. The content of Nietzsche's thought was spiritual, according to Iqbal, but his evaluation was anti-spiritual, and therein lay the tragedy. Nietzsche was probably right when he saw the germs of the decay of European civilization in the undue emphasis on intellect and the consequent underestimation of the role of feelings in the scheme of life. Nietzsche was also right when he railed against the dead fossilized religions of the world, particularly those that were negativistic and refused to acknowledge the importance and the significance of the mundane existence. But he was totally wrong in suggesting that the salvation of humanity lay in the evolution of Supermen who realized their Will to Power through the accumulation of technological and other material resources. In Nietzsche's philosophy there could be found no reference to those spiritual and moral forces in the absence of which the material modes of existence not only become rudderless but also assume diabolical forms and cause destruction in all aspects of human existence.

That God is needed in some form or another to normalize human relations is the feeling of a great many people today. This was understood by Iqbal as well. His Perfectman, instead of rising on the sheer strength of the material modes of existence, has a sense of direction that comes from knowing the "whence and whither of life." His Perfectman resembles Nietzsche's Superman inasmuch as he is not oblivious of the power that science has and is therefore very eager to harness the physical forces for his benefit, but in contradistinction to Nietzsche's Superman's, Perfectman's glory lies in becoming the vicegerent of God. As vicegerent of God, he cannot shut his eyes to the laws of justice that operate in the universe as surely as do the physical laws. The moral order is not so obvious in its operations as the physical order is, and therein lies the reason that it is often ignored and even denied. But those people who take a long-range view of the human situation cannot fail to be convinced of the law of justice, working sometimes directly and sometimes indirectly. In the rise and fall of civilizations, one can discern, though dimly, the operations of the laws of God.

It seems to me that Albert Schweitzer struck a true note when in diagnosing the nature of the disease of present-day civilization, he noted what he called the optimistic-ethical interpretation of the world and suggested in its stead the adoption of the world-affirming, ethical-active mysticism. In his Preface to *Civilisation and Ethics*,[7] Schweitzer says:

> Ethics grow out of the same roots as world and life affirmation, for ethics too are nothing but reverence for life. This is what gives me the fundamental principle of morality, namely, that good consists in maintaining, promoting and enhancing life, and that destroying, injuring and limiting life are evil. Affirmation of the world which means affirmation of the will to live that manifests itself around me is only possible if I devote myself to other life. From an inner necessity I exert myself in producing values and practising ethics in the world and on the world even though I do not understand the meaning of the world. For in world and life-affirmation and ethics I carry out the will of the universal Will to Live which reveals itself in me. I live my life in God, in the mysterious Divine Personality which I do not know as such in the world, but only experience as mysterious Will within myself.

Schweitzer feels that no civilization can survive without a world view and a moral basis for its day to day activities.

What Schweitzer calls the ethical basis of existence is really the moral order we have been talking about, for unless there is a firm conviction that the universe is founded on principles of justice, though it may not be possible for the puny intellect of man to grasp their significance in full, there is no sense in talking of the ethical basis of existence or of making it the ground of life. Schweitzer thinks that reverence for life is the supreme virtue, the recognition of which not only can save European civilization from annihilation but can also rid the world of wars.

There is a lot of wisdom in what Schweitzer says. It goes without saying that modern civilization, with its faith in technology, that is to say, in the machine, has lost sight of the fact that human beings are more than machines and that they cannot be understood through statistical averages and functional laws. Both the Marxists and the Existentialists have noted with horror the fact of depersonalization and dehumanization that is going on in the world of today and have prescribed remedies in their own way. The Communists work for the liberation of workers, the masses, in communist terminology, and their sovereignty. The Existentialists try to save the individual and reassert his dignity through their doctrine of freedom with or without God and also through their philosophy of Absurdity. But the communist strategy leads to indoctrination and dictatorship, and the Existentialists fail to offer any philosophy of society. Communism is based on the rejection of God; existentialism, by its too great emphasis on the individual and his plight in what its proponents call the alien world, ignores the requirements of corporate existence. True, there are certain flashes in existentialism that can be helpful in building up a society in which each individual feels free and lives free. But these flashes are not enough. For instance, Gabriel Marcel and Martin Buber talk of the relation of I–Thou that should regulate human relations instead of the I–It relation that governs the machine man of today. In the I–It relation the other person is treated as a means to be exploited and made use of. His status is no better than that of a machine utilized for the benefit of the entrepreneur. In an authoritarian or dictatorial state, the individuals forming the state are treated as instruments for the stability and the glorification of the state. In a bureaucratic form of government, where law and order are given precedence over other things, the people are no better than pawns and can be disposed of to suit bureaucratic ends. In I–Thou relations, one comes near to Kant's ideal, where each person is treated as an end and never as a means and where every person is a member of the kingdom of ends.

Martin Buber, a dialogical philosopher, recognizes the fact of sociality. In *Between Man and Man,* he observes that "The individual is a fact of existence in so far as he steps into a living relation with other individuals. The aggregate is a fact of existence in so far as it is built up of living units of relation." Buber recognizes a category of the "essential we." "The 'essential we' includes the 'Thou' potentially, for only men capable of truly saying 'Thou' to one another can truly say 'We' with an other." Through this essential "We," and only through it, can man escape from the impersonal "one" of the nameless, faceless crowd. Buber therefore distinguishes between the "social" in general and the togetherness of true dialogue. In the "social," many individual existences are bound into a group with common experiences and reactions, but no personal relation necessarily exists between one person and another within the group. Rather, the membership of a group tends toward the suppression of personal relations in favor of the elements of pure collectivity.

Martin Buber is, consequently, in favor of the dialogical social principle rather than the political. The former means free fellowship and association; the latter, which means the necessary and ordered realm of the world of "It," tends toward domination and compulsion. The dialogical philosophy of "togetherness" is the same as the philosophy of "being with" that Sartre has rejected in favor of "conflict."

Unfortunately, Sartre believes in unlimited freedom—a reaction against the total determinism of the physical and psychological sciences. "Togetherness" or "being with" requires the willing surrender of one's liberty in the interest of accommodation, adjustment, and understanding.

IV

Martin Buber is certainly right in recognizing the reality of "We" along with the reality of "I." But it seems to me that it is not possible to use "We" meaningfully in the absence of a certain frame of reference, whether defined or undefined. How can a person use "We," which includes the speaker as well as the persons addressed, without relating himself to others in some understandable manner. To the Moslem, the context is provided by the notion of vicegerency. This state is not given to man from the beginning but has to be achieved through righteousness and purification. Human beings as vicegerents of God will be faithful to the divine covenant and address each other as "We" within the framework sanctioned and ordained by the Almighty God.

This may sound bizarre to the European and American ear, because it recalls to his mind the idea of theocracy with all its attendant evils in the form of church control and priesthood. Westerners cannot conceive of a religiously motivated and religiously oriented state without that state assuming some form of theocracy and admitting some type of priesthood. Luckily this is not the case with Islam. The theocracy of Islam recognizes neither church nor priesthood, it is simply an assertion of the sovereignty of God, which in turn is the sovereignty of values. God is a Person and a repository of all the excellences that the human mind can conceive of. The Koran mentions several attributes of God, thus presenting God as an Ideal to be copied and to be realized. True, a limited and a finite individual cannot hope to realize all the excellences that constitute, as it were, the nature of God, but he can be deputy of the Lord according as he, in his endeavors and achievements, approximates the Ideal One.

The idea of the sovereignty of God is, I think, very useful for peace. As observed already, the sovereignty of God is, in fact, the sovereignty of values, or what amounts to the same thing, the sovereignty of man, for values have no meaning except in a human situation that is enriched and ennobled by their adoption and infusion. This idea stresses the accountability of man to the Ultimate Reality, which is essentially good—being the repository of all excellences that man can conceive of—and therefore suggests that in the final analysis it is not the material or the physical order that reigns supreme but rather the moral and the spiritual one that, though not so obviously, governs the scheme of the universe.

From the sovereignty of God follows the idea of the brotherhood of man. Oneness of God implies oneness of mankind. A sound political outlook can harbor no racial, geographical, or materialistic conceptions. Such conceptions disrupt the essential unity of mankind and narrow down the cosmopolitan outlook of people. It is indeed a sad commentary on the affairs of the world that with the weakening of the hold of religion, the God of nationalism reared its head and demanded as much loyalty as the God of religion did, and in some respects more. Whereas the God of religion could be appeased by occasional prayers, the God of nationalism desired active warfare for His glory, aggrandizement, and what may be called, for want of a better phrase, the extension of His sphere of influence. All European nations and now the Asiatic ones, after a long struggle involving "toils and tears," have developed militant types of nationalism. Each nation believing "My country, right or wrong," has cultivated an outlook in which whatever truth the other side possesses disappears altogether. Each nation builds its strategy on the hatred of its near or remote neighbor and accuses it through the mass media of perfidy, aggression, and violation of international commitments. Nationalism is a fulfillment of Sartre's philosophy of conflict, inasmuch as each nation guided by what we have called "enlightened self-interest" thinks that the other nation is out to disintegrate it and what it stands for. Thus modern conflicts assume the shape of ideological conflicts and adherents fight as if they are crusaders working for the vindication of right and the suppression of evil.

Disgusted by nationalism and also what may be called political fragmentation of the world, some people have thought of one world government very much on the analogy of one world culture or one world religion. It is supposed that as a result of speedy means of communication and transport, distances have shrunk and people have come out of their narrow grooves. Consequently, petty prejudices are giving place to a broad universal outlook, and there is emerging a world culture that, though not antagonistic or partial to any one culture, transcends them and presents a fine amalgam of them all. Likewise, a world religion is emerging that transcends all the existing religions, though canceling or vindicating none of them. These world phenomena may be conceived on the analogy of homes in a country: every home is independent and yet in the larger interests of political stability and socioeconomic welfare, the homes accept the suzerainty of the state. The world culture or the world religion would attempt a synthesis and present the minimum essential of either culture or religion in the interest of world peace. Such a thing is already evident in the assembly of educated, sensible people who, while retaining their individualities, exhibit a broad understanding of the cultural or religious standpoints of the others. Gone are the days when votaries of a particular religion or culture conceived themselves the monopolists of spirituality or graces. Exigencies of time and of international situation demand the existence of much broader sympathies and the adoption of a far greater liberal attitude than is the case at the present moment.

The idea of a world government is commendable. Some people think that the skeleton of this form of government can be seen in world bodies, particularly the United Nations and its various agencies. The aim of these world organizations is to weld different interests together and to bring about unity of thought and feelings where discord or imbalance prevails. All right-thinking men and women believe that the establishment of the United Nations with its various agencies is a step in the right direction. But notwithstanding its utility, there are serious doubts in the minds of people of the underdeveloped nations regarding the motives that underlie this organization and the way in which it comes into action. It is thought that the United Nations exists for the benefit of the erstwhile imperialistic nations and the new powers that have emerged on the ruins of the old ones. Moreover, the organization comes into action when the interests of a bigger nation are at stake and remains inactive when the interests of weaker nations are in danger. Again, it is feared by a large majority of the "have-nots" that the organization has constantly worked to the detriment of certain sections of the world. This shows that a good thing may turn out to be bad, if the intentions are not above reproach. I think that no organization, much less a world organization, can work if it is not grounded in some kind of broad based or universal ethics.

To be a success the world government should recognize the sovereignty of God and should work to dispel doubts and fears. It should aim at the betterment of mankind and shed all ideas of exploitation or domination of one section over another, however powerful or wealthy any one section be.

It may be said that the above is merely a counsel of perfection, that all three, the world culture, the world religion, and the world government, are simply dreams like the utopias of the previous thinkers, incapable of being realized in this world of dirt and filth. To a large extent the fears are correct. I again refer to the dialogue of God and the angels with which this chapter commenced. God did not reject the fear of the angels, which shows that the tendency to create disorder—in psychological jargon, the aggressive tendency—is a part of human nature. Hence there can never be a complete realization of dreams. Areas of tension will be found here and there. But these areas should not prove major disturbing factors once it is understood that the source of all power is God, who is vitally interested in the well-being of His creation.

Acceptance of the religious view would not mean total abolition of war. But let it not be forgotten that wars can be fought in diverse ways. They may not involve the massacre and the worldwide misery of the last two world wars. Already, in the opinion of Arnold Toynbee, World War III is going on in every nook and corner of the world. Only its tactics have changed and its severity lessened. Each day's newspaper bristles thicker than yesterday's with headlines reporting worldwide trouble. There may be student agitations, protests, strikes on the part of industrial units, separatist movement by minorities here or there, political scuffles, police actions, or just the extension of spheres of influence—in all of them you witness man creating disorder. World War III scattered, as it is, over the different parts of the world is a novel type of war. It combines the fascination of wars of the traditional type with the advantage of being very much less destructive of lives and property.

Yet it seems that the world has understood the foolishness of world-engulfing wars. For this reason, efforts are being made to restrict the quantity of armaments that any country should have lest it become a danger to others. Also, there is an attempt to control the production and use of the atom bomb. But all these things will remain fruitless if people do not learn to live together, or, what amounts to the same thing, do not adopt the philosophy of "being with." This philosophy, in order to become a practical code of living, should not simply be understood as a cold logical truth, it should be emotionally backed. Spinoza wanted "intellectual love" for God; the same intellectual love is needed for "being with." It would thus be possible to decrease the frequency, the severity, and the geographical extent of wars. Total abolition of wars may not be possible —perhaps this abolition is not a part of God's design—but if human beings are able to save themselves by lessening the amount of tension that exists at the present moment, they should not consider themselves as having failed in human history.

NOTES

1. Voltaire, *Candide*, trans. John Butt (Hammondsworth: 1947), p. 96.
2. *L'Être et le néant: Essai d'ontologie phénoménologique* (Paris, 1943), p. 481.
3. *Ibid.*, p. 349.
4. In Radhakrishnan & Muirhead (eds.), *Contemporary Indian Philosophy*, 3rd ed. (London: 1958), pp. 565–592.
5. Vol. I (Wiesbaden: 1963).
6. Lahore: 1962.
7. London: 1961.

CHAPTER SIXTEEN

Pacifism and Law

Harrop A. Freeman

Professor of Law,
Cornell University

There can be no adequate philosophy of war and peace except as it also embraces a philosophy of conflict and law. And there can be no adequate philosophy of law that does not address itself to the place of violence and nonviolence. I am a pacifist and a lawyer precisely because I believe that these two professions hold the greatest promise of a consistent and socially responsible philosophy.

Law is, by derivation and definition, the institutionalized nonviolent method of formulating the rules of relationship between men or between associations of men and of settling disputes and conflicts. It comes into existence wherever and whenever men are no longer willing to leave these matters to naked power and violence. Violence is lawless. Law should not be violent (though it may be coercive). In the rarified atmosphere of philosophies of law and in the mire of law enforcement by police, these basic presuppositions are constantly forgotten or overshadowed. Law can then be defined as the edict of the state backed up by the force of the state, and police enforcement becomes paramilitary, with helmets, dogs, armored personnel carriers, submachine guns, and gas. It is likewise then easy for a nation to assert that it engages in war to enforce legal rights such as self-determination, the repulsion of aggression, and the fulfillment of treaty obligations. Suddenly, any amount of violence is asserted to be legitimate if an opposing violence exists or can be conjured up. All that is necessary is a claimed right and an allegedly opposing violence.

Let us briefly examine what one traditional philosophical concept—absolute sovereignty (internal and external)—does with regard to law and war. It is doubtful that absolute sovereignty ever existed as a *fact* any more than Kant's "pure reason." Instead, it was an hypothesis, a theory, used to back up a seizure of power and give it the semblance of legality. Bodin's thesis was used originally within the state to undergird France's monarch ("The State [law], it is I"). Hobbes and Austin likewise developed the theory to support the British crown in Parliament (which is asserted to have power to make anything true—even that a woman is a man). The net result has been the absolutist value upon law and government no matter how contrary they be to truth or justice. Similarly, Grotius defined external sovereignty legally to place beyond challenge the power-grab of the mercantile and colonial nations. The United Nations today is an organization of sovereign nations, over 130 of them, many with no functional reason for being. Though all are sovereign, some are more sovereign than others and retain total supremacy over even international government, for example, through the veto. The World Court has no binding authority, being subject to the sovereign reservation of the independent nations. War itself is the ultimate proof of international sovereignty—the ability to impose one's will on another state or to resist its will. Though the exigencies of modern life have caused a considerable inroad on sovereignty by functional international organs, the philosophy of sovereignty is shouted even more stridently from the nations' capitol-tops. In fact, it ought to be recognized that sovereignty of both types is dead; what is needed is a burial.

I propose that we get back to some fundamentals and construct a philosophy of law and order, both intranationally and internationally, attuned to the forthcoming century, one that is in harmony with humanity rather than an argument for power seizure. In 1960, in *Dear Mr. President, An Open Letter on Foreign Policy*,[1] I suggested some of the worldwide revolutions shaping our world:

> . . . (a) *the nuclear revolution*, similar to the industrial revolution, in which nuclear and solar fuels replace solid and liquid fuels, (b) *the military revolution* wherein destructive power has so increased as to no longer permit action to "defend" or "decide" anything, (c) *the political "power" revolution* in which "balance of power" or making of decisions through exertion of military or other power has little chance because nations find it difficult to "confront" each other and a small nation can launch or threaten to launch world devastation without itself having a substantial stake, (d) *the colonial (freedom) revolution* in which "colonialism" is disappearing and nationalism is the pattern, (e) *the geographic revolution* in which emphasis has shifted from Europe to Asia, to Africa, to South America (the problem is North–South rather than East–West), (f) *the nonviolent revolution* which is demonstrating that political change (India) and social change (southern U.S.) can be achieved by nonviolence, (g) *the administrative revolution* by which national governments have turned to functional or administrative law over court or legislative law and by which demand is being made for international government on the same pattern, (h) *the human rights revolution* in which it is recognized that every man in the world has a right to food, work, health, dignity and freedom, and that fulfillment of these demands is more required of government than are the original "liberties" of free press, religion and discussion, (i) *the socialist revolution* in which

all economic systems are being socialized and in which unrestrained private ownership and management is being replaced everywhere, and in which government is increasingly the capital-former and planner, (j) *the population-possessions revolution*, by which the population explosion is increasingly highlighting the inequitable distribution of the world's products and facilities.

Some of these revolutions (for example, the nuclear, the geographic, the colonial, the population-possessions, and the administrative revolutions) are recognized by any serious thinker today. Although every piece of evidence—from Watts and Harlem, Berkeley and Washington, Korea and Vietnam—underlines the existence of military, power, human rights, and nonviolent revolutions, the Establishment, entrenched in outmoded philosophies of law and order, refuses to devise a new philosophy to take account of these revolutions and meet mankind's basic demands. Yet I sense, particularly in the Vietnam War and in the malaise of the inner city and the Negro ghetto, a wide popular understanding of the need for change. Whereas in the past we concerned ourselves primarily with our own history, institutions, law, language, culture, economics, we now perforce find that all our associations are supranational and that we are joined in the human race in whatever strata of society or part of the globe it is found. Our balance of payments, our cost of defense, our priorities in research and education are determined by events halfway around the world. And we cannot morally or physically escape from the two-thirds of the human race that are ill-educated, ill-clothed, ill-used, ill-fed, and just plain ill.

Of all others, the problem of violence is the most important to our new-forming communities, supranational and interhuman. There was a time when those in power could suppress the demands of the serf or the aspirations of a rising nation by violence. Now we find that the closeness of living together, the stake of the power group itself in the institutions and property that may be destroyed, and the changed nature of violence render the use of violence unacceptable. Great superiority in force on which the power structure always relies is not really able effectively to overcome a much smaller but more justified violence, as Korea and Vietnam and Watts have demonstrated. Violence is so threatening and destructive that it no longer is a tool of defense, foreign policy, bargaining, or social change. This century has been a record of great violence as though we had repeatedly to go through this awful demonstration before we could learn its true nature. But it has also been a century of experimentation—and success—with nonviolence, from Gandhian independence to Southern civil rights.

It is precisely at this point that pacificism offers the philosophy necessary to organize and develop the emerging revolutions in the way least disruptive of society and most committed to the development of community, law, and justice. Pacifist philosophy embodies (1) an end view of man united in nonexploitive community, (2) a revolutionary theory of change, and (3) a commitment to nonviolence as means. It asserts that all men are brothers, that each man is in and part of his brother. Or, if you prefer religious pacifist language, that there is something of God in each unique individual, that God cannot be fulfilled except as He is fulfilled in each individual. Pacifism is extremely revolutionary, urging that almost all of our institutions are and have been exploitive, violent, unjust, and inhuman. It recognizes that the tempo of demand has so accelerated that gradual revolution cannot meet the requirements and that society must be overhauled from top to bottom. Pacifism insists that the only appropriate method for this revolution is nonviolence.

This insistence on nonviolent means holds the greatest truth for society. If violence has become so destructive that it can no longer be tolerated as a defender of society or a tool of social change, then some other instrument must be found, for it would be an immoral *and* stagnant society that allowed its citizens no way to press for change, particularly when the demand is revolutionary in timing and scope. Philosophers and even courts are recognizing that violence is always outside the law, violative of law and order, destructive of community. The corollary is also being accepted and is even more important: if violence is illegal, then a democracy must provide means for nonviolent revolutionary change (as the Supreme Court did in *Cox v. Louisiana,* 379 U.S. 559 [1965], and other cases); for nonviolence is *within the law*, a form of legal confrontation such as democratic dialogue and free speech that builds respect for law, justice, and community. Pacifism is anti-war, anti-power, anti-injustice; it is community-building, humanitarian, global, and nonviolent. This is why it offers a philosophy in harmony with the needs of our times.

Now, I would be the first to recognize the dangers that hover just behind pacifism. But I deny that pacifism must be responsible for them. It is often said that nonviolence works exactly because potential violence is in the background, and that society accepts the demands of the lesser of two evils, though not freely. That may be true. But even this forced choice between violence and nonviolence is a preferred form of dialogue or persuasion. Secondly, it is quite possible that since pacifism advocates two doctrines—one of ends and the other of means—a listener may hear the call for ends loud and clear, for his ear is already tuned to revolutionary change. But the hearer might reject the means of nonviolence. His ear could be deaf to this plea because of his experience of persistent violence. The fault lies with the existing violent society that has taught him only the language of violence, not with the philosophy that seeks to reverse this state of affairs.

In illustration of the way a nonviolent humanist philosophy may handle the problems of current society I shall briefly discuss four interrelated concepts that involve the very core of emerging humanity: (1) *civil disobedience,* (2) *rule of law,* (3) *war,* and (4) *a mature society.*

1. *Civil Disobedience.* The utilization of civil disobedience as the tool of the civil rights and anti-Vietnam War movements is well known. It was formulated in the pacifist movement and sparked by pacifist leaders. It is defined as a public, nonviolent protest against basic illegality and injustice through the disobedience of some specific law. It generally arises only when evils protested against are so intolerable and so contrary to the basic principles of law and justice that to obey would be in the deepest sense to disobey the essence of law and therefore illegal. When these evils are such that demand for change cannot and ought not be stilled, the choice is between civil disobedience (nonviolence) and civil disorder (violence). The pacifist argues that it is best for law to recognize civil disobedience as within the law and to condemn only violent protest. Civil disobedience has been formulated by legal theoreticians and lawyers, for example, Gandhi, as a means of effectuating change within the law when law's normal procedures are inadequate, misused, or held captive by anti-legal forces, or when law enforcement agencies themselves engage in violence and thus lose the protection of law.

Civil disobedience is sometimes the *only* legal procedure to raise constitutional and other legal issues. It may be required by law itself as the Nuremberg principles require an American to refuse participation in the Vietnam War if that war is against the established principles of international law. Civil disobedience may be a form of free speech (like picketing) protected by the First Amendment; it may be the assertion of the validity of a higher law over a lesser law (federal constitution over city trespass law); it may even be a challenge to a previously upheld law, recognizing that legal principles do change through continuous dialogue (*Brown v. Board of Education*, 347 U.S. 483 [1954], overruling *Plessy v. Ferguson*, 163 U. S. 537 [1896] on segregation). Much of this argument has already been accepted by the U.S. Supreme Court and the highest courts of other countries.

It is my belief that to avoid civil disorder the legal nature of civil disobedience should further be recognized. There will obviously be times when the breach of law is so tangential to the issue protested that some acts of civil disobedience will be held to be illegal. Then, and only then, pacifist philosophy asserts, must the civil disobedient willingly pay the penalty society demands. This is the ultimate test that proves the pacifist's legality: his final support of law in its totality even when he feels the present interpretation of law is wrong. In the end, the demands of obedience may not take precedence over man's deepest philosophical insights in religion, morality, and humanism. This is pacifism's offer of a philosophy to avoid government without dissent, which would be tyranny, to preserve democracy, which is a government of dialogue, to allow for revolutionary change, to ward against violence, which prevents true confrontation, to place men's bodies nonviolently on the line in support of men's ideas, to preserve society under a rule of law, and to achieve justice therein.

2. *Rule of Law.* Often set off against any right of civil disobedience is a certain concept of the rule of law. It is argued that law is to be distinguished from politics: politics is the place for debate; law is not the place for debate. Once law is enacted or adopted it must be supreme; therefore *all* law must be obeyed—bad law as well as good law. Law is absolute so that obedience to it must be absolute. Any rule of law stated in this way is equivalent to the defense of war

and patriotism as "my country, right or wrong." This cannot be the true concept of rules of law. It does not square with the history of the development of law. It is disproved by the thousands of cases that reach the courts each year and the very profession of lawyers engaged in challenging and avoiding laws.

A great deal of legal philosophy has been wasted in proving the origins of law and order and such concepts of law as property and contract. The real origin and development of law look like this to me: All law is in fact political, private as well as public law. Law starts as a protection of the interests of the power structure—its property, slaves, investments, contracts, business, levies, etc. Property originates out of seizure of wild animals on unoccupied land and the addition of something of value by the seizor (at least, exclusion of others). This concept extends all the way to legalized monopolies, colonization, and the recent national seizure of the continental shelf. Law also establishes rules of the game (such as cricket or football) within the power structure, concerning what consideration is necessary for a contract, what notes are negotiable, what liens have priority, etc. These are important only to those engaged in the game. Semi-legal institutions are recognized to further their purposes: corporations, monopolies, patents, mergers, associations, unions, cartels. These are all claimed by the power structure to be law and appeal is made to the rule of law to gain obedience. But no rule of law is yet in existence; there is still only rule of power or rule of the game.

During this period, constitutions begin to establish a new organization of the power structure—government—and to give legislative, executive, and judicial powers to its branches. The persons not holding power are persuaded to accept these institutions by reference to already accepted legal concepts: that government is a contract or that they had something to do with its creation (as our Constitution states: "We the people . . . do ordain"). In fact the government is always set up by the élite power structure, and its powers are only those deemed safe. Gradually, law, often through the judiciary, builds a legal system, a set of principles and rules to hold all parts of the Establishment together consistently. Slowly, the persons outside the power structure find rules therein that they can utilize in achieving a right they claim *against* the power structure of government. In the interest of consistency and its own preeminence the judiciary asserts authority to bring the power structure and the governors under law. Then, and only then, is the rule of law in effect. The rule of law occurs when the king is under the law. It is not the court's power of enforcement that makes the rule of law effective. The court cannot enforce against the power structure, which has a monopoly of power. Its opinion is merely persuasion, but it relies on the inherent support of those within power who need the law and those out of power whose sense of morality and injustice applauds the decision.

The rule of law is a rule against absolutism, not a rule *of* absolutism. It affirms that the government is a government subject to rules, not a government of the private whims of individuals, that the President can be called to account for the illegality of his action in Vietnam as fully as the lowliest debtor must pay his debt. When he in fact is so called to account, we shall have a rule of law.

3. *War.* War is defined as a *legally* accepted method for the *violent* resolution of conflicts or controversies between *political groups.* The philosophy back of war is peculiar, if not absurd and illogical. As Millis and Real have pointed out, we have largely abandoned "the acquisition or defense of *things,* [and have] begun to fight for *theory,*" for national honor, democracy, communism, etc. This concept does not, however, as is claimed, provide philosophical and

sociological support for war but rather for war destroyed, *reducto ad absurdum;* for when the battle is one of ideas for "the minds and hearts" of man, violence cannot convince or persuade. This is why many of us now observe that war is philosophically dead, *kaput*.

Legal philosophy early went to work on the subject of war. When man could no longer be allowed to seize what he needed for survival, or what his hot anger impelled, these acts were branded as hostilities or violence and illegal. But when a state of war was declared to exist, and this was a label placed on it by the power structure, the law permitted political groups to contend by force. From this theory a series of legal rules developed for trading, blockade, land warfare, etc. The definition was of legal status, not merely of physical power. The parties were *legally* equal, and non-participating states were to treat belligerents impartially. External sovereignty was recognized, and states could initiate war for reasons of state, which became a political question not to be reviewed in court.

By World War II legal philosophy had swung almost 180 degrees, still bent on protecting the power system. War was catalogued as just and unjust (nonaggressive and aggressive). Aggressive war was outlawed. In the U.N. Charter a new obligation was spelled out to take action against aggressive war, and war was to be made an enforcement process of the United Nations. Finally, to reach certain individuals, the Nuremberg and Tokyo trials sought to destroy the protection of the act of state doctrine and make individuals criminally guilty for acts of improper war. Some persons look upon these theory developments as pie in the sky, wishful thinking; for great nations continued to wage war, small and large, without interference. But is that so? Are not these rules, originally intended to protect the power structure, now being used to call that structure to account? Is not this what the Lord Russell war crime trials, the draft case pleading of Nuremberg theory, the wars of liberation are all about? We may even yet use the legal rules of the system to bring the rule of law to the international order.

You may ask how I can imply that war is *legally* buried when it apparently is so much alive, destroyed by neither logic nor philosophy. It may be argued that war originally was a tool that got us what we needed and we will not face its obsolescence; it is the subject of 90 per cent of our history and we will not abandon history; it is an exciting alternative to the humdrum of life and we have never been able to find a moral equivalent; it created one of the largest and most powerful classes in our society, which became the military-industrial complex; it still is a legal institution.

But I would reply that war is legally ripe for burial because it is *in fact dead*. It can no longer decide an issue. It can no longer win but only destroy. The world is so small, the population growing so rapidly, the resources so limited that mankind, "for realistic as well as spiritual reasons, must come to the abandonment of the use of force." World cooperation is functionally developing world community and will not allow the community to be broken. The power structure has now become supranational and must work out rules within the expanded structure. The war system is being challenged internally as never before, and law has already begun the delegalization of war. War is factually and philosophically dead. I have tried to show that processes of legal change may bury it.

4. *A Mature Society*. What has been said above envisions society as maturing, just as an individual matures. In this process old myths are discarded in favor of more sophisticated philosophical, sociological, and psychological principles. Maturity is a person's ability to manage his own affairs, not on the basis of external commands and directions, but in response to inner conscience. And a mature society, according to Erich Fromm, is one that is based on man's conscience and allows it full play. The time is crucial for a turn to conscience. Social historians such as Toynbee

and Sorokin, as well as pacifist philosophers, diagnose the present illness of society as decay of moral integrity or conscience. The most brutal of wars, response to the Negro and the poor by increased police power, imprisonment of our most conscientious young people suggest our present crisis of conscience.

Law has a particular interest in conscience. Criminal responsibility is imposed on the basis that the individual knows the difference between right and wrong. Conscience is precisely "that moral sense in man which dictates to him right and wrong." It is time the law recognize that it cannot make criminals of those who most actively follow conscience while it still depends upon conscience to give morality to its criminal law.

Conscientious objection is often used as a synonym for pacifism, though in fact it is much more restricted. But the philosophy of pacifism rests on conscience, and it offers the most extensive development of the theory of conscience. We therefore assert that this philosophy holds the greatest promise in creating the mature society. The pacifist conscience must be kept alive and encouraged—to lend content and adaptation to religion, morals, and ethics, to prevent a decline of civilization and a return to barbarism, to furnish a conscience for the state, to undergird the law, to produce good citizens and public officers, to vitalize democracy and freedom, to end the system of war.

I am aware that I claim much for the pacifist philosophy in all its tasks—but I see no other way for us to go in our choice between law and war.

NOTE

1. Ithaca, N.Y.: Norton. P. 21.

CHAPTER SEVENTEEN

The Technique of Nonviolent Resistance

R. Balasubramanian

Reader in Philosophy,
University of Madras, India

I

My aim in this chapter is to show that the technique of nonviolence as advocated by Gandhi is the most effective and the least expensive weapon for fighting against destructive war and violent conflict, and that it is only possible through individual commitment.

Gandhi provides us, not only with a blueprint for the internal organization of society, but also with an effective means, a novel technique by which it is to be implemented. The latter is more important than the former. It is no use to think of a new organization or transformation of the existing setup into something different and better unless one is very sure of the means, the technique, the strategy through which it is to be realized. Gandhi, therefore, is more concerned with the means than with the goal, without, however, losing sight of the goal. It must be emphasized that Gandhi does not view the problem of war and violence from the standpoint of national sovereignty or prestige, the art of diplomacy or statecraft. It is not a problem of the organization of one nation *vis-à-vis* another involving a clash of ideologies. It is basically a moral problem. Gandhi attempts to solve a political problem involving the destinies of the nations at the moral plane. If every society is properly and morally organized at the national level on the basis of nonviolence, there will be peace not only within among the people who constitute the society but also without with other neighboring nation-states.

To the question: "What is the cause of war?" Gandhi's unambiguous answer is exploitation. He points out that all activity for stopping war must prove futile so long as the causes of war are not understood and readily dealt with. According to his analysis, the prime cause of modern wars is the inhuman race for exploitation of the so-called weaker races of the earth.[1] He thinks that the motive of exploitation accounts not only for the outbreak of war between two states but also generally for the chaotic situation that prevails at the national and international levels.

A careful analysis of the Gandhian position will show that at a still deeper level there is another factor that serves to explain the inhuman race for exploitation, and that factor is selfishness. Exploitation is only the outer manifestation of the inward selfishness of the individual. When the selfishness of the individual is organized, systematically pursued, and given institutional form by a group of individuals of kindred interests, it culminates in class antagonism and class exploitation with all the attendant consequences.

War is a visible symbol of the physical force and violence in which the individual believes as the effective instrument for settling disputes and controversies that he thinks cannot be solved otherwise. Whether it is a physical fight between two individuals or groups of individuals, or whether it is a large-scale war involving nations, war must be traced to the individual who alone is responsible for it. It is not what takes place in spite of the individual and without an active participation by him. Gandhi attributes war to the brute in man, the lower nature that for the time being overwhelms the spirit that constitutes his higher nature and serves to distinguish him from other animals. The essential difference between man and the brute, according to Gandhi, is that the former can rise superior to the passions that he owns in common with the brute and, therefore, superior to the selfishness and violence that belongs to the brute nature and not to the immortal spirit of man. He says:

> Nonviolence is the law of our species as violence is the law of the brute. The spirit lies dormant in the brute and he knows no law but that of physical might. The dignity of man requires obedience to a higher law—to the strength of the spirit.[2]

II

Philosophers and peace lovers are earnestly in search of a moral equivalent of war that would embody the technical features of war minus its violence as the surest way to establish peace. The technique of *satyagraha* proposed by Gandhi with a view to meet the challenge of war operates on the basis of nonviolence. The guiding principle in his approach is that the means must be as good as the end. Since the means-end relation forms one continuous process, no true good can result from an immoral means: hence the appropriateness of nonviolent resistance as the alternative to war.

The nonviolent resistance that is the characteristic feature of *satyagraha* shares certain common features with the method of war, except for its violence, and is, therefore, a fit candidate to take the place of war. Since war is ultimately resorted to on the ground that it is an effective way of deciding issues, the alternative to it must have the required merits to face the challenge and pave the way for deciding the issues effectively. And the technique of nonviolent resistance fulfills the requirements. Four important features contribute to the effectiveness of the method of war: (1) force, (2) direct action, (3) organization, (4) number. The Gandhian technique of nonviolent resistance has all these features, and an intelligent and planned coordination of these factors is bound to prove successful.

1. Gandhi is of the view that nonviolent resistance is the mightiest force on earth. Being the force of the inward spirit in man, it knows no limit and requires no support or assistance from any quarter:

> It is a force that may be used by individuals as well as communities. It may be used as well in political as in domestic affairs. Its universal applicability is a demonstration of its permanence and invincibility.[3]

With that one can defy the whole might of an unjust empire.

2. It is a way of direct action. The expression "pacifism" or "passive resistance" does not bring out the full significance of the Gandhian technique. Gandhi is not in favor of the expression "passive resistance" because it conveys the idea of inaction on the part of the individual and also because it is interpreted as a weapon of the weak. It may sound paradoxical when Gandhi uses the expression "active nonviolence." What he means is that a champion of nonviolence cannot be indifferent to evil and injustice wherever they may be; his love of truth must find concrete expression in his activity. That is why he says that "no man could be actively nonviolent and not rise against social injustice no matter where it occurred."[4] With a deep insight into the sociology of conflict, Gandhi proposes direct action in a nonviolent way in order to bring about a radical change in the existing setup. This aspect of his technique is undoubtedly what brings him close to the revolutionaries who believe in direct action. But the difference between Gandhi and other revolutionaries is that, while he swears by nonviolence as the safest course, others preach the cult of violence as the unfailing weapon. Gandhi remarks:

> Those who have to bring about radical changes in human conditions and surroundings cannot do it except by raising a ferment in society. There are only two methods of doing this, violent and nonviolent. Violent pressure is felt on the physical being and it degrades him who uses it as it depresses the victim, but nonviolent pressure exerted through self-suffering, as by fasting, works in an entirely different way. It touches not the physical body, but it touches and strengthens the moral fibre of those against whom it is directed.[5]

3. Though nonviolent resistance can be practiced both by an individual and a group, organization is necessary when it is to meet an injustice affecting a vast number of individuals. Consider the magnitude of the task when it is a question of resisting unjust constituted authority or the aggression from a neighboring state. It is then a question of mobilizing the people to fight against the authority or the aggressor—which is similar to mobilizing the citizens in times of war. Educating the people in the practice of nonviolent resistance and organizing them into one disciplined unit are the essential prerequisites for the successful launching of *satyagraha* on a mass scale. In short, the organizational aspect of the *satyagraha* movement is closely parallel to that in the army. Gandhi's faith in organization, training, and discipline for starting a mass movement on a large scale is well brought out in his declaration: "I am not going to take a single step in noncooperation unless I am satisfied that the country is ready for the step."[6] It is his conviction that without proper discipline nonviolence can only be a veneer.

4. Though resistance on a large scale is necessary in order to meet aggression or to overthrow foreign domination, *mere number* is not going to add strength to the movement. *Satyagraha* is a *clean* fight and so it requires *clean* fighters. "In *Satyagraha* it is never the numbers that count; it is always the quality, more so when the forces of violence are uppermost."[7] Number is bound to be a decisive factor in

achieving the goal, if care is taken at the same time that the quality of the fighters is of a very high order.

There are more critics than admirers of the Gandhian technique; there are more admirers than sincere adherents of it. It is, therefore, necessary to examine this technique not only from the theoretical aspect but also from the standpoint of what it presupposes on the part of the individual who is to practice it.

No less a thinker than Karl Jaspers, who with a remarkable insight understands the basic position of Gandhi, has his own misgivings about the success of the Gandhian technique in the struggle against totalitarianism. He points out that we have reached a political situation where politics miserably fails us and that the way of politics needs another guidance. Our present political thinking, according to Jaspers, is radically wrong. The threat of the atom bomb cannot be met by removing the bomb alone; it can only be met by removing war, by establishing world peace. He argues that the ideal that in the long run wars might be waged without atom bombs, but with intimidation by the atom bomb, is an illusion.[8] Since there is a limit to pure politics, mankind can survive only if it allows itself to be guided by the *suprapolitical* element. Gandhi, says Jaspers, stunned the world as he fought force with nonviolence, basing his politics on religious, suprapolitical grounds. But according to Jaspers, the Gandhian method could succeed only in the atmosphere of British rule and for the limited purpose of Indian liberation. He concludes that "for the extremity of present world-wide realities Gandhi gives us no answer," and that "in the struggles against totalitarianism Gandhi's procedure would not be a political way but a way to certain doom."[9] Kingsley Martin voices the same difficulty. He asks: "Would Gandhi's technique have achieved the same measure of success if it had been the Germans or Japanese who occupied India?"[10] Since the success of Gandhi's technique depends at least in part on its moral effects on the enemy, it is to be doubted, according to Martin, whether it will be effective against an enemy who is ruthless.

Gandhi is not unaware of this criticism. There are two ways in which a nation can try to defend itself when it faces the threat of extermination by a mighty, unscrupulous power such as that of a Hitler: the ways of violence and of nonviolence. The folly of resistance by violence is obvious. Hitler cannot be defeated by counter-violence without a good deal of preparation for war, which means a heavy military budget and considerable loss of life. And still there is no guarantee that Hitler will be defeated. Further, the possibility of survival is very remote when there is nuclear warfare. But let us suppose that a nation that is pitched against Hitler offers nonviolent resistance, and that he has occupied the country without a bloody fight. He cannot, according to Gandhi, continue to stay on in that country if the people offer total noncooperation to him. Gandhi observes:

> At the back of the policy of terrorism is the assumption that terrorism if applied in a sufficient measure will produce the desired result, namely, bend the adversary to the tyrant's will. But supposing people make up their mind that they will never do the tyrant's will, nor retaliate with the tyrant's own methods, the tyrant will not find it worth his while to go on with his terrorism.[11]

The critics proceed on the assumption that dictators such as Hitler have no conscience and that they are incapable of moral response. But Gandhi argues that belief in nonviolence is based on the assumption that human nature in its essence is one and therefore unfailingly responds to the advances of love. It would be a novel experience for the Hitlers to face unarmed men, women, and children offering nonviolent resistance without any bitterness in their minds. It is sure to bring about a desirable change in their attitude.

Gandhi has another argument. "If Hitler is unaffected by my suffering, it does not matter. For I shall have lost nothing worth. My honour is the only thing worth preserving."[12] To Gandhi, nonviolence is a matter of principle, and so nonviolent practice is extremely significant to him. Either one resorts to the Machiavellian method of violence, brutality, and treachery, or one follows the path of nonviolence at all stages. There is no middle ground between the two. There is nothing that would suggest that the Gandhian method is theoretically unsound. Nor can it be ruled out on the hypothetical ground that it is unsuitable to meet the threat of totalitarian regimes without actually trying it out.

While admitting that violence is wrong as a matter of principle, Gandhi also maintains that it is the duty of everyone to resist it. But what is profoundly significant in the Gandhian position is the *manner* of resistance to violence. Resistance to violence by counter-violence is obviously wrong. A wrong cannot be righted by another wrong. The addition of another wrong does not diminish but adds to the evil already in existence. So violence must first be resisted by persuasion, and when persuasion fails, it must be resisted nonviolently. Critics very often fail to understand that nonviolent resistance of the Gandhian type is also a *force,* which is different from violence. The two words "violence" and "force" are used so frequently as interchangeable words that we fail to understand that force need not always be violent, that it can also be nonviolent. To Gandhi, nonviolent resistance is a force that repels force which is violent.

III

To Gandhi the individual alone is the one supreme consideration and all other things are valuable not in themselves but only as related to the personality of the individual.

Though an individual may aim at the personal good, he cannot realize it in isolation from the good of others. The good of the individual is not what is private to him; it is what is good to him as a member of the community of persons. It is a good to others as well, for they are also rational and moral agents like him. There is reciprocal relation between the individual and society. A society cannot advance unless the units composing it advance, and, conversely, no individual can advance without the society of which he is a part also advancing.[13]

Without being swayed by narrow prejudices and restricted loyalties, man, according to Gandhi, must show his allegiance to the entire humanity. It does not mean that one can ignore the claims of the immediate neighborhood, from the family to the nation. There is nothing in the logic of events that compels us to think in terms of one nation versus another. Every individual is called upon to play different roles—as a member of a family, of a working group, of a society that is politically organized, as a member of humanity. The claims of a higher group tend to fulfill and not to frustrate those of a lower. Nothing less than the ideal of universal human fellowship can satisfy the rational and moral agent. What is required in order to realize genuine human achievement is mutual service. The ideal that is worthy of human achievement is such that in its pursuit there can be no competition of interests.

If Gandhi declares that human society is one and undivided, whatever may be the social, political, economic, and religious compartments into which it is divided, it is because of his deep-rooted faith in the truth of nonduality (*advaita*).[14] He believes that all life in its essence is one, and that the human beings are working consciously or unconsciously toward the realization of that identity. The ideal that he envisages is universal interdependence, a federation of interdependent nations. No individual and no group of men could remain exclusive. Nor could they pursue a course of action destructive of the interests of others without jeopardizing their own interests. The first concrete step toward the realizing of the ideal is a willing and pure sacrifice for the betterment of the world by the individual. The ideal society can be brought into existence only on the foundation of responsible individuals devoted to truth and love and adhering to nonviolence. In short, individual commitment is what is presupposed by him, and if this requirement is fulfilled, neither the realization of a perfect society (or at least a near-perfect society) nor an effective nonviolent resistance to external aggression when it unfortunately takes place is impossible.

According to Errol Harris, the nonviolent approach to political issues is fallacious on the level of ethical principle insofar as it presupposes a morally regenerated individual, a perfected individual capable of acting on the basis of love and self-sacrifice, whereas such a being can come into existence only as a result of the proper maintenance of social and political order. Nonviolence, so he thinks, can be practiced only by a saint, a man of perfection. The level of morality on which he functions presupposes social and political order, but it can only be its culmination. In other words, what presupposes social and political order cannot be used to set right that very order. Harris concludes that nonviolence, pacifism proper, is beyond the realm of politics and is in effect the abandonment of political methods altogether. He thinks that we should have a political solution practicable in our time among fallible men and self-seeking nations.[15]

The objection seems to be convincing. But before we answer his criticism, it is worth considering the presupposition that lies hidden in the solution that he puts forward in order to face the challenging situation. Harris is convinced that world government is the solution to interstate war and international problems. Let us assume for the sake of argument that Harris's contention is sound. The important question to be considered then is: How are we to realize that ideal? Obviously, it cannot descend all on a sudden from the blue sky. It can be made a reality only when people with vision and a sense of realism work for it through stages. Harris suggests that we have to work for it through the modification of the doctrine of national sovereignty and the formation of regional organizations at the intermediary level between the nation-state and the world authority. He himself admits that this ideal of world government is bound to remain the most unpractical utopianism so long as people believe that their salvation and welfare depend on their sovereign independence. What, then, is the remedy? A change of attitude on the part of the people is necessary, but that is not sufficient. What is required in addition to this is sincerity to work it out. It may be called, in existential language, commitment on the part of the individual. But whose commitment is that? Though it cannot be denied that it is the commitment of fallible men, it is the commitment of those individuals who want to realize an ideal in which disinterested service must find an important place. If so, this phase of morality, contrary to what Harris maintains, is the precondition of any well-ordered social and political framework. It is not the case that men to start with are in a moral vacuum and that through the social order they acquire a moral stature. It is the capacity to conceive of, and contribute to, the common good that entitles the individuals to membership in a society, and this capacity, which is at the basis of social and political order, is undoubtedly moral as well as rational.

Whether the formation of world government is the effective solution to international tension is another issue. Since a very important source of trouble arises from centralization of authority in one place, it is to be seriously doubted whether it will be conducive to the preservation of the freedom and personal worth of the individual as well as the promotion of world peace. Our experience so far at the national level does not encourage us to think favorably of world government. If the centralization of power and authority in one place makes those who run the political machinery inefficient, indifferent, corrupt, and above all violent in all their practices, it is not going to make the position different when the authority of nation-states is replaced by the authority of world government. What is required is not a unitary authority but a plurality of authority functioning on the basis of nonviolence in all matters in harmony with one another. The ideal to be pursued is a federation of friendly interdependent states where the entire setup will be based on the principle of decentralization with nonviolence as the principle of action.

It is futile to think of institutional changes without changes in the attitude and conduct of the individuals. Institutional changes cannot be brought in by a few individuals. If they are bent on introducing those changes, they could do so only by violence, by making use of the political machinery. Such a radical change with a view to realizing some utopian ideal will be neither peaceful nor beneficial to the people at large. And also, how far the people at large are prepared for such a change is a question to be considered. Instead of starting with institutional changes of a radical nature in pursuance of some utopian plan, a beginning must be made to bring about a change in the outlook and conduct of the individual. This is necessary because the successful implementation of any social and political program depends upon the part to be played by the individual. It is necessary to bear in mind that the human factor is the ultimately uncertain and wayward element in social and political life. And so we must work for a steady and slow change in the attitude and conduct of the individual, for everything ultimately depends upon the actions and interactions, thoughts and aspirations of individual men. The successful implementation of the Gandhian technique depends on the willingness of the individual to commit himself for the chosen ideal with the attitude of "one step is enough for me." His manner of living will indicate his commitment. What he is and does are not without significance. The way to peace lies through peace.

NOTES

1. *Young India,* May 9, 1929.
2. *Ibid.,* Aug. 11, 1920.
3. *Selections from Gandhi,* ed. N. K. Bose (Ahmedabad: Navajivan Publishing House, 1948), p. 183.
4. *The Harijan,* Apr. 20, 1940.
5. Quoted in K. Sridharani, *War Without Violence* (Bombay: Bharatiya Vidya Bhavan), p. 255.
6. *Young India,* Aug. 18, 1920.
7. *The Harijan,* Mar. 25, 1939.
8. Karl Jaspers, *The Future of Mankind* (Chicago: The University of Chicago Press, 1961), p. 28.
9. *Ibid.,* p. 39.
10. Kingsley Martin, *War, History, and Human Nature* (Bombay: Asia Publishing House, 1959), p. 77.
11. *The Harijan,* Dec. 24, 1938.
12. *Ibid.,* Oct. 15, 1938.
13. *Young India,* Mar. 26, 1931.
14. *Ibid.,* Dec. 4, 1924.
15. Errol E. Harris, *Annihilation and Utopia* (London: George Allen & Unwin, 1966), pp. 132–133.

CHAPTER EIGHTEEN

The Revolution Against War

Robert S. Hartman

Research Professor of Philosophy, National University of Mexico, Mexico

I

It seems paradoxical, but the times of both war and peace are behind us. The time of war is behind us, for what threatens the human race is not war but extinction. War, according to Clausewitz, is the pursuit of national goals by force. National goals cannot be pursued by nuclear weapons that wipe out all nations. War thus has become self-contradictory, a self-contradiction epitomized in the already classic words: "It became necessary to destroy the town to save it." As the time of war, so the time of peace is behind us. What lies ahead—if anything does—is not the opposite of war, peace, but the opposite of death: life. To rid humanity of war there must be a new awareness, almost an explosion, of man's will to live. There must be an existential awakening.

Of the three riders of the Apocalypse, Pestilence, Famine, and War, the first is a natural evil to be overcome, and being overcome, by natural science. The second is partly a natural, partly a social, evil, to be overcome, and being overcome, by both natural science (revolutionary agricultural techniques) and social revolution. The third is a purely human evil, created by man, to be overcome by a revolution of man's own self-awareness, a moral revolution that must produce a new man, sensitive to the immorality of war and not deceived by the slogans used to justify it.

Even this revolution is on the way. Mankind is revolting against, and being revolted by, war as never before in history. The reason is in part technological—television has brought the horrors of war into the living room—and in part moral. There is an awakening to the futility of violence in general, and an understanding of the suicidal nature of nuclear violence in particular. There is an awareness that the life of mankind, its existence, is in the balance. The revolution against war thus is an existential revolution, born out of the anxiety for the life of man on earth.

The natural dangers of life, even its social dangers, are being contained by powerful ramparts of human organization, especially the state. But the state is a gigantic Dr. Jekyll and Mr. Hyde. While it is a fortress against natural and social evil, it is at the same time the creator of human evil. While the Department of Health, Education, and Welfare develops ingenious means for prolonging life on earth, the Department of Defense, with the same ingenuity, develops the means for its destruction. While the Department of Agriculture advises farmers how to improve their livestock, the Pentagon kills 6,000 sheep with a wind-borne nerve gas.

This poses a clear lesson: We have to develop the civil departments of the state while getting rid of the military. We have to kill Mr. Hyde and help along Dr. Jekyll. And we must be more successful than Stevenson's hero. We must, first of all, learn clearly to distinguish between those of the state's features that are beneficial and those that are detrimental; between the state as an administrative unit and the state as "sovereign," as supreme ruler of our lives and deaths, above the moral law. We must learn to understand that while the civil function of the state is legitimate, its military function is illegitimate. If the state is to grow today, it must do so intensively, not extensively, qualitatively, not quantitatively. In the first sense, it is the servant of the people and its welfare; in the second, it is the manipulator of its life and death. The latter is the function of sovereignty. Secreted away in the landscape and cityscape of the nations are the instruments of war, and among their peaceful citizens walk those who serve these machines. The combination of men and machines of the sovereign state is the most powerful complex in the world. It is geared to death, and it can turn everything state and society stand for to ashes in the wink of an eye. It is a vehicle of catastrophe. Thus, and this is the second thing we must be clear about, as long as the state continues its sovereign function we are living under the shadow of instant catastrophe. Our life is poised on a sword's tip. The old Socratic word that the unexamined life is not worth living is literally true today. Unless we examine this precarious life of ours, we may lose it any moment, and such a life *is not* worth living.

The Greek word "catastrophe" means "sudden turn": the sudden turn that ends everything. Only in a few situations are we conscious of the possibility of catastrophe, as in an airplane. Sometimes, as in the Greek tragedy, we see the noose of fate being tied slowly, knot by knot, and although we see with clear eyes the threatening fate, we feel powerless to escape it. Generally, however, we live without the presentiment of catastrophe. Our life goes its tranquil course—or at least we think it does.

Actually, we are too busy with the tasks of everyday life to have either time or desire to reflect on what a shaky base rests our daily life, how finely all its elements are balanced, how exactly the earth must circle around the sun, how precisely the currents of air and water, how sun and rain, and the whole of nature must keep itself in balance to make possible our existence. A little more heat and we burn up;

a little more cold and we freeze to death; a small fissure in the crust of the earth and we fall into the abyss and our houses bury us.

All these are natural risks of our existence. We all unite in order to prevent such disasters or, if they happen, to soften their impact. The state is nothing but an insurance company that mobilizes the means of all in order to help those in misfortune. We all pay the policeman at the street corner in the hope that we shall never need him, just as we pay our insurance premiums in the hope never to have to claim them. We are happy when our money profits others. On some of the houses in my village in Bavaria is written: "Saint Florian, protect our town, pass by my house, burn others down." ("*Oh heiliger Sankt Florian, verschon' mein Haus, zünd and're an.*") We want to have nothing to do with disaster, we leave it to the others. We recognize its possibility theoretically and protect ourselves routinely. We leave its coming to statistics and are convinced that it does not concern us. Our own life is well ordered, somehow protected, we believe, through the rationality that, thank God, is inherent in the world and the course of our own life. We take the good times as our due and are desperate when misfortune hits, instead of being grateful for every minute of happiness. We believe that our life is safe. In this belief rests our security and our happiness.

Suppose we would start with the thought that our existence is precarious, uncertain, and that every happy moment is an unexpected present. In this case, we would not take the everyday occurrences of life as matters of course. Our whole life would take on a new dimension, one of gratitude toward a kind fate or God or a Power that watches over us and protects us against evil. We would not only live but experience every moment; we would be aware continuously of the limits that are set to our existence. We would perceive our existence as a limit situation in the sense that every moment could be the last—although, thank God, it is not. Limit situations, say the existential philosophers, are situations in which man collides with the inevitable, final, and inexplorable limits of his being: guilt, death, fate, chance. In such situations, we become conscious of our own existence, which otherwise we take for granted, and all our values take on a different hue. Our whole life, as a limit situation, would be under the species of eternity—in the consciousness of the infinity that surrounds our own finiteness.

When we ask people what they think is the main thing in their lives, we get all kinds of answers. Knowledge, love, money, success, health, but rarely the answer that existentially is the only correct one: *the main thing of my life is that I live it,* the fact that *I am,* that I was born, brought into this world. This *substance* of our existence we forget and are content with some *qualities of* this existence: money, love, success, etc. But all these are possible only under the condition that *I am.* If I am not, all these qualities and gifts are not either. Qualities *of* existence are only possible when there is existence itself. Therefore, to concentrate on qualities and forget the substance that alone can have these qualities means concentrating on the nonessential and forgetting the essential. He who lives a life that forgets existence and concentrates on not life itself but its accessories does not truly live; in the existential sense, he vegetates. Instead of living, as the existential philosophers say, he is merely around, he has not life but *Dasein,* being there, being thrown into this world by chance. And when he dies he has contributed nothing to the world. He will, after a longer or shorter presence here, simply disappear, eliminated from the world, so to speak, as indigestible; for the world is one large organism that is being existentially nourished by those who truly live. If such nourishment through true living does not take place, if people are just around, like things, then the world itself dies off. We call this degeneration, decadence, decline, and historically it has happened to all civilizations—Egypt, Greece, Rome—and it may now be happening to us.

It is therefore not a matter of indifference how we live; for our true life is a contribution to the life of all. If we are not concerned about our own selves, we neglect not only ourselves. We neglect in ourselves all others. If we do not love ourselves, says Jesus, we cannot love our neighbors either. And if, says Kant, we neglect humanity in our selves, we neglect humanity in all.

At the times of Jesus and Kant, these admonitions were just as true as they are today, but they were not of vital necessity in the sense that today my neglect of myself could mean literally the death of all my fellow men, of my own family, my children, and my children's children. Then I could neglect myself and waste my life and yet not immediately drag down the whole world with me. The welfare and misery of my fellow men were not immediately dependent upon my own spiritual well-being—unless I was a leader of peoples, a general, or a politician whose moods and caprices could lead thousands and millions into misery and disaster. And even in such situations, the individual had always the possibility of avoiding the disaster. As Hegel has said, the juggernaut of history destroys only those who don't get out of the way. Almost the entire population of North America consists of the offspring of those who got out of the way of the juggernaut of European history. The human situation, in other words, up to now never was a limit situation. What was limited were the catastrophies. And even though there often were some sudden turns, through natural or historical powers, even though often hundreds of thousands, indeed millions, had to die together, even though their individual death, the most private act there is for each of us, was a spectacle of collective powers, there have always been places on this globe where the quiet, well-thought-out plan of daily life, the sequence of day and night, the rhythm of the seasons went its balanced course, through the months and years, and where men, women and children could live their daily lives for three and four score years.

All this has now ended. All of us are in a limit situation in which we depend so much one on the other that, if we do not all see the existential dimension of our situation, we shall all die together. As in Greek tragedy, the fates are spinning the thread and, turn by turn, are entwining us in the web. And, as in the tragedy, we are all either too blind to see the unavoidable fate that is being prepared for us, or, if we see it, too powerless to avert it. Unlike the persons of the Greek drama, however, we are not the creation of a poet, we make the drama ourselves. We are ourselves the poets of our fate. And with open eyes and hearts we could, through our own action, ward off the disaster and turn what threatens to be catastrophe into abundant life.

II

The catastrophe that threatens to engulf us is the result of a well-defined shortcoming of man, an incapacity of organization that philosophers for two and a half millennia have clearly seen. Unfortunately, philosophers have never yet had the power to do anything about it. They have never been able to influence the state, our insurance against disaster and organ of our disaster. Socrates's words in the *Republic* are as true today as they were then: "Unless either the philosophers are kings in the states or the rulers of the states have the spirit and insight of philosophers, and thus both coincide, the power in the state and philosophy, there will be no end to the misfortunes of the states nor, I believe, of the human race." States, says Plato, must be built on *dikaiosyne*—justice, as it is often translated. A better translation would be "correctness," for *dike* means "correct judgment." States must be built on correctness, and correctness, in the Platonic definition, means everyone doing his own. Everyone should dedicate himself to one activity in the service of the state, to that, namely, to which he is best suited. Unfortunately, and that is the core of the evil that overtakes states, the most important places in the state are occupied by those who are least capable to fill them. The reason for the misfortune of states, says Plato, is that two types of persons are wrongly placed, the politicians and the philosophers. The politicians are people with small thoughts in big situations, and the philosophers are people with big thoughts in small situations. The education of the philosopher-statesman, or statesman-philosopher, is the solution to this unhappy situation. It puts the man with big thoughts into the big situation and the man with small thoughts into the small situation. In the transposition of these two types and their places in the state lies the necessity of catastrophe. This is the moral of the parable of the pilot. The ship of state is being thrown hither and yon on the waves of the sea, between the rocks of the narrows and the whirlpools of the deep, and there is nobody who can steer it. The captain is taller and fatter than the rest of the crew, but somewhat deaf and near-sighted and equally defective in the art of navigation. The sailors fight for the wheel, each thinking he can steer the ship, although he has never learned the art of navigation and cannot name a master who could have taught him. Indeed, they proclaim that the art of navigation cannot be learned on principle and tear to pieces everyone who says the opposite. They fight among themselves, fetter each other in red tape, hit each other over the head with bottles, throw each other overboard, overpower the captain with beer and wine, tear the steering wheel out of his hand, plunder the stores, and make the trip a wild orgy. The ship groans and creaks and desperately plows its way through the waves until it founders on the rocks and sinks into the deep. There is only one man aboard who is unconcerned about it all. He sits in a corner, his knees pulled up to his chin, looking up to the sky. Nobody bothers about him, and he is thought the ship's fool. He is the philosopher. He is the only one who could steer the ship, for he studies its course in the stars. He is the pilot.

The whole gigantic work of Plato consists in inventing methods by which the philosopher could take the wheel of the state and in planning the education the philosopher must have for this purpose. It makes nice reading, and a hundred generations have had their pleasure with it while the politicians were busy ruining the states. Not one state since antiquity has lasted until today. One after another has gone down in the waves of history. Today, humanity itself faces extinction. The world situation has become so big that politics and philosophy cannot be separated anymore. The politician, in order not to see his state annihilated, must be a philosopher, and the philosopher, in order not to allow his politicians to annihilate him, must be a statesman. *The situation of the philosopher, the universe itself, has become the situation of the state,* and thus that of the politician. This situation, up to now, had been limited to small states, from the Greek *polis* to the City of Rome and its empire, which still was only a small part of the world, to the feudal rules and the national states, still only fragments of humanity. All these forms of states are today fused into a unity, a comm*unity,* linked together for better and for worse. The inventions of the natural philosophers, from Galileo to Einstein, have produced weapons that do not stop at the borders of their own states or those of their enemy states; they expand over the whole world of mankind. We are all, not legally but actually, members of one single community, linked together in one common fate, for life and for death.

In this new situation the old organization of states and nations is obsolete. We have to think in new categories. The sanction for our failure to do so is that we will all die together, in the collision of nations with which our own state may have nothing in common except that it exists on the same earth with them. The whole earth in its course around the sun is the new ship of state. Who can and should steer it? Where is the stellar map that charts the *political* course of the planet? What is the accident that may cause the death of all of us, and how can it be avoided?

Plato's solution was fundamentally simple and easy to realize. But nobody took it seriously. The Athenian cities, the Roman so-called empire, the feudal and the national states, all were too small to recognize the necessity of the philosopher-statesman. But today it is obvious that the situation is so tremendous that it can no longer be mastered by politicians. During the Cuban crisis, Kennedy and Khrushchev wrote each other letters actually imploring the other to restrain himself and not lose control of the situation. The situation was in imminent danger of getting out of their control. They were both at the terrible threshhold of catastrophe when the rational is being overtaken by the irrational, the horrible situation of the pilot who suddenly feels that his plane does not obey him and, uncontrolled, an object of gravitation, is crashing to earth. In natural catastrophies, it is the force of natural gravitation that brings the disaster. In artificial situations, as those of the state, it is the force of artificial gravitation that brings the disaster. *The total situation of artificial gravitation is war.* It transforms everything into throwing and falling, makes the whole machinery of the state into a gigantic slingshot, a catapult of projectiles and grenades, fires and gases. Into this machinery Kennedy and Khrushchev saw their state disintegrate. It was in the process of slipping into the control of the masters of gravitation: the military. Both Kennedy and Khrushchev made desperate and only just successful attempts to keep the control of the situation in their own civilian hands and not let it fall into the hands of the military, the professionals of destruction. With one single accidentally or intentionally loosed atom bomb the whole world would have gone up in flames. As a result of this situation we have today the partial nuclear test ban and the direct so-called hot line between Washington and Moscow, an almost desperate recognition of the threatening danger and the uncontrollable machinery of the state—a thin lifeline of our civilization.

The Cuban crisis was for Khrushchev and Kennedy the limit situation in which they saw the abyss, the end of the world, open under their feet. Perhaps it changed them from politicians to statesmen. In any case, it gave them the existential dread. When we later read their correspondence, we learned that they were almost helpless—pilots of the ship of state that they had never learned to steer, engineers of a machinery of cosmic range the laws of which they did not understand. The present rulers of the state are in no better position; they are all in the position of Plato's captain. We are all ruled by the machinery of the state, servants of the megamachine, instead of being its masters and ruling it.

III

We shall now describe this machine.

During Hitler's war, bombs with the explosive power of one million tons were dropped *on Germany* alone. In all World War II, on *all* fronts, in seven years, five million tons of explosives were exploded out of rifles, guns, planes, and tanks.

The United States today has in stock, ready for use, bombs with an explosive power not of one or of two Hitler wars, not of five or of ten, of fifty or a hundred, not of five hundred or one thousand, not of two thousand or three thousand, but of four thousand Hitler wars.[1] Russia will soon match this capacity. Together, the United States and Russia have or will shortly have the explosive power of eight thousand Hitler wars. This explosive power grows every moment, it has been growing since you began reading. In Hitler's war, fifty-four million men, women, and children were killed. In order to annihilate the whole of humanity the explosive power of sixty Hitler wars would be sufficient. Instead of this, we have eight thousand Hitler wars in stock. The world can be destroyed by the United States and Russia today some one hundred and sixty-seven times. According to the Pentagon, it takes four hundred megatons to wreck Russia. The United States thus can annihilate Russia not once or twice, or twenty, but fifty times. Americans have an overkill capacity of 5,000 per cent.[2] And Russia can, or soon will be able to, destroy the United States often, with the same overkill capacity. Moreover, the nuclear weapon is only one of the three ABC weapons stockpiled by the state: atomic, bacteriological, chemical. The so-called scientists of war do not speak anymore of deaths and of losses in war, but of megadeaths, corpsemillions, or millioncorpses. A single Polaris submarine missile has the explosive power of one million tons of TNT, or as much explosive power as was dropped over Germany in the whole of Hitler's war. A Polaris submarine has sixteen such missiles. A single Polaris submarine thus has the firepower of more than three total Hitler wars. The United States alone has been building about fifty such ships, so that the entire Hitler war is represented by less than 1 per cent of the American Polaris fleet, and the Polaris fleet is only a small part of the U.S. nuclear weapons arsenal. Yet its power is not big enough for the admirals; the new Poseidon missile will *multiply* the striking force of Polaris.

At the same time, the Russians are building the same kind of ships with the same kind of bombs. Hitler in all his fiendishness had yet only a fraction of the destructive power that good men and earnest politicians, such as Kennedy, were in all seriousness and all goodwill prepared to shoot off in the name of freedom—as would Breshnev and Kosygin and Nixon. And the partial nuclear test ban was only possible because it did *not* limit the production of these bombs.

Once exploded, these bombs destroy not only the country against which they are directed but the whole world. In particular, like a boomerang, because of the air currents in the northern hemisphere, they destroy the country that fires them. Thus, if the United States were ever to use its arsenal against Russia, Russia would not have to retaliate in order to destroy the United States. The air currents would do the job. The same goes for Russia. Thus, if war is the pursuit of national goals by force, it is obvious that we cannot speak anymore of war. National goals cannot be pursued by nuclear weapons. Rather, we are involved in the preparation of a suicide, indeed a murder orgy; for innocent and uninvolved countries would be destroyed: Canada, Iran, Sweden, Mexico. In the words of Dr. Sandoval Vallarta, the head of the Mexican Atomic Energy Commission: "Mr. MacNamara is very optimistic. He says that in an atomic war nine out of ten Americans will die. No, ten out of ten will die—and six out of ten Mexicans." At a simulated atomic attack on the United States ten years ago, on October 17, 1958, with only fifteen hundred megatons—and Russia has already ten times that many nuclear weapons stockpiled—the winds over Mexico were so full of radioactive fallout, of 600, 400, and 200 roentgen Strontium 90 (each of these doses is fatal to the population) and covered the country so completely that only a minority would have survived. There is actually no salvation in the case of such a war for any country in the northern hemisphere. We would all die together. In this small attack, according to the calculations, 90 per cent of the American people died. A nuclear attack, let alone an exchange of medium intensity today, would kill more than nine-tenths of all people in the northern hemisphere, communists and capitalists without distinction.

Such a mass destruction of humanity, of course, can no longer be called "war." War up to now has been a well-defined act between the military forces of two nations, the aim of which was to destroy the military forces of the enemy. Hitler's was the first war where large parts of the civil population were destroyed, the first genocidal war. In an atomic war not only the civilian population of the war-making powers but also those of the non-warring would be destroyed. Such a war then would not be a war between two nations but a crime against humanity. It is therefore nonsensical to speak of nuclear "war." There is only nuclear world destruction. The notion of war is not usable anymore. There is a sickness of rats where a tooth grows through the palate into the nose, through the nose into the eye, through the eye into the brain, killing the animal. Such a monster tooth of course cannot be called a "tooth." Its gigantic growth destroys its purpose. So it is with the weapons of today. Their gigantic growth has destroyed their purpose.

It is also nonsensical today to speak of defense in connection with nuclear weapons. We can only speak of destruction. When, for example, we say that Berlin, Korea, or California would be "defended" with nuclear weapons, what we actually say is that they would be destroyed by nuclear weapons; for after such a "defense" what we would want to defend would not exist anymore. Consider Vietnam, where not even nuclear weapons have been used. One one-hundred-megaton bomb over Germany, one over France, and one over Britain, strategically placed, would destroy the whole of Europe. It is nonsense for NATO to speak of the nuclear defense of Europe. Nuclear "defense" can only destroy the "defended." When Confucius was asked how he thought to create order and morality in the state, his answer was: "By correcting names," meaning, by calling each thing by its correct name. This is the same that Plato meant when he gave the prescription that everyone should do and think his own. To every situation we must give the corresponding concept. What is called *defense* today is *destruction.* Whenever we hear or read the word "defense," we should put instead the word "destruction." And whenever we hear or read the word "war," we should put instead "the end of the world." Then we would see that we are speaking not of the defense of freedom, but of its destruction; not of the defense of our country, but of its destruction; not of war, but of the end of the world. The war ministries are ministries of the end of the world, the defense ministries destruction ministries and, in particular, self-destruction ministries.

A nuclear policy for a big country such as the United States and Russia is suicide; for a small country such as France or Germany, hardly larger than Nevada or Wisconsin, it is a folly that is greater even than Hitler's. During the aerial attacks on Dresden and Hamburg there arose fire storms that sucked the air out of the air-raid shelters, tore the children from the hands of their parents, and seared the lungs of those who believed they had escaped the flames. In these fire storms three hundred thousand men, women, and children died in Dresden, in Hamburg, eighty thousand. The fire storms were the result of attacks with fifteen hundred tons of TNT, that is, of attacks that had 7 per cent of the power of the Hiroshima bomb—and one thousandth of 1 per cent of the power of one one-hundred-megaton bomb. The fire storm caused by a hundred megaton bomb would have a diameter of one hundred miles. Two such bombs exploded over Philadelphia would burn out Philadelphia, New York, Harrisburg, Baltimore, and Washington. They would make the ocean boil fifty miles from shore. Two such bombs would be sufficient to burn out the state of Tennessee. The Pentagon calls such destruction of all life and civilization "considerable thermal damage," and in the Kremlin they have similar euphemisms. They serve to build these figments of hell into the system of power politics, and to dim the minds of the nuclear citizens.

The fiendish evil of an atomic war is either not being recognized or being passed over in silence or trivialized. Thus, for example, A. F. Shinn, radiation ecologist of the Civil Defense Research Project's Agriculture Team, whose work began in 1965, said in Oak Ridge on February 3, 1968, after two years of intensive study, that "freshwater fish may be one answer to a sufficient protein diet for the U.S. population following a nuclear attack, research indicates. Although no prolonged shortage of raw or processed food stuffs is likely in such an emergency, temporary deficits will occur in some areas." He forgot to mention only two details: (1) that the freshwater fish will be radioactive, and (2) that there will be no people left to enjoy them.

Another so-called expert on nuclear war, Herman Kahn, in discussing the genetic dangers of fallout says in his *On Thermonuclear War* that it is not so important if a few million children in future generations would be born with withered limbs *"if that meant not giving up Europe to Soviet Russia."* "War," says this expert, "is a terrible thing; but so is peace."

IV

Obviously, we have here a very special kind of mind and morality: the so-called *raison d'état*, the reason of state, that is diametrically opposed to common sense judgment and human morality. The reason of state is the morality of those who put the state above people; human morality is the morality of those who put people above the state. Jefferson once said there never is so much wrong arithmetic used as in the justification of war. This is especially true today. Thus, an atomic physicist, Edward Teller, in his book *The Legacy of Hiroshima*, in all seriousness makes the following so-called calculation: The total national wealth of the United States is fifteen hundred billion dollars. The United States can produce five hundred billion dollars' worth of goods a year. Therefore, if the nation should be wiped out in an atomic war, the survivors could in three to five years restore what has been lost. Teller does not see the development of thousands of years that led to the tremendous productive apparatus of five hundred billion, now eight hundred billion, a year, nor can he imagine the miserable plight of the survivors, if any. They, as President Truman said, would envy the dead. Teller believes quite simply that these crazed and wandering hordes could keep up the production of the vanished United States. Another atomic physicist, Ralph A. Lapp, in his book *Kill and Overkill*, says one can only admire the elegant simplicity of Teller's arithmetic. According to Teller's argument, the old Greeks, with what they knew and just a few essential instruments, would have been able within five years to jump into the twentieth century.

What is amazing is that thinking such as Teller's is being printed, read, and believed. Such thinking is an example of what Ortega y Gasset calls the thinking of the "specialized barbarian." In *The Revolt of the Masses*, Ortega says that scientists and politicians live in our civilization as unconcerned as savages in the primeval forest. Like the savages, the politicians take everything around them for granted. They do not stop to realize that it was the thought and sweat of millions of people through hundreds of generations that created today's civilization. These scientists and politicians live, Ortega says, without the sense of time, like savages—and, we may add, like criminals. The criminal has no sense of time. What others have achieved in the long and hard labor of a lifetime they believe they can seize in a short and violent act and hold with the same justification. They have no respect for the past and no concept of the future. To build up, says Ortega, one needs the sense of time, the feeling of what he calls the Project, the plan to be worked out in a lifetime. The good takes time, the bad can be done in a moment. To create a life takes nine months and many years of growth and education; to snuff it out takes a second.

What is true for the life of the individual is also true for the life of collective bodies. He who does not have the sense of time believes that civilization grows by itself like the primeval forest. In Chapter X of his book, entitled "Primitivism and History," Ortega says that those who enjoy the blessings of civilization without bothering to maintain civilization will at the flick of a hand be left without civilization. The modern barbarian believes that the civilization into which he was born is as spontaneous and self-producing as is nature, "and ipso facto he is changed into primitive man." For him, civilization is the forest. The basic values of culture are of no interest to him, and he has no contact with them. Hence the disproportion between the complex subtlety of the problems and the coarseness of the minds that should study them. It is painful, says Ortega, to hear relatively cultured people discuss the most elementary problems of the day. They seem like rough farmhands trying with thick, clumsy fingers to pick up a needle lying on the table. Political and social subjects are handled with the same rude instruments of thought as served two hundred years ago to tackle situations two hundred times less complex. In Chapter XII, "The Barbarism of 'Specialization,' " he speaks of the so-called intellectuals, educated professionals who believe that because they understand one subject, they understand all. Today's scientist, says Ortega, is the prototype of the mass man. The scientific man, because he has to reduce the sphere of his interest, progressively loses contact with other branches of science and thus the integral interpretation of the universe that alone deserves the name of science.

As a specialist, the scientist becomes the modern barbarian, a knowledgeable ignoramus who hides behind his specialty. Knowing well his own tiny corner of the universe and being radically ignorant of the rest, he is particularly dangerous today because he can use the state itself for his barbaric ends. The state, says Ortega, has in our time become a tremendously powerful machine that, owing to the quantity and precision of its means, works with marvelous efficiency. The mass man will be inclined more and more to use the machine for his own ends. The state is as soulless as himself, and thus he is convinced that he is the state. What is good for him and his corporate masters is good for the state. He confuses the state with society. He will more and more tend to set its machinery in motion, on whatsoever pretext, to crush beneath it any creative minority that disturbs him—politically, ideologically, or economically. Since, however, the state is in the last instance only a machine the maintenance of which depends on precisely these creative powers of society, the state itself, by misusing and sucking the marrow out of society, will die the rusty death of a machine—a death, says Ortega, that is more cadaverous than that of a living organism. The state will become one gigantic junk pile.

All this, says Ortega y Gasset, has happened before. It was the pitiable fate of antiquity.

> Already at the time of the Antonines [2nd Century], the state overwhelms society with its anti-vital supremacy. Society

> begins to be enslaved, to be unable to live except *in the service of the state.* The whole of life is bureaucratized. What results? The bureaucratization of life brings about its absolute decay in all orders. Wealth diminishes, births are few. Then the State, in order to attend to its own needs, forces on still more the bureaucratization of human existence. *This bureaucratization to the second power is the militarization of society.* The State's most urgent need is its apparatus of war, its army. First of all, the State is the producer of security (that security, be it remembered, of which the mass-man is born). Hence, above all, an army. The Severi, of African origin, militarize the world. Vain task! Misery increases, women are every day less fruitful, even soldiers are lacking. After the time of the Severi, the army has to be recruited from foreigners.
>
> Is the paradoxical, tragic process of Statism now understood? Society, that it may live better, creates the State as an instrument. Then the State gets the upper hand and society has to begin to live for the State. . . . This is what State intervention leads to: The people are converted into fuel to feed the mere machine which is the State. The skeleton eats up the flesh around it. The scaffolding becomes the owner and tenant of the house.

What happened in Rome and brought about the fall of the Roman Empire is, says Ortega, also the greatest danger for human society today: the state itself. The title of Chapter XIII is "The Greatest Danger: The State." The greatest danger that threatens society—and this was written forty years ago, before World War II—and civilization today is the state. It meddles with everything, absorbs all spontaneous social life, especially in the militarized countries, where opposition to the state's often ill-advised and ruinous adventures is called treason. Ortega's analysis was clairvoyant. Today, in Russia and in the United States, one sees exactly the same development as in Rome. The apparatus of the state sucks into itself the life of society and its vital resources. What was means becomes end. The state, founded in order to enhance the life of society, draws the forces of society onto itself to expand its own existence. Bureaucracy becomes its own end. The military apparatus grows only in order to grow, like the rat's "tooth." Such transposition of means and end is in ethics called *metentelosis*, the means becoming end. In the United States and in Russia the military apparatus devours the society that it is supposed to defend.

Both the Western and the Eastern nations today use a large percentage of their internal capital formation for military purposes. In Mexico, a sane country, this expenditure amounts to 5 per cent. In the United States, it is 60 per cent, in Great Britain 42 per cent, in France 35 per cent, in the Soviet Union 34 per cent, and in Greece, Czechoslovakia, Poland, East Germany, West Germany, etc., between 30 and 16 per cent. Both the Eastern and the Western worlds today are warfare states. The military budgets of the five nuclear nations are as big as *the total gross national product of all the world's developing nations together*. All this can only lead, as in the case of Rome, to bankruptcy or to war, or to both. As in Rome, we see how the value of money declines, the balance of payments worsens, hidden unemployment increases; for in spite of unheard-of production the largest part of it is unproductive and consists of arms. The civilian society stagnates; schools, hospitals, roads, housing, all that makes the life of the individual materially worth while is sucked up by the behemoth of war—and more and more it sucks up life itself. At the same time, the production of weapons increases, by up to 40 per cent a year. On August 13, 1963, the Secretary of Defense (that is, of Destruction) of the United States told a Senate committee, in order to justify the partial nuclear test ban, that production of nuclear bombs in the last two years had risen by 100 per cent. What did this mean? It meant that two years before the United States could destroy Russia only twelve times and that then it could do so twenty-four times. It meant that in 1961 the United States had stockpiled only one thousand Hitler wars and in 1963 two thousand. In the same way, the Soviet Union doubled its intercontinental ballistic missile force in 1966. In 1967, it could destroy the United States twenty times while it could do so only ten times at the beginning of 1966.

This mad logic is the logic of the reason of state. It is a logic of irrationality, that is, of rationalization. Those who are caught in it have their own jargon. They speak of survivability and *vitality,* not of people but *of bombs.* Our hardened nuclear missile sites have survivability and vitality, that is, they are capable of surviving *us.* When we are all dead, our desolate land will be capable of spitting out bombs against Russia, and we will have the consolation of dying in the knowledge that the others will die too.

So-called nuclear politics rests on a fundamental contradiction. We trust that the enemy will be deterred by our weapons from making war. But this can only be the case if he is rational. And if he is rational, he can be persuaded. We don't need weapons; we can make treaties with him. However, even if he is rational, he *may not* be deterred, as Russia could not deter Kennedy in 1962 (even though the Cuban missiles were no closer to us than the Turkish missiles were to Russia). *The reason of state itself is irrational, so that no rational argument holds within it.* Nuclear power cannot be "balanced," just as the balance of power has failed throughout history, most recently in 1914 and 1939. If ever a madman, such as Hitler, came to power in a nuclear nation, he would only have to push a button in order to have his boldest dreams of chaos surpassed by mad reality. The situation, far from being one of deterrence, is, on the contrary, an irresistible invitation for madmen—for the crew of Plato's ship of state.

The whole history of so-called power politics rests on a logical fallacy and its course has been correspondingly disastrous.

V

In the Preamble to the Constitution of UNESCO, the United Nations Educational, Scientific and Cultural Organization, we read the famous words: "Since wars begin in the minds of men, it is in the minds of men that the defences of peace must be constructed." Pope John XXIII says in *Pacem in Terris* that braking the armament race and eliminating it is impossible unless disarmament is so complete and efficient that it includes the minds of men. Every single person, says the pope, must in his own heart stamp out the fear and nightmare of war. This, he says, is only possible if it is understood that true and secure peace between nations consists not in a balance of terror but in mutual trust. In other words, the battlefield of peace is in the heart of man.

When the United States was founded, it relied on its distance from power politics represented by the Atlantic Ocean. Today this distance has shrunk. The distance from power politics must now be found in the heart of each of us. Peace now is a matter of morality, not of weaponry. Politics itself must be overcome. The sovereign national state is obsolete both in concept and in reality. Its power consists exclusively in the obedience of its own citizens. As soon as the citizens understand completely the suicidal game that is being played with them, they will simply refuse to play. At that moment the military state will break down and the civil society, human life itself, will become sovereign. Existence itself will come into its own. As Jacques Maritain says in his book *Man and the State*, every citizen of a warlike nation-state is a vassal of this state. He must liberate himself from it and not lend it the force of his life. The sovereign of life is not the state but the individual person under God.

The sovereign state is a fetish that puts the state in the place of God—the same lethal blasphemy committed by the Roman Emperors, and particularly by Constantine, who put himself at the head of the Church—a lure and a trap from which Christianity has never recovered. Reason of the state must be replaced by moral reason, the immorality of the state by the morality of the human person. We must put ourselves consciously above the military state and make the state our servant, not our master. We must think in civilian, not in military, terms. Thus, instead of spending thirty billion dollars a year for the destruction of the South Vietnamese, we could spend this amount for their instruction and production. This would give $2,000 to every man, woman, and child, in a country where the average annual income is $113. We could make them all rich—and rich people don't become Communists. But such creative solutions are beyond the military mind that rules us, indeed, beyond our own military-mindedness. We would never give thirty billion dollars to a tiny country such as South Vietnam. It just isn't worth it. But it *is* worth it if we can use the money to destroy it. Then, suddenly, South Vietnam is a very important country.

In a word, we love war better than peace.

There are two reasons for this, one of cognition and one of will. The first is that we do not really know what peace is. We know what war is because natural science today is largely the science of war. We know how to wage war, but we do not know how to wage peace. There is no science of peace. The reason is that the philosophers of the Renaissance and the Enlightenment developed only natural, but not moral, philosophy into science. Yet their true purpose was moral knowledge. Before the minds of the philosophical interpreters of natural science and its mathematical foundations, Descartes and Leibniz, there stood with great clarity the vision of a Science of Value, or as it was then called, a Moral Science, to be established by the side of natural science and based, like it, on the *mathesis universalis,* which today is called logic. Descartes's goal was to reformulate not only a natural science but also a "mathematical morality: that was the bold program. Nothing in the development and the system of Descartes can be rightly understood unless this is understood." For Leibniz the differential calculus was only part of a large calculus of universal logic applicable to all the sciences and humanities, so that "two philosophers who disagreed about a particular point instead of arguing fruitlessly would take out their pencils and calculate." As for Descartes and Leibniz, so for the other philosophers of that great age: the science of morality presented itself based on the methods of natural science. Spinoza applied the geometrical method to the whole of ethics. Locke wrote his *Essay* as prolegomena to "a subject very remote from this," namely, morality and revealed religion, and showed "that moral knowledge is as capable of real certainty as mathematics." The full title of Hume's Treatise is *A Treatise on Human Nature. Being an Attempt to Introduce the Experimental Method of Reasoning into Moral Subjects.* And even Berkeley used epistemology only as a tool for theological ethics, the rules of which "have the same immutable universal truth with the propositions of geometry."

What made the natural philosophers soar ahead and the moral philosophers stagnate was that the former did and the latter did not understand the Newtonian method. This was the paradox of the Newtonian achievement. Natural philosophy became science; moral philosophy, in spite of all the attempts of Renaissance and Enlightenment and even of Newton himself, remained philosophy and degenerated into ideology. As a result, while the natural philosophers brought about the scientific revolution, the moral philosophers only brought about political revolutions. And while the scientific revolution changed the earth, the political revolutions changed fundamentally nothing. The great evil of absolutism, the sovereignty of the state over the moral law, is today stronger than ever. As a result, we have today the combination of natural science with the amoral sovereign state.

The first task of the revolution against war is an intellectual one. We must bring about the moral science our predecessors intended but failed to achieve. At the end of his *Optics*, Newton says, after describing the method of analysis and synthesis: "And if natural philosophy in all its parts by pursuing this method shall at length be perfected the bounds of moral philosophy will also be enlarged." Unfortunately, in his studies in morality and religion—which took many more years of his life than his studies in nature—Newton himself did not use this method: instead of applying number to observation, he applied it to speculation; instead of mathematical, he made numerological studies. Some philosophers have discussed what the Newtonian method would mean when applied to morals. Yet nobody has so far realized that, though it is relatively easy to state, *to apply the Newtonian method of analysis and synthesis to social and moral phenomena means to break down these phenomena into their primary qualities and reconstruct the latter in a coherent formal system.* Primary qualities of society and man, as Susanne Langer has stated long ago, will resemble the obvious properties of man and society as little as the obvious properties of things resemble protons and electrons. We have to get away, thus, from the obvious properties of social and moral phenomena, as Galileo got away from the obvious properties of things in motion. Much of our present-day psychology, sociology, philosophy, and so-called political science will then turn out to be ideology, just as the Aristotelian–Aquinian dogma of Galileo's time turned out to be ideology—thought constructions, that is, without counterparts in reality.

What we have to do, therefore, is to bring about the

complement of Renaissance and Enlightenment: we must apply the Newtonian method to human values. The result will be a moral science by the side of natural science—a science of peace by the side of the science of war. Thus we would bring about the union of cosmic conquest and moral insight that is the intellectual task of our age.

How can this be done? Ethics, which today is still as archaic as Aristotelian physics, must leap forward not only to the modern age but beyond it to the age of planetary humanity. Moral philosophers, not yet able even to define the nature of goodness or to influence, let alone guide, human fellowship on earth, must produce the tools of planetary ethics. Yet we are not entirely unprepared. Philosophers, from Plato to Whitehead, have charted the course, projecting to join mathematics with the good. George E. Moore approached the definition of the primary properties of value, and Bergson, in *The Two Sources of Morality and Religion*, worked out the cosmic program. What is left to do is to pull the strands together and create a science of ethics as precise and universal as the science of nature. Even this task is well on the way. We can already see what these philosophers divined: that the science of ethics has indeed its exact laws, that they can be formulated with precision and applied to social and moral phenomena. It is not utopian, then, to believe that a science of morality is possible. Indeed, if we did not, we would have to hold that all philosophers from Plato onward had been mistaken and that a few modern sophists are right. Once we believe, however, that a science of ethics is possible, we are obliged to work for its realization. The future of peace will see Institutes of Value Research on many a campus, institutes that will have the exact function that Plato outlined for *his* research institute, the Nocturnal Council, in *The Laws:* "To grasp the laws which control the stars and to apply them harmoniously to the institutions and rules of ethics" —to combine, that is, cosmic order with human morality and to find the *logic* that rules the universe without and within us. This logic will be a new specialty, that of axio-logic or value logic, which will structure and suffuse all humanistic and social subject matter, as today mathematics structures and suffuses all natural science subject matter.[3]

Once this science is on the way, the same will happen as happened in the development of natural science: a refinement and deepening of human sensitivity. Natural science refined and deepened our understanding of the problems of nature to the very limits of the sensitivity of our measuring instruments—down to the quantum and up to the pulsar. Moral science ought to deepen and refine our understanding of moral nature, to the very limits of our own sensitivity, down to the suffering of an ant and up to the agonies of war. In this way the fulfillment of our intellectual task will make possible that of our volitional task: as natural science led, through its inherent method, to technology, in particular that of war, so moral science should lead, through its inherent method, to the techniques of goodness, in particular those of peace.

Clarity of moral purpose, therefore, would lead to decisiveness of moral action, and the moral revolution lead necessarily to the existential revolution. As the scientific revolution of the Renaissance and the Enlightenment was accompanied by an exhilarating rise of extensive vitality, an explosion of the will to *act,* so the moral revolution of the future ought to be accompanied by a similar rise of intensive vitality, an explosion of the will to *live*. This awareness of life, and the circumstances of life, ought to be coupled with an awareness of death and the circumstances of death. It will then be possible clearly to distinguish between the two kinds of state and society, the natural of life and the artificial of death: the family of man and the military state. We have discussed the latter; we must now examine the former.

The natural society of man, to which belongs the civil

function of the state, is based on the laws of the universe itself: the earth's circling around the sun, the currents of air and water, sun and rain, the sequence of day and night, the rhythm of the seasons, the whole balance of nature that makes possible our existence. Each of us is the offspring of a long chain of generations, created in billions of years out of primal matter, each of us a progeny of the universe, in the sense of Walt Whitman:

Immense have been the preparations for me,
Faithful and friendly the arms that have help'd me.
Cycles ferried my cradle, rowing and rowing like cheerful boatmen,
For room to me stars kept aside in their own rings,
They sent influences to look after what was to hold me.
Before I was born out of my mother generations guided me.
My embryo has never been torpid, nothing could overlay it.
For it the nebula cohered to an orb,
The long slow strata piled to rest it on,
Vast vegetables gave it sustenance,
Monstrous sauroids transported it in their mouths and deposited it with care.
All forces have been steadily employ'd to complete and delight me,
Now on this spot I stand with my robust soul.

In this soul I know what is right and what is wrong, I know that all men are brothers with me on this planet.

This natural society is so obvious as never to become visible; it is a truth in the depth of our spirit. But it is overlaid by the slogans and divisions of history. The split between the two societies is a split within us. With our minds we are in the fragmented society of a national state, with our soul we live in the oneness of humanity. Each of us is victim, or potential victim, of the one and harbinger of the other. In all of us is the transposition between man and what used to be the citizen but is rapidly becoming the subject. This transposition is found strikingly, even amusingly, illustrated in the book *Five Journeys from Jakarta* by Maslyn Williams, a book on a new nation still smarting from the indignities of the old colonialism. Williams attended a meeting where a lovely young girl made the predictable speech: "Crush Malaysia and free our neighbors from British imperialism" and all that. He was incensed at the "worn-out phrases . . . falling from her pretty lips." He "wished for a hysterical second that someone would kiss her and stop the flow of words, words, words . . . give her a baby, make her a mother, turn her back into a pretty girl instead of a robot with a tape recorder for a brain." But a moment later the mask fell, and the girl was revealed. Her brothers were making plans for a feastday dance. "I wondered why they should die in Malaysia, and who will gain," she says. "She stopped," Williams notes, "and looked down as if she had run out of words, and there was quiet."

All over the world people feel the moral antagonism between system and life that splits mankind into states and a man himself into allegiances. There is a new sensitivity abroad, found in various degrees not only in individuals but in large groups of society. We could mention the Negro revolution that is an awakening to human dignity and expectation on a large scale. We could mention the new, and it seems definite, awareness of the clergy, of their own independent moral role against the immorality of the state, returning to the pre-Constantinian awareness of the early Church, after centuries of subservience to the state. In the words of Dr. Eugene Blake, Secretary of the National Council of the Churches of Christ:

> In World War II we were asked to regard as the ultimate fiends of humanity the Germans and the Japanese against whom we fought by the side of our great and good friends, the

> Russians and the Chinese. Today we are asked to regard these same Russians and Chinese as the ultimate fiends and accept the former fiends as our great and good friends. We may be stupid, but not that stupid.

In this confusion, he says, there is only one truth, that of Jesus Christ: "Love your enemies, do good to those that hate you." Christianity, says Dr. Blake, is radical, though Christians are often docile and conservative. The same should be said of science and the scientists and of education and the educators. Their work is the future, but many live in the past. Yet it is the educators who will be put to the test; for, important though the two groups mentioned are, more important is a third group awakening today to moral awareness: the group of those who carry the future and will be filling colleges and universities in the years to come, today's youth. They see—and this is a peculiar phenomenon common to the young people all over the world, but especially to those in the two great nuclear nations, the United States and Russia—that the old forms of thought and society are *outmoded because they are immoral.* These rebels have grown in the last ten years in both countries, from about 1 per cent to about 5 per cent of all youth. If the trend continues they will, in another ten years, grow to 25 per cent. Although this awakening sometimes takes peculiar forms, one should not be misled by outer appearances. There is a serious and profound core in this sudden rally of the young.

These young people are not political; they are moral revolutionaries. And they are not really revolutionaries, for they are rediscovering some very old truths. They are only trying to bring society up to date, to elevate it to its own professed moral standards. They are discovering the inalienable moral truth within, and of, their own selves. This awakening is called the New Left in the United States and may be called the same in Russia. Both movements go back to the original inspiration that formed their states and are opposed to its later perversions. Their unrest is not an ordinary generational rebellion, it is the "existential" politics, unideological and hence really neither left nor right, the moral revolt that happens when a dominant system of society has come to seem senile and absurd. It seeks existential truth, *pravda.* The Russian young men and women say, *mutatis mutandis,* the same that a high school girl, Sara Greenfelder, says in the Life-Time Special Report *The Young Americans:*

> I'm sort of sick of the United States [of Russia]—not my immediate environment, but the moral standards of most people. Adults in this country are always playing games. They can't do or say what they want. In public they're forced to be hypocrites by our system, which is all based on money [on power, the Russian young people say].

In both countries the young rebel against their elders' conformity, and it is this conformity that the military state thrives on. Hence the rebellion is largely directed against this state. It is a true revolution against war, but against war as the symptom of a moral disease. In the words of David Harris, former student-body president of Stanford, who has refused induction: "No new policy or no new politician is going to bring an end to what we object to in this country. *What we need is a new way of life, a brotherhood of men.*"

Thus, there is already more to the new moral humanity than the call for the development of a new science to create it. There is the commitment of an increasing part of humanity to this new vision. Once it is joined to intellectual understanding, the methods of peace will unfold as elaborately and efficiently as those of war. This will bring about a change deeper than any that has ever taken place in history. It will lead to the emancipation of the individual person from the state, the emancipation of the civil society from the military apparatus. Peace has nothing to do with capitalism, communism, or any other ism, any economic or ideological difference. The democratic and the totalitarian citizens die for the same kind of fiction, of "sovereignty," as did their medieval ancestors. *"Ce sont toujours les mêmes qui se font tuer."*[4] The revolution against war is a rebellion of the *morituri* who have stopped to salute Caesar. The subjects of the military system have suddenly become conscious of their fetters. They want to live.

The rebellion of the young is nothing but the first rumbling of the explosion of the will to live that will sweep away the third rider of the Apocalypse.

To give this movement power, to lead it from utopia to science, philosophers must concentrate as thoroughly, and as ingeniously, on the essence of man as our predecessors—at the beginning of the modern age—concentrated on the essence of nature. The Renaissance was a new beginning, born from external and internal events, the exploration of the globe and the feeling of individual independence. The new epoch into which we are entering is born from external and internal exploration: we are the generation that has seen a man floating above the terrestrial globe in outer space, and our youth is exploring, often desperately, the expanses of inner space. But the feeling of individual independence is now one of individual interdependence. We have seen this earth as one from above, we must now form it as one from within.

NOTES

1. I.e., 10,000 warheads at 2-megaton average, though the average tonnage is probably higher.

2. Actually, at 1 ton of TNT per 10 people, a generous allotment, the United States only needs 30 megatons to do away with all the Russians. We thus have an overkill capacity of 67,000 per cent.

3. For details see the present author's *The Structure of Value* (Carbondale, Ill.: Southern University Press, 1967, 1969).

4. "It is always the same ones who get killed."–*Jacques Maritain.*

A Bibliography of the Philosophy of War in the Atomic Age

Addison, James Thayer. *War, Peace, and the Christian Mind: A Review of Recent Thought.* Greenwich, Conn.: Seabury, 1953.

Adler, Mortimer J., *et al.* "War and Peace," *The Great Ideas: A Syntopican of Great Books of the Western World,* Vol. II, pp. 1010–1037. Chicago: Encyclopædia Britannica, 1952.

Arendt, Hannah. *On Revolution.* New York: Viking, 1965.

Aron, Raymond. *The Century of Total War.* Boston: Beacon, 1955.

———. *Peace and War: A Theory of International Relations.* New York: Praeger, 1967.

———. *On War.* New York: Norton, 1968.

Bainton, Roland H. *Christian Attitudes Toward War and Peace: A Historical Survey and Critical Re-evaluation.* New York: Abingdon, 1960.

Bennett, John C. (ed.) *Nuclear Weapons and the Conflict of Conscience.* New York: Scribner's, 1962.

Bennett, John C., *et al. The Road to Peace: Christian Approaches to Defense and Disarmament.* Philadelphia: Fortress, 1966.

Bernal, J. D. *World Without War.* London: Routledge & Kegan Paul, 1958.

Bloch, Ernst. "Widerstand und Friede," Peace Prize Address. Frankfurt: Börsenverein des Deutschen Buchhandels E.V., 1967.

Bohannan, Paul (ed.) *Law and Warfare: Studies in the Anthropology of Conflict.* Garden City, N.Y.: Natural History Press, 1967.

Bondurant, Joan V. *Conquest of Violence: The Gandhian Philosophy of Conflict*. 2nd ed. Berkeley: University of California Press, 1965.

Braden, Charles Samuel. *War, Communism, and World Religions*. New York: Harper Brothers, 1953.

Bramson, Leon, & Goethals, George W. (eds.) *War: Studies from Psychology, Sociology, Anthropology*. 2nd ed. New York: Basic Books, 1968.

Brownlee, Ian. *International Law and the Use of Force by States*. Oxford: Clarendon Press, 1963.

Buchan, Alastair. *War in Modern Society: An Introduction*. New York: Harper & Row, 1968.

Butterfield, Herbert. *Christianity, Diplomacy, and War*. New York: Abingdon-Cokesbury, 1953.

———. *International Conflict in the Twentieth Century: A Christian View*. New York: Harper Brothers, 1960.

Cantril, Hadley (ed.) *Tensions that Cause Wars*. Urbana, Ill.: University of Illinois Press, 1950.

Carlston, Kenneth S. *Law and Organization in World Society*. Urbana, Ill.: University of Illinois Press, 1962.

Chagin, B. A. "The Role of the Subjective Factor in the Prevention of World War," *Soviet Studies in Philosophy*, III (Winter, 1964–1965), 3–8.

The Christian Faith and War in the Nuclear Age. New York: Abingdon, 1963.

Clancy, William (ed.) *The Moral Dilemma of Nuclear Weapons: Essays from Worldview*. New York: Council on Religion and International Affairs, 1961.

Clark, Grenville. *A Plan for Peace*. New York: Harper Brothers, 1950.

Clark, Grenville & Sohn, Louis B. *World Peace Through World Law*. 3rd ed. Cambridge, Mass.: Harvard University Press, 1966.

A Constitution for the World. Santa Barbara, Calif.: Center for the Study of Democratic Institutions, 1965.

Cordier, Andrew W. & Foote, Wilder (eds.) *The Quest for Peace*. New York: Columbia University Press, 1965.

Cordier, Andrew W. & Maxwell, Kenneth L. (eds.) *Paths to World Order*. New York: Columbia University Press, 1967.

Delos, J. T. "The Sociology of Modern War and the Theory of Just War," *Cross Currents,* VIII (Summer, 1958), 248–266.

Deutsch, Morton. "Psychological Alternatives to War," *Journal of Social Issues,* XVIII, 2 (1962), 97–119.

Diwakar, R. R. *Satyagraha: The Power of Truth.* Hinsdale, Ill.: Regnery, 1948.

Douglass, James W. *The Non-Violent Cross: A Theology of Revolution and Peace.* New York: Macmillan, 1968.

Einstein, Albert. *Einstein on Peace* (eds. Otto Nathan & Heinz Norden). New York: Schocken, 1968.

Ewing, A. C. *The Individual, the State, and World Government.* New York: Macmillan, 1947.

Falk, Richard A. *Law, Morality, and War in the Contemporary World.* New York: Praeger, 1963.

———. *Legal Order in a Violent World.* Princeton, N.J.: Princeton University Press, 1968.

Falk, Richard A., & Mendlovitz, Saul H. (eds.) *The Strategy of World Order.* 4 vols. New York: World Law Fund, 1966.

Fedoseev, P. N. "Contemporary Sociological Theories Concerning War and Peace," *Soviet Studies in Philosophy,* I (Winter, 1962–1963), 3–24.

———. "The Peace Problem in Contemporary Social Thought," *Soviet Studies in Philosophy,* VI (Summer, 1967), 3–15.

Fischer, Louis (ed.) *The Essential Gandhi: His Life, Work, and Ideas.* New York: Random House, 1962.

Fleischmann, Rudolf, *et al.* *Kann der atomare Verteidigunskrieg ein gerechter Krieg sein?* Munich: K. Zink, 1960.

Frank, Jerome D. *Sanity and Survival: Psychological Aspects of War and Peace.* New York: Random House, 1968.

Freeman, Harrop A. *Road to Peace.* Philadelphia: Pacifist Research Bureau, 1945.

Fried, Morton, Harris, Marvin, & Murphy, Robert (eds.) *War: The Anthropology of Armed Conflict and Aggression.* Garden City, N.Y.: Natural History Press, 1968.

Friedrich, Carl J. *Inevitable Peace.* Cambridge, Mass.: Harvard University Press, 1948.

Fromm, Erich, & Herzfeld, Hans (eds.) *Der Friede: Idee und Verwirklichung; The Search for Peace.* Heidelberg: L. Schneider, 1961.

Gangal, S. C. *The Gandhian Way to World Peace.* Bombay: Vora, 1960.

Gray, J. Glenn. *The Warriors: Reflections on Men in Battle.* New York: Harper & Row, 1967.

Gregg, Richard B. *The Power of Nonviolence.* 2nd ed. New York: Schocken, 1966.

Grob, Fritz. *The Relativity of War and Peace: A Study in Law, History, and Politics.* New Haven, Conn.: Yale University Press, 1949.

Harris, Errol E. *Annihilation and Utopia: The Principles of International Politics.* London: Allen & Unwin, 1966.

Hoffmann, Stanley. *The State of War: Essays on the Theory and Practice of International Politics.* New York: Praeger, 1965.

Hollins, Elizabeth Jay (ed.) *Peace Is Possible: A Reader on World Order.* New York: Grossman, 1966.

Horowitz, Irving Louis. *The Idea of War and Peace in Contemporary Philosophy.* New York: Paine-Whitman, 1957.

Howe, Günter (ed.) *Atomzeitalter, Krieg, und Frieden.* Witten: Eckart-Verlag, 1959.

Hula, Erich. "The Revival of the Idea of Punitive War," *Thought,* XXI (September, 1946), 405–434.

Hutchins, Robert Maynard. *The Atomic Bomb Versus Civilization.* Washington: Human Events, 1945.

Jack, Homer A. (ed.) *Religion and Peace: Papers from the National Inter-Religious Conference on Peace.* Indianapolis: Bobbs-Merrill, 1966.

Jaspers, Karl. *The Future of Mankind.* Chicago: University of Chicago Press, 1961.

John XXIII "Pacem in Terris," *The Encyclicals and Other Messages of John XXIII* (with commentaries by others) (ed. by the Staff of *The Pope Speaks Magazine*). Washington: TPS Press, 1964, pp. 327–373.

Kahn, Herman. *On Thermonuclear War.* Princeton, N.J.: Princeton University Press, 1960.

———. *Thinking about the Unthinkable.* New York: Horizon, 1962.

Kendall, Willmoore, & Sibley, Mulford Q. *War and the Use of Force: Moral or Immoral, Christian or Unchristian; A Debate*. Denver: Swallow, 1959.

Keys, Donald (ed.) *God and the H-Bomb*. New York: Macfadden-Bartell, 1962.

Khadduri, Majid. *War and Peace in the Law of Islam*. Baltimore: Johns Hopkins Press, 1955.

Knudson, A. C. *The Philosophy of War and Peace*. New York: Abingdon, 1947.

Kovalev, A. M. "War and Revolution," *Soviet Studies in Philosophy*, IV (Fall, 1965), 43–49.

Lentz, Theo. F. *Towards a Science of Peace: Turning Point in Human Destiny*. New York: Bookman Associates, 1955.

Lewin, L. (ed.) *Report from Iron Mountain on the Possibility and Desirability of Peace*. New York: Dial Press, 1967.

Lorenz, Konrad. *On Aggression*. New York: Harcourt, Brace & World, 1966.

Lynd, Staughton (ed.) *Nonviolence in America: A Documentary History*. Indianapolis: Bobbs-Merrill, 1966.

McClure, Wallace. *World Legal Order: Possible Contributions by the People of the United States*. Chapel Hill, N.C.: University of North Carolina Press, 1960.

Mangone, Gerard J. *The Idea and Practice of World Government*. New York: Columbia University Press, 1951.

Maritain, Jacques. "The Problem of World Government," *Man and the State*. Chicago: University of Chicago Press, 1951.

Martin, Kingsley. *War, History, and Human Nature*. New York: Asia Publishing House, 1959.

Martin, Thomas Owen. "Problems in the Morality of Warfare," *Proceedings of the Catholic Theological Society of America*, II (1947), 47–71.

Mayer, Peter (ed.) *The Nonviolent Tradition*. New York: Orion, 1964.

———. (ed.) *The Pacifist Conscience*. Chicago: Regnery, 1967. Includes an extensive bibliography by William Robert Miller on "War, Pacifism, Non-Violence, and Related Studies."

Mendlovitz, Saul H. (ed.) *Legal and Political Problems of World Order*. New York: World Law Fund, 1962.

Merton, Thomas, *et al.* *Breakthrough to Peace*. Norfolk, Conn.: New Directions, 1962.

Miller, William Robert. *Nonviolence: A Christian Interpretation*. New York: Schocken, 1966.

Millis, Walter, *et al.* *A World Without War*. New York: Washington Square Press, 1961.

Mills, C. Wright. *The Causes of World War Three*. New York: Simon & Schuster, 1958.

Morgenthau, Hans J. *Politics Among Nations: The Struggle for Power and Peace*. 4th ed. New York: Knopf, 1967.

Mumford, Lewis. *Atomic War: The Way Out*. London: National Peace Council, 1948.

Munk, Arthur W. *A Way of Survival*. New York: Bookman Associates, 1954.

Murphy, Gardner (ed.) *Human Nature and Enduring Peace*. Boston: Houghton Mifflin, 1945.

Murty, K. Satchidananda, & Bouquet, A. C. *Studies in the Problems of Peace*. New York: Asia Publishing House, 1960.

Muste, A. J. *The Essays of A. J. Muste* (ed. Nat Hentoff). Indianapolis: Bobbs-Merrill, 1967.

Naess, Arne. *Gandhi and the Nuclear Age*. Totowa, N.J.: Bedminster, 1965.

Nagle, William J. (ed.) *Morality and Modern Warfare: The State of the Question*. Baltimore: Helicon, 1960. Includes an extensive bibliography by Noel J. Brown on "The Moral Problem of Modern Warfare."

Narain, Shiv. *Outlines of World Peace*. Delhi: Sarover Prakashan, n.d.

Narveson, Jan. "Pacifism: A Philosophical Analysis," *Ethics*, LXXV (July, 1965), 259–271.

Nef, John U. (ed.) *Towards World Community*. The Hague: Dr. W. Junk N.V., 1968.

———. *War and Human Progress: An Essay on the Rise of Industrial Civilization*. New York: Norton, 1968.

Niebuhr, Reinhold. *The Structure of Nations and Empires: A Study of the Recurring Patterns and Problems of the Political Order in Relation to the Unique Problems of the Nuclear Age*. New York: Scribner's, 1959.

Northrop, F. S. C. (ed.) *Ideological Differences and World Order: Studies in the Philosophy and Science of the World's Cultures.* New Haven, Conn.: Yale University Press, 1963.

Park, No-Yong. *The White Man's Peace: An Oriental View of Our Attempts at Making World Peace.* Boston: Meador, 1948.

Parsons, Howard L. "Human Nature and the Causes and Cures of War: Can Christians and Marxists Agree and Cooperate?" *Proceedings of the XIVth International Congress of Philosophy,* Vol. II, pp. 649–655. Vienna: Herder, 1968.

Pauling, Linus. *No More War!* Enl. ed. New York: Dodd, Mead, 1962.

Pear, T. H. (ed.) *Psychological Factors of Peace and War.* New York: Philosophical Library, 1950.

Ramsey, Paul. *The Just War: Force and Political Responsibility.* New York: Scribner's, 1968.

———. *The Limits of Nuclear War: Thinking about the Do-Able and the Un-Do-Able.* New York: Council on Religion and International Affairs, 1963.

———. *War and the Christian Conscience: How Shall Modern War Be Justly Conducted?* Durham, N.C.: Duke University Press, 1961.

Read, Herbert. *Education for Peace.* New York: Scribner's, 1949.

Reed, Edward (ed.) *Beyond Coexistence: The Requirements of Peace.* Papers of the 2nd *Pacem in Terris* Convocation. New York: Grossman, 1968.

———. (ed.) *Peace on Earth, Pacem in Terris: The Proceedings of an International Convocation on the Requirements of Peace.* New York: Pocket Books, 1965.

Reves, Emery. *The Anatomy of Peace.* 10th ed. New York: Harper & Brothers, 1946.

Richardson, Lewis Fry. *Arms and Insecurity: A Mathematical Study of the Causes and Origins of War.* Pittsburgh: Boxwood, 1960.

Russell, Bertrand. *Common Sense and Nuclear Warfare.* London: Allen & Unwin, 1959.

———. *Fact and Fiction,* Part IV. London: Allen & Unwin, 1961.

———. *Has Man a Future?* New York: Simon & Schuster, 1962.

———. *New Hopes for a Changing World,* Part II. New York: Simon & Schuster, 1951.

Saiyidain, Khwajah Ghulamus. *Education for International Understanding*. Bombay: Hind Kitabs, 1948.

Sartre, Jean-Paul. *On Genocide: And a Summary of the Evidence and the Judgments of the International War Crimes Tribunal* (by Arlette El Kaïm-Sartre). Boston: Beacon, 1968.

Schlissel, Lillian (ed.) *Conscience in America: A Documentary History of Conscientious Objection in America, 1757–1967*. New York: Dutton, 1968.

Schweitzer, Albert. *Peace or Atomic War?* New York: Holt, 1958.

Sibley, Mulford Q. (ed.) *The Quiet Battle: Writings on the Theory and Practice of Non-Violent Resistance*. Garden City, N.Y.: Doubleday, 1963.

Somerville, John. "Democracy and the Problem of War," *The Humanist*, XXVII (May–June, 1967).

———. *The Philosophy of Peace*. 2nd ed. New York: Liberty, 1954.

———. "World Authority: Realities and Illusions," *Ethics*, LXXVI (October, 1965), 33–46.

Speier, Hans. *Social Order and the Risks of War: Papers in Political Sociology*. New York: Stewart, 1952.

Smith, T. V. *Atomic Power and Moral Faith*. Claremont, Calif.: Claremont College, 1946.

Strachey, Alix. *The Unconscious Motives of War: A Psycho-Analytical Contribution*. London: Allen & Unwin, 1957.

Teilhard de Chardin, Pierre. "Some Reflections on the Spiritual Repercussions of the Atom Bomb," *The Future of Man*, pp. 145–153. New York: Harper & Row, 1969.

Thomas, Norman. *The Prerequisites for Peace*. New York: Norton, 1959.

Thompson, Charles S. (ed.) *Morals and Missiles: Catholic Essays on the Problem of War Today*. London: Clarke, 1959.

Toynbee, Arnold J. *War and Civilization*, Selected from *A Study of History* (ed. Albert V. Fowler). New York: Oxford University Press, 1950.

Tucker, Robert W. *Just War and Vatican Council II: A Critique* (with commentary by others). New York: Council on Religion and International Affairs, 1966.

———. *The Just War: A Study in Contemporary American Doctrine.* Baltimore: Johns Hopkins Press, 1960.

Vyas, Ramnarayan. *Peace, Philosophy, and Progress.* Jullundur City, India: Sterling, 1966.

Wallace, Victor Hugo (ed.) *Paths to Peace: A Study of Wars, Its Causes, and Prevention.* Carlton, Australia: Melbourne University Press, 1957.

Waltz, Kenneth N. *Man, the State, and War: A Theoretical Analysis.* New York: Columbia University Press, 1965.

Wasserstrom, Richard. "Three Arguments Concerning the Morality of War," *Journal of Philosophy,* LXV (October 3, 1968), 578–590.

Weinberg, Arthur & Lila (eds.) *Instead of Violence: Writings by the Great Advocates of Peace and Nonviolence Throughout History.* Boston: Beacon, 1965. Contains an extensive bibliography.

Weizäcker, Carl-Friedrich von. "Bedingungen des Friedens," Peace Prize Address. Göttingen: Vandenhoeck & Ruprecht, 1963.

———. *Ethical and Political Problems of the Atomic Age.* "The Burge Memorial Lecture." London: SCM Press, 1958.

Wells, Donald A. *The War Myth.* New York: Pegasus, 1967. Contains an extensive bibliography.

Woodward, Ernest Llewellyn, *et al. Foundations for World Order.* Denver: University of Denver Press, 1949.

Wright, Quincy. *The Role of International Law in the Elimination of War.* New York: Oceana, 1961.

———. *A Study of War.* 2nd ed. Chicago: University of Chicago Press, 1965.

———. (ed.) *The World Community.* Chicago: University of Chicago Press, 1948.

Wright, Quincy, Evan, William M., & Deutsch, Morton (eds.) *Preventing World War III: Some Proposals.* New York: Simon & Schuster, 1962.

Zahn, Gordon. *An Alternative to War.* New York: Council on Religion and International Affairs, 1963.

———. *War, Conscience, and Dissent.* New York: Hawthorn, 1967.

Index of Names and Concepts